Eric Butcher
Trace Elements

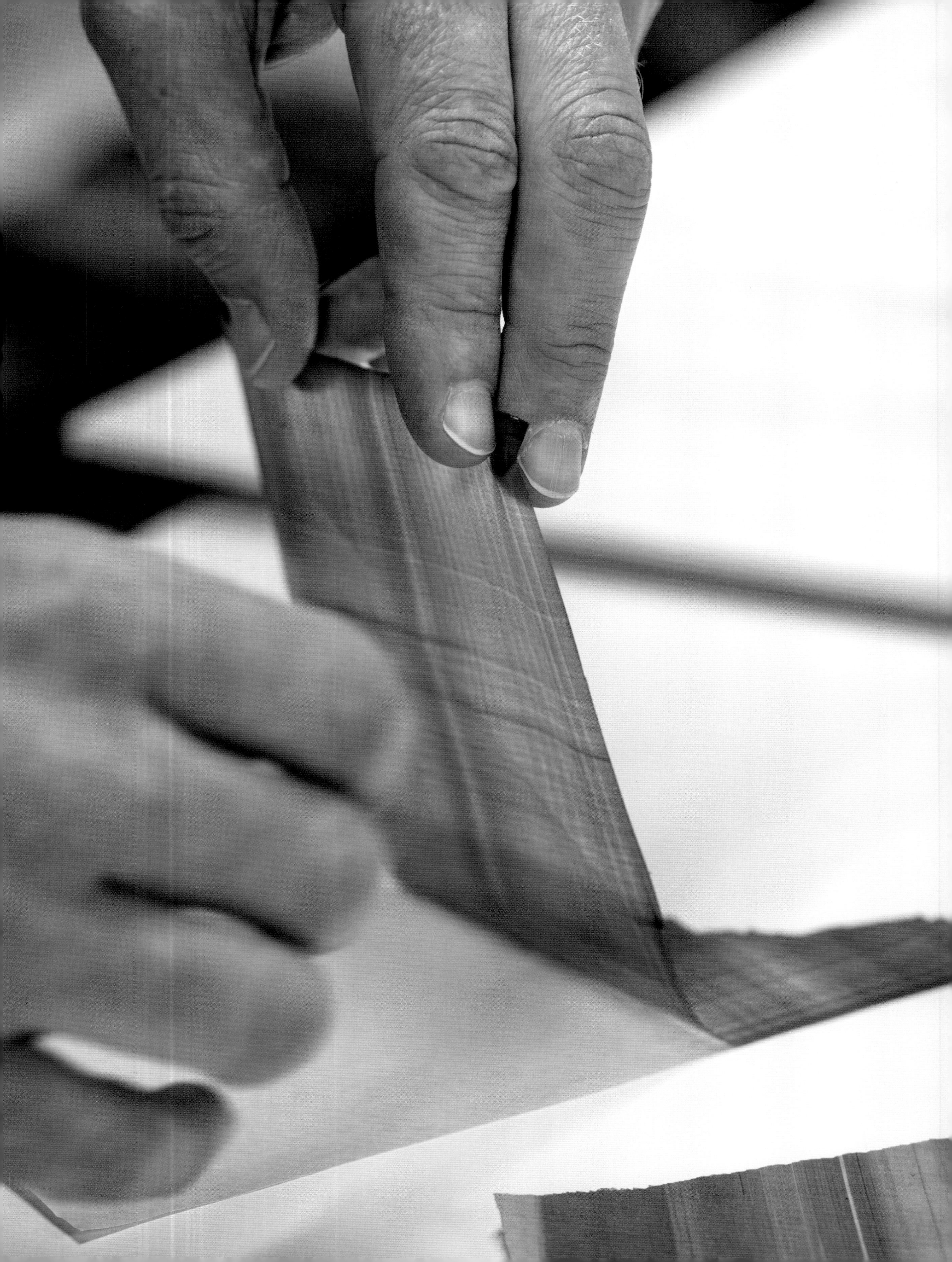

Eric Butcher
Trace Elements

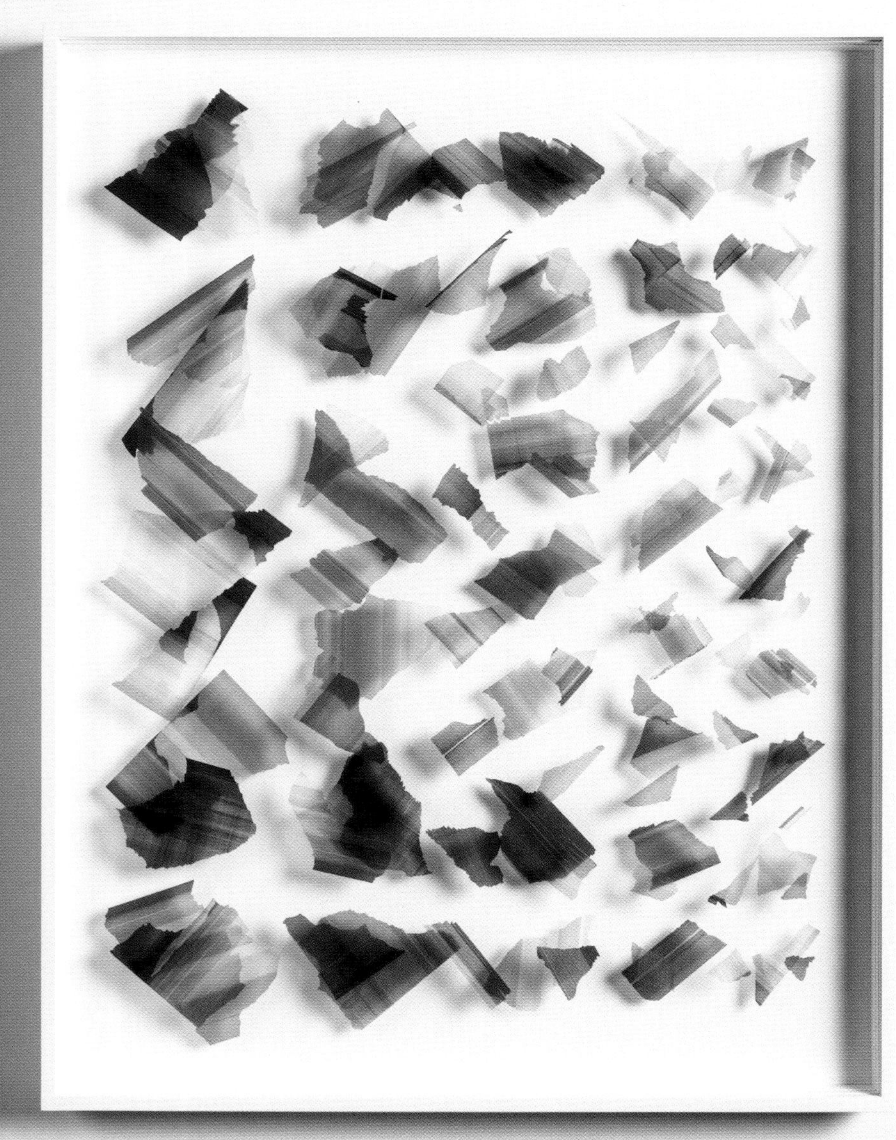

Contents

T/R.1058, Recycled Paint Fragments: Acrylic, Graphite + Acrylic Gel on Glass, 109×86 cm, 2025

Cover Image: *T/R.1067* (detail), Recycled Paint Fragments: Acrylic, Graphite, Tin + Acrylic Gel on Glass, 55×44 cm, 2025

The artist who wants to stop making art

Jonathan Watkins

It depends on how you define being an artist.
Do you need to produce stuff to be an artist?

I don't think I'll be an artist when I stop making art.
I think I'll be creative about the things I do,
like other people. And I'm looking forward to it.[1]

Eric Butcher

Not so long ago, British artist Eric Butcher had been "devoted to the patient and incremental development of a practice of reductive, self-referential process-based painting".[2] Often, oil paint mixed with resin or graphite with acrylic medium applied to geometric aluminium panels, it was then scraped away to leave thin residues of transparent colour. The result was a glowing abstraction – with light reflected by the metallic ground, or underlying surface – engaged with its architectural circumstances, very carefully installed, asserting itself as part of our object world, rather than being representational. It was ostensibly accessible, but not everyone's idea of art.

This was the kind of work that featured in Butcher's solo exhibition, *Sweet Heresy*, opening at Patrick Heide Contemporary Art, London in January 2020. It was a good looking show, smart in its responses to details of the gallery interior – boxed plumbing and radiators, even – and sensitive to the play of light. This was artwork that took its cues from its setting whilst insinuating itself back into it, confusing artistic gestures and context to the extent that they were inseparable. Butcher explains: "Once you start to consider the painted surface as just one surface of a three-dimensional object, you start to think about the transitions between surfaces, and from the object to wall, and once you consider the wall as being part of the work that leads you to think about the whole environment of the piece."[3] The idea of a work of art as something self-contained was effectively contradicted by this exhibition, as it had been by many others previously that had involved Butcher either as an artist or artist/curator.[4]

Saturation Point, a "curatorial and editorial project for systems, non-objective and reductive artists working in the UK", published two texts on *Sweet Heresy* (January 2020). One was an interview with Butcher by young artist Karen Loader.[5] In answer to a question

1 All quotations are from an unpublished conversation with the artist, 2 May 2025, unless otherwise indicated.
2 Artist's statement accessed 14 July 2025, https://www.ericbutcher.com/statement/
3 Karen Loader, 'Interview with Eric Butcher', saturationpoint.org.uk/Eric%20Butcher.html. Accessed 16 July 2025
4 For exhibitions curated by Eric Butcher, see www.ericbutcher.com/curating/. Accessed 14 July 2025
5 Karen Loader, Op.cit.

about the exhibition's title, Butcher explained that it signified a distinction between his practice and "a certain sort of work, mainly issues-based work which is politically or socially engaged, [that has had] a lot of media and art world attention." He elaborated:

> *What I do is not preoccupied with what is going on in the world in terms of current affairs, which feels slightly heretical and so it's really a reference to that. It's not that I have anything against this sort of work, but we're members of a broader church than you might think if you look at the shortlists for major art prizes or the preoccupations of superstar curators. I feel the work I do, and so many others is marginalised in the current climate and I wanted to reflect that impression.*

He goes on to describe his preoccupation with the way things look, for example, "the relationship between the size of the wall and the size of aluminium panels and the size of the gap between the panels. They're rather modernist, formal concerns and of course that's not all there is to the work, nevertheless I spend quite a lot of time thinking about these things." The art of *Sweet Heresy* might have been formalist, but, at the same time, it was subverting the exclusivity of art for art's sake. Engaging, with both its environment and those who encountered it; yes, it was about the way things look, but also it was about ways of seeing.

The second *Saturation Point* text was a review by Clare French, another artist, very much on Butcher's wavelength. His wit was not lost on her: "These [works] are fun and bright, and Butcher is not afraid to reference IKEA-esque interior design, hobby painting and the decorative." She goes on to explain that, despite such references, the "art credentials" of Butcher's work are impeccable: "displaying high levels of technical and curatorial skill, and a wonderful use of colour and natural light".[6]

For French, the non-artistic references enhanced Butcher's artistic achievement, but equally there is an argument that such an insinuation of everyday life into art, and vice versa, eventually will lead to the undoing of the latter. There were many societies, prior to western contact, that had no concept of art – Japan being a notable example, with no word for 'art' before the mid-nineteenth century – but culturally were no poorer for it. William Morris in *News from Nowhere* was dreaming of a new England in which art was made redundant due to high levels of technical skill (and, no doubt, a wonderful use of colour).

* * *

In tune with Morris, I imagine a human race several generations hence that will look back on our obsession with art and wonder what it was all about. Why did we think we needed it? Painting, sculpture, video installation and all other media of creativity fine, but why art? From my point of view, art is like religion, a placebo effect. We have artistic experience because it is what we are conditioned to expect.

* * *

A few weeks after *Sweet Heresy* closed, in March 2020, the UK was locked down due to the COVID-19 pandemic. It was traumatic, intense, a time for review for many and, with respect to his artistic practice, Butcher had a Damascene experience, as he has recently described:

> *I've always struggled with being an artist. I've always felt two contradictory things at the same time. One is that you feel incredibly lucky, lucky to pursue your creative endeavours, whatever they might be, without somebody breathing down your neck … I've always thought that was a privilege. At the same time, I've always struggled with legitimising this to*

6 Clare French, 'Eric Butcher/Sweet Heresy', saturationpoint.org.uk/Eric%20Butcher%20review.html. Accessed 16 July 2025

T/R.1058, Recycled Paint Fragments: Acrylic, Graphite + Acrylic Gel on Glass, 109×86 cm, 2025

> *myself. I feel that pushing funny coloured bits of mud around a two-dimensional surface for a living is such a long way from a real job. And it does often feel indulgent, and vain and selfish. It really came to a head during lockdown… I'd come into studio and hear what the death toll was – I've got friends [doctors] who literally save lives for a living, every day. They'd go into a hospital and save lives and I'd be pushing funny coloured bits of mud around… It all seemed a bit irrelevant.*

Suddenly, this was a far cry from the *Saturation Point* assertion that he was distanced from current affairs. The pandemic itself did not become a theme, but rather he assumed an explicit environmentalist stance. It was the deliberate amplification of a tendency evident in all his previous work – involving, as it did, recycling, reusing and repurposing – and so his studio activity was to become aligned with the urgency he now felt: "Confronted by the devastating impact of human behaviour on the planet, my former studio practice seemed deeply problematic and indulgent. What was it that my work consisted of but taking precious resources and turning them into useless objects?"[7]

And so started *Endgame*, the modus operandi of all Butcher's current and future creative work. From his website: "[Butcher] has committed to use only those materials already available in the studio; using up, repurposing and recycling what he already has without consuming more. He will draw out his use of current resources for as long as possible, being as frugal as he can and when he has run out of materials he will simply stop making art." In the light of my longstanding scepticism with respect to art as an institution and, incidentally, my attraction to work that is process-based, driven by logic, how could I not be more interested when Eric Butcher announced that he wanted to stop making art?

* * *

Arguably it is more heretical for an artist to stop making art, than it was to be an artist swimming, however "sweetly", against a tide of issue-based art in the new year of 2020. Artists make art, and art is made by artists. Art is assumed to be a vocation, or a calling, and so Butcher's proposed retirement suggests renunciation. Having been brought up in the Roman Catholic faith, certainly he understands the significance of his gesture, and how it contradicts conventional ideas of artistic identity.

For Butcher, the studio has become a closed system, and his artistic practice now feeds on itself. He "[pulls] his previous works apart, both intellectually and physically, peeling the skins of paint from their supports and categorising them according to a basic taxonomy. In short, he [subjects] his entire practice to a sort of forensic examination. The resulting skins, fragments and traces of paint are presented sandwiched between sheets of glass like specimens. They provide a record or index of past artistic endeavours, a 'natural history' of his creative self."[8]

The process of *Endgame* has been consistent from the beginning, involving a recycling of peeled skins of paint from earlier works for their presentation, glazed and framed, but the work itself has gone through changes. Early on it was one peeling per frame, then constructivist-style collages to be superseded by a format inspired by entomological collections: "I wanted to present [the peelings] as they were, rather than turning them into a work of 'art'." To this end, to start with, Butcher would present sandwiched rows of peeled skins of paint with a typewritten index, numbers referring to a list of works from which the paint was extracted – in other words, paintings he had destroyed. Then he made work without text, grids of released brushstrokes. Despite the scientific format, and true to form (pun intended), he was enjoying making juxtapositions of their translucency, at once reflecting and

7 From the artist's website: www.ericbutcher.com/endgame-2024/
8 Ibid.

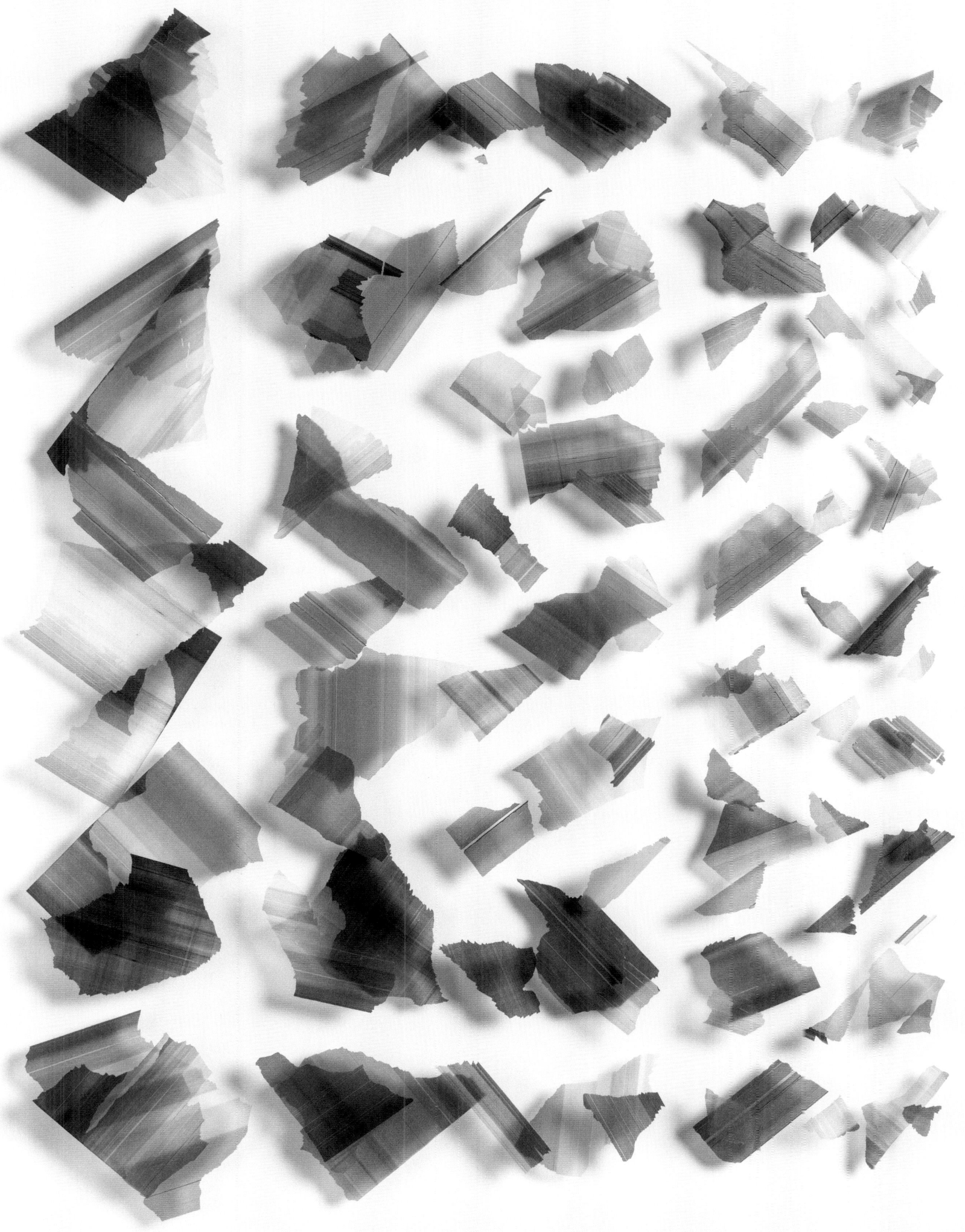

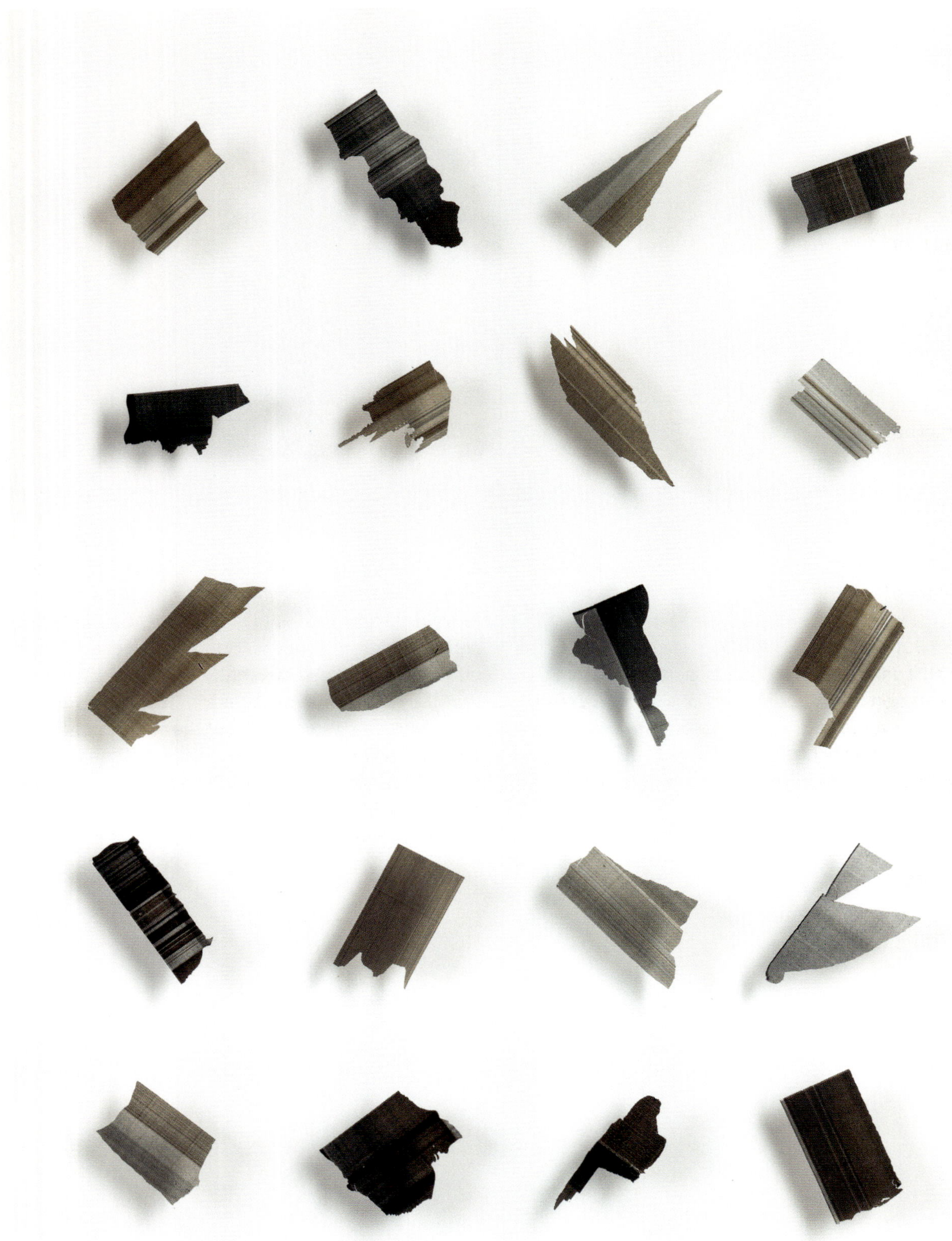

T/R.1033, Recycled Paint Fragments: Graphite, Bronze + Acrylic Gel on Glass, 55×44 cm, 2023

refracting light, throwing coloured shadows onto a white backboard. Aesthetically contrived, of course, and he is unapologetic: "I can't help myself. By having removed so many creative decisions/choices through the imposition of a process – a system – I allow myself a chance to play."

The business of recycling skins of paint is painstaking. Butcher fixes them to a sheet of transparent adhesive – pH neutral, non-yellowing – and then he cuts around each one, meticulously, with a scalpel. Boring? No: "I like the mindlessness of it […] I've always enjoyed that. Even when I was painting. It's a kind of Jekyll and Hyde experience. I'd lose myself in whatever I was doing, perhaps not really thinking about it all, and then I'd stand back and ask myself, 'What am I going to do with this now? What happened here? What's good about that?'"

And about framing? Butcher explains: "From my perspective there's something quite satisfying about having [the paint skins] safe in a frame where they can't get damaged. My previous work was rather delicate and potentially vulnerable; it needed constant cleaning. Whereas the new work, being behind glass is safe, fixed, in a sense eternal. It no longer needs me to install it, make decisions about it, so I feel I can move on."

* * *

I'm hardwired as a Catholic.

Arguments for the correspondence between art and religion have been rehearsed many times. Art, as we now know it, was invented in the west in the 18th century, and exported to the rest of the world through colonialism and trade expansion. With no intrinsic quality, art has all the hallmarks of sophistry, requiring faith, chosen ones with a special calling and sensibility (artists as prophets) revered relics (works of art) and places of worship (museums and galleries). Art is acquired usually with the assumption that it will enhance the quality of life, that life lived with art will be better somehow; this in spite of the fact that we know that there is a lot of bad art, and that there are a lot of good things in life which aren't art. Ideas that equate art with goodness, truth and beauty or some kind of transcendental experience – an epiphany perhaps – run counter to common sense, and yet they persist in our (postmodern) society. Art is all-too-human and the key to understanding why it exists at all probably lies in fields of psychology, sociology and anthropology – certainly not on some moral high ground or in realms of aesthetic refinement.

Eric Butcher knows all this. Like Michael Craig-Martin, also brought up a Catholic, he acknowledges the transubstantiation that transforms a glass of water into an oak tree,[9] the kind of faith required to apprehend an everyday object as a work of art, despite the fact that nothing has changed materially. His pre-pandemic work, such as that shown in *Sweet Heresy*, is a case in point, daring us to identify his constructions as art without the conventional means of display to signify its presence – no frames, no plinths, for example – although of course they were fixed on the walls of an art gallery. That is key. Butcher likens his painted aluminium pieces to the contents of a tool-box. There were dozens of them "that would come together for a particular site, be de-installed and then coalesce in another site […] I've always thought, where one work stops and another one starts is always entirely arbitrary."[10] Not discrete works of art, the painted aluminium pieces were elements in equations devised to suit a variety of dedicated art spaces, and now they are the source of material for another artistic project, the *Endgame*.

In an evocative essay, written in 2019, critic Paul Carey-Kent describes the artist in his studio: "Butcher is there five days a week,

9 Michael Craig-Martin's An Oak Tree (1973) is a two-part work. A glass of water on a glass shelf is accompanied by a text in which the artist explains that he has changed "a glass of water into a full-grown oak tree without altering the accidents of the glass of water […] the actual oak tree is physically present but in the form of a glass of water."

10 See Karen Loader, Op.cit. Butcher explains, "Once you start to consider the painted surface as just one surface of a three-dimensional object, you start to think about the transitions between surfaces, and from the object to wall, and once you consider the wall as being part of the work that leads you to think about the whole environment of the piece."

as he has been for twenty years: isolated without distraction in a rural setting in Oxfordshire. Every day the same routine, the same basic materials and process. It sounds monastic …"[11] And, well, that's how it occurred to me when I visited six years later. The solitary, careful and repetitive nature of Butcher's current practice is conducive to (mindless) meditation, and his archival method, whereby peeled traces of his own paint strokes are isolated and sealed within a frame, has clear religious connotations.: "I like the idea of relics, the idea that I'm preserving something…" The vaguely visceral quality of the peelings, like skin, only serves to reinforce our understanding of his new works as reliquaries.

Butcher's proposition is as existentialist as it is ecological. Significantly he chose the title *Endgame* because of its reference to Samuel Beckett's play of the same name, in which four characters await an ending that is at once unspecified and ominous. Like much post-war drama and literature, it derived its dramatic tension largely from a "locked room" scenario; all action happens within one stage set. It is a place of confinement, providing physical protection whilst being a prison. Outside, in Beckett's *Endgame*, is a post-apocalyptic wasteland; outside Butcher's studio – a closed system, a locked room – is a world increasingly warning us of the effects of human-induced climate change.

Art is like religion. Art is a religion. Eric Butcher, having entertained ideas of entering the priesthood as an adolescent, has been an atheist – "aggressively so" – for more than 35 years. He now imagines a life after art as he works away in his studio, recycling, glazing and framing paint strokes he made before his pandemic conversion. The twist in this existentialist tale, as it nears its end, is that Eric Butcher is now making art, artistically, more than ever.

Jonathan Watkins

[11] Paul Carey Kent, 'Richness in Rightness', *Eric Butcher: Time Trial*, Galerie Robert Drees, Hanover and Patrick Heide Gallery, London 2019

T/R.1028, Recycled Paint Fragments: Acrylic, Graphite, Bronze, Acrylic Gel, Oil + Resin on Glass, 109 × 86 cm, 2023

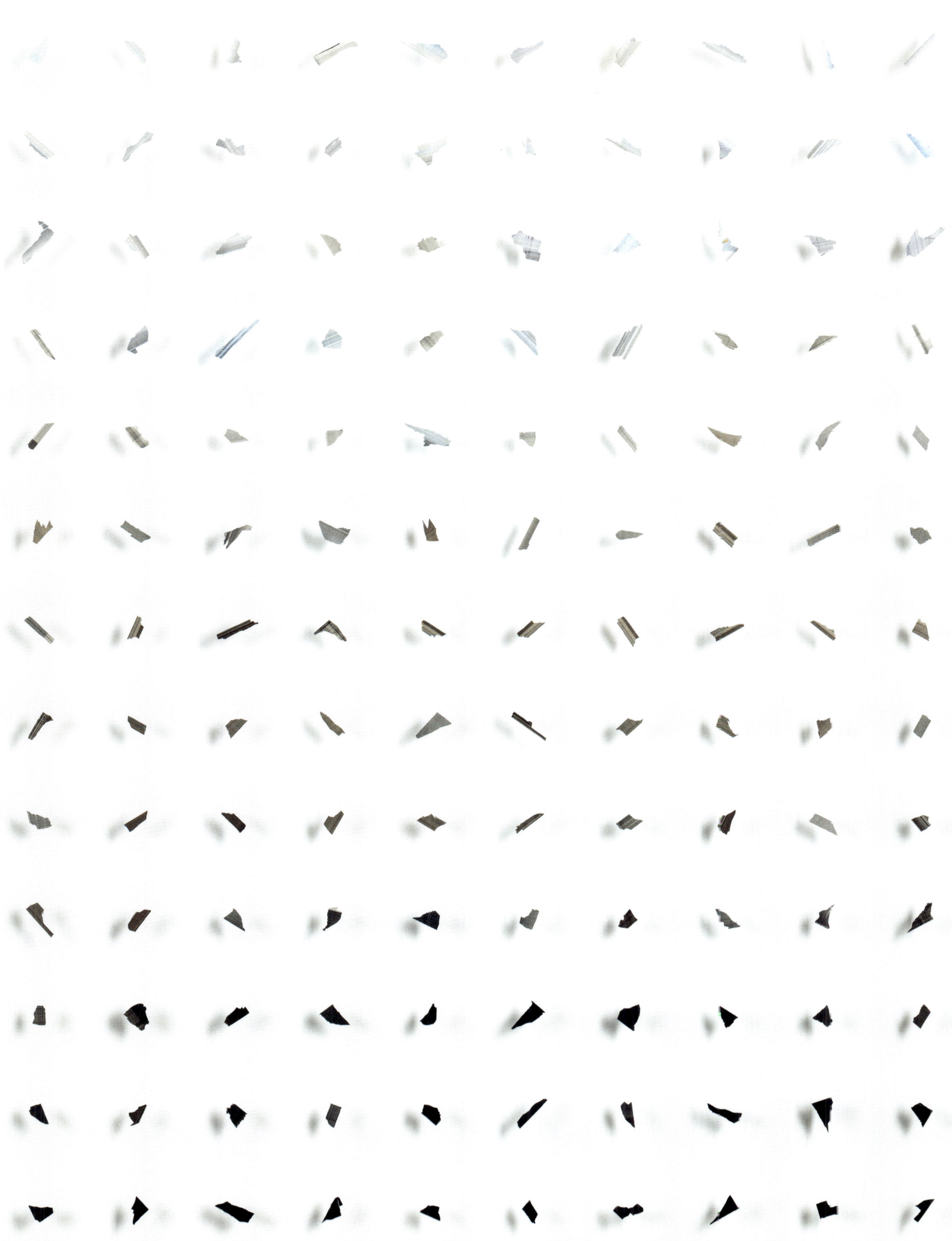

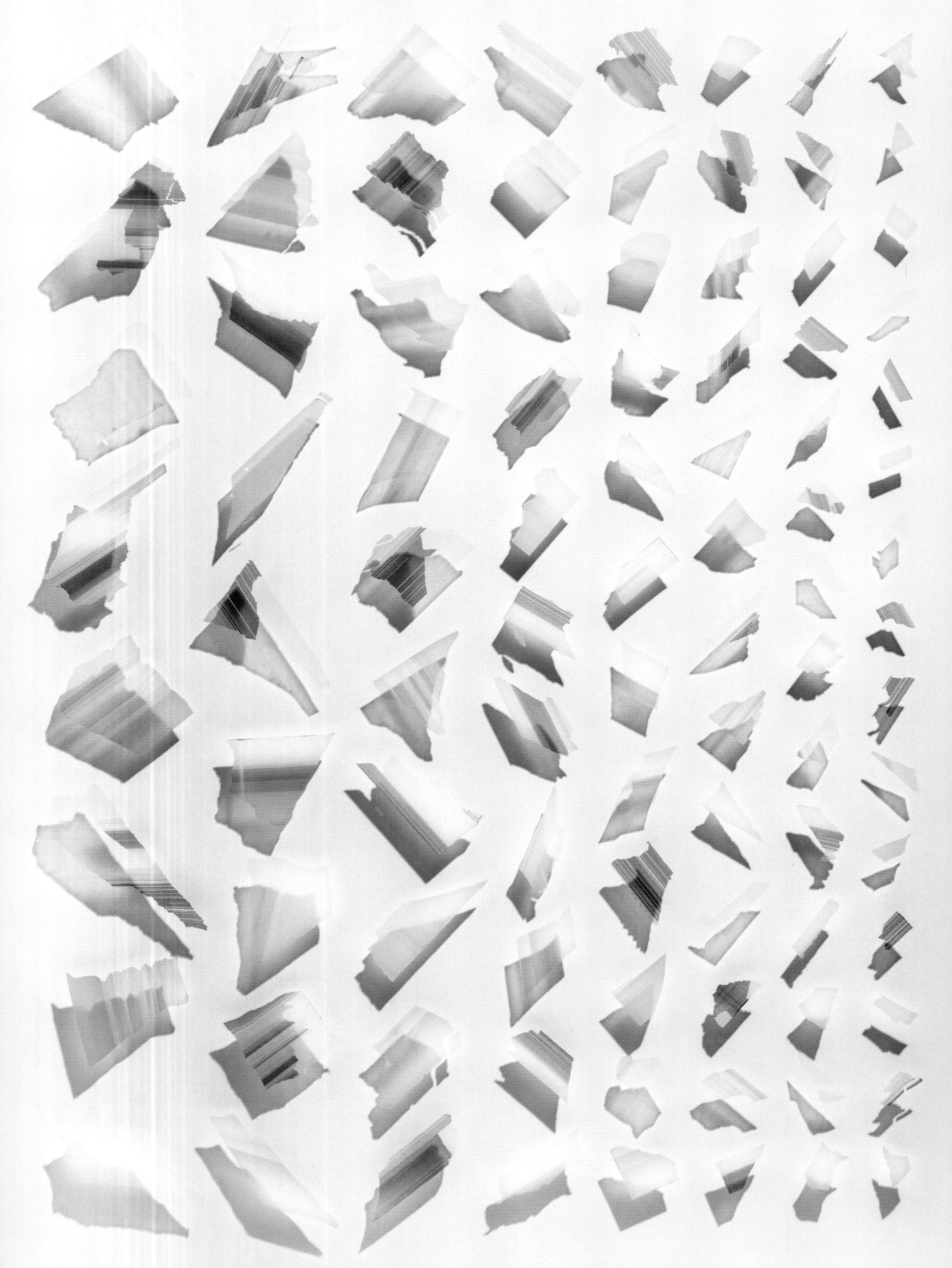

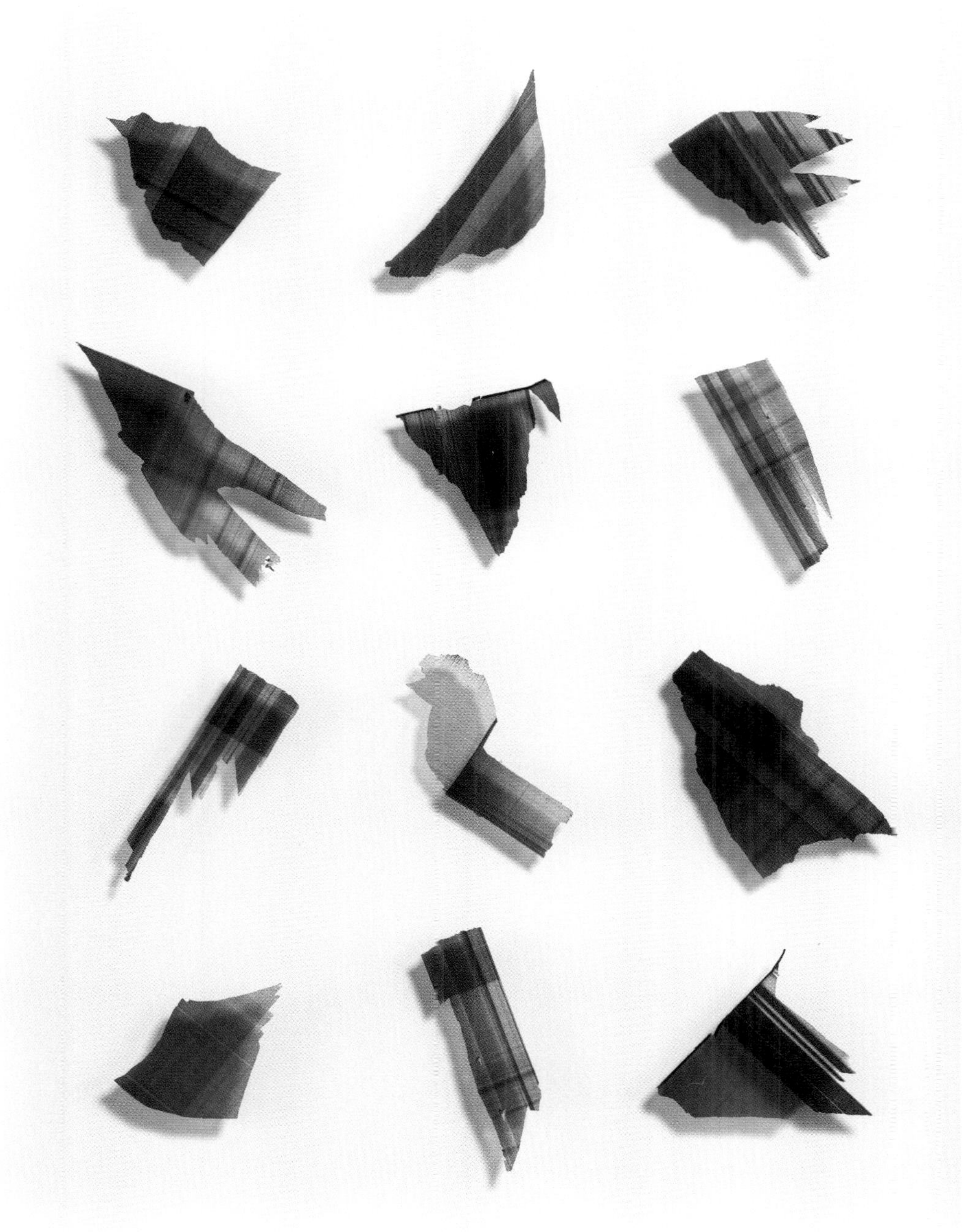

T/R.1114, Recycled Paint Fragments: Graphite, Tin + Acrylic Gel on Glass, 140 × 104 cm, 2025

T/R.940, Recycled Paint Fragments: Graphite, Bronze + Acrylic Gel on Glass, 55 × 44 cm, 2020

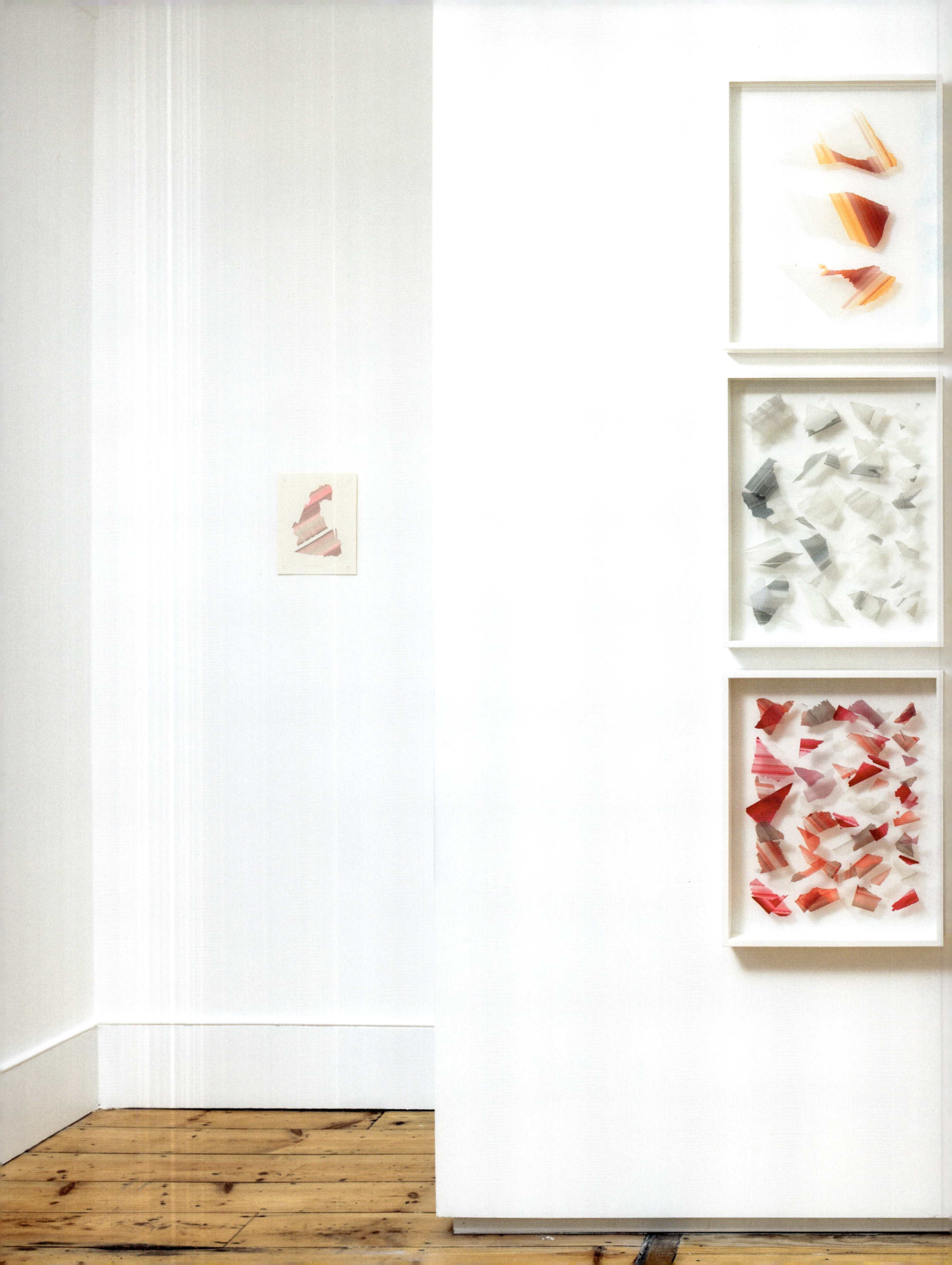

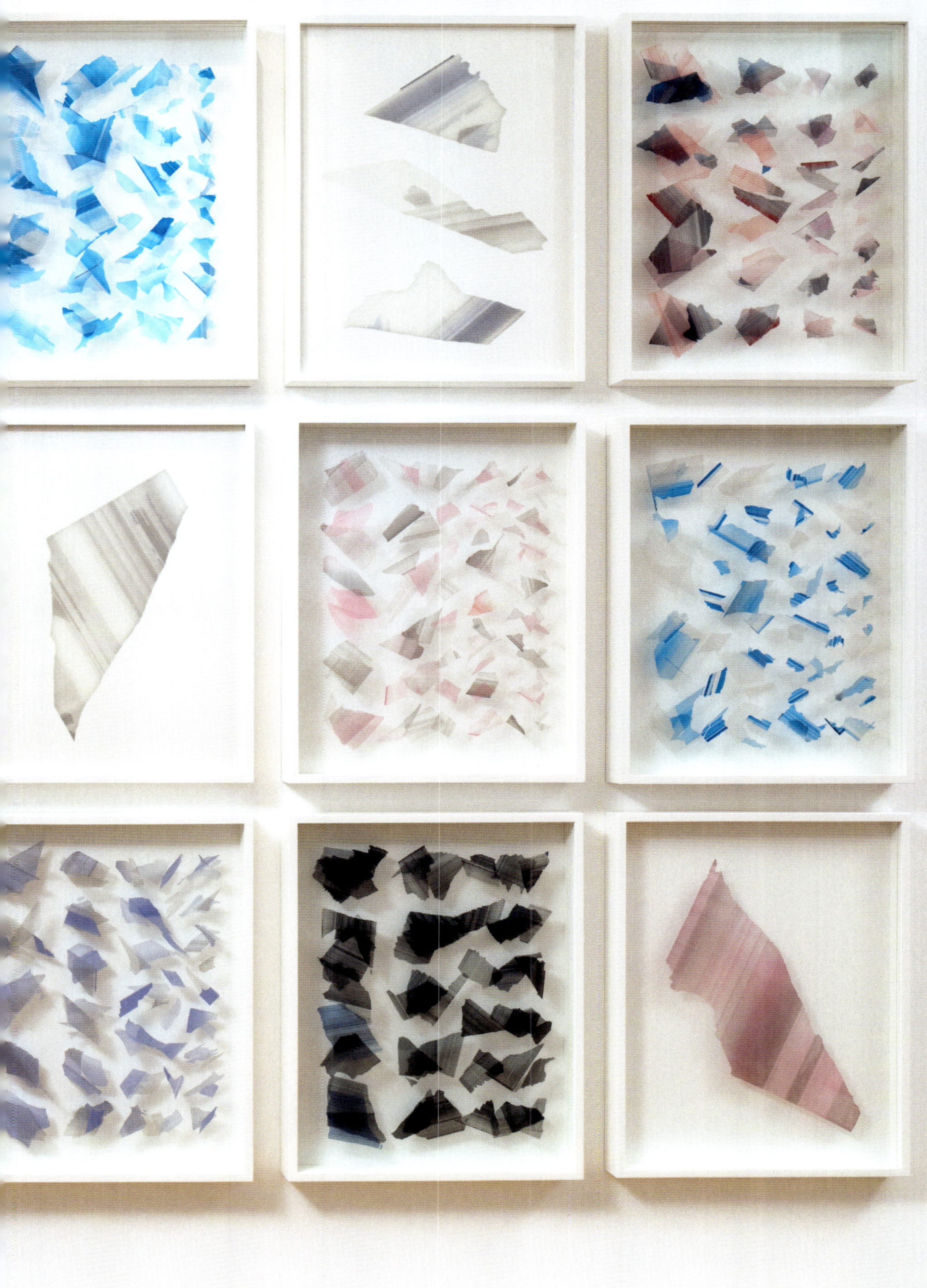

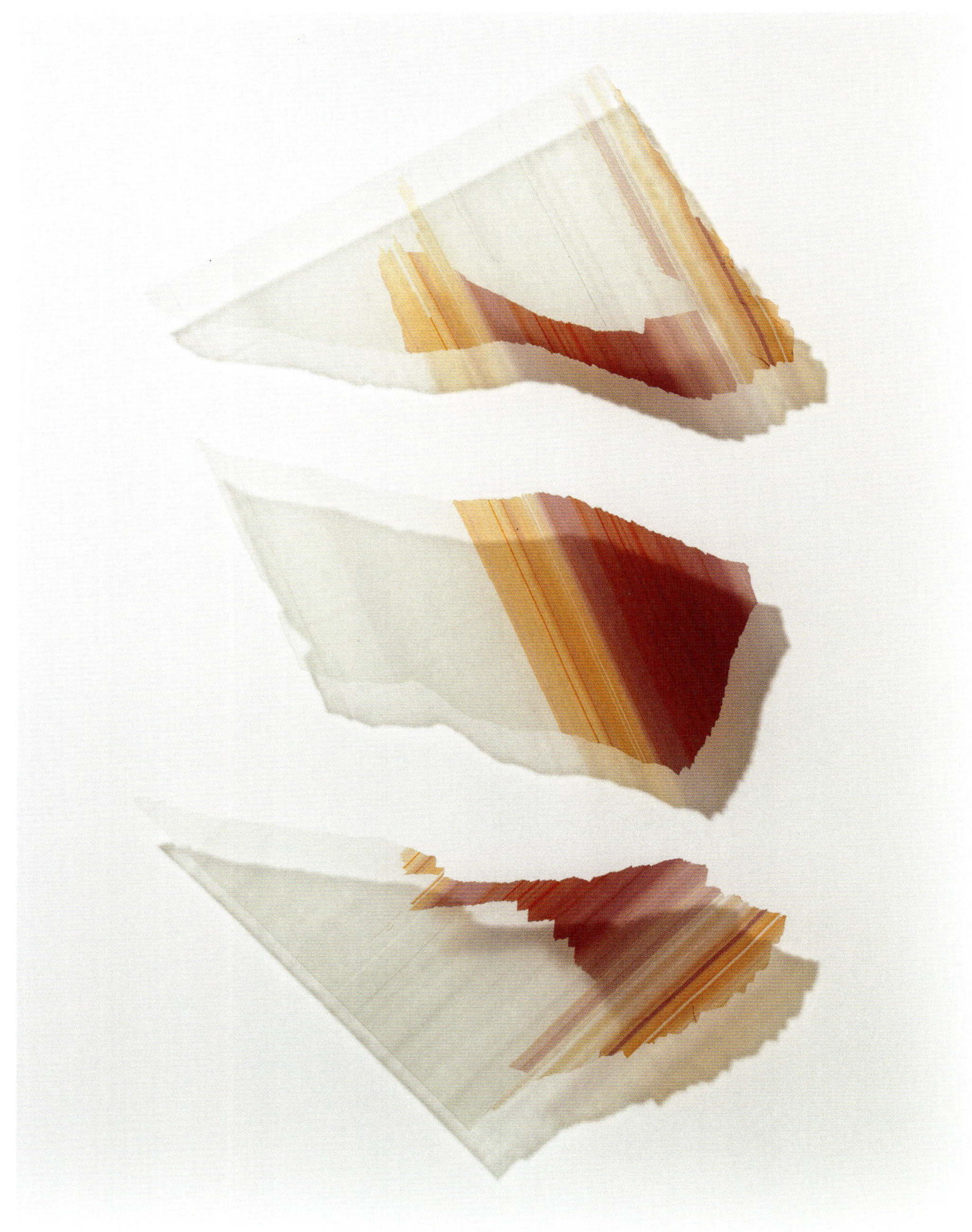

T/R.1072, Recycled Paint Fragments: Acrylic, Graphite, Tin + Acrylic Gel on Glass, 55×44 cm, 2025

T/R.1067, Recycled Paint Fragments: Acrylic, Graphite, Tin + Acrylic Gel on Glass, 55×44 cm, 2025

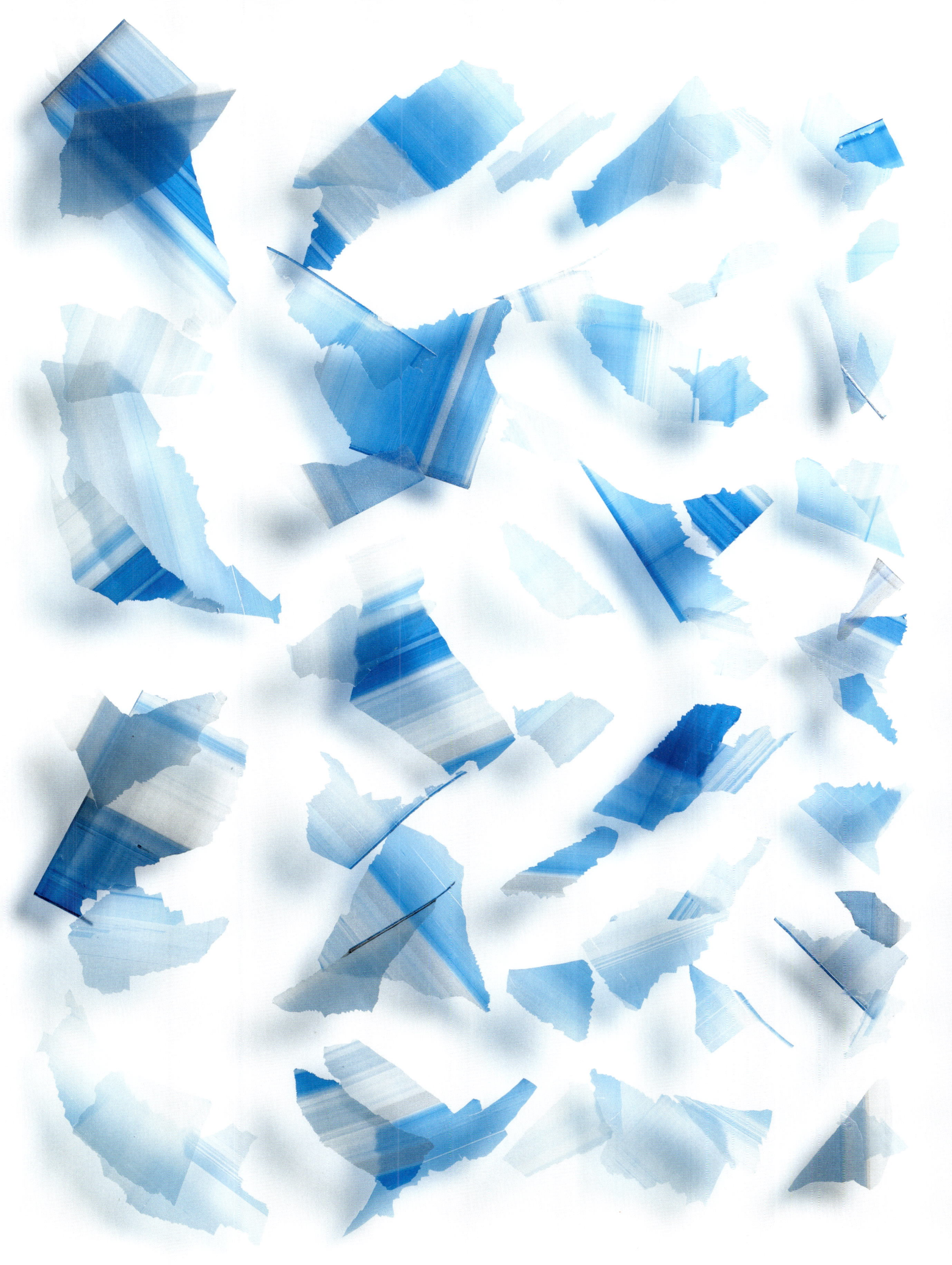

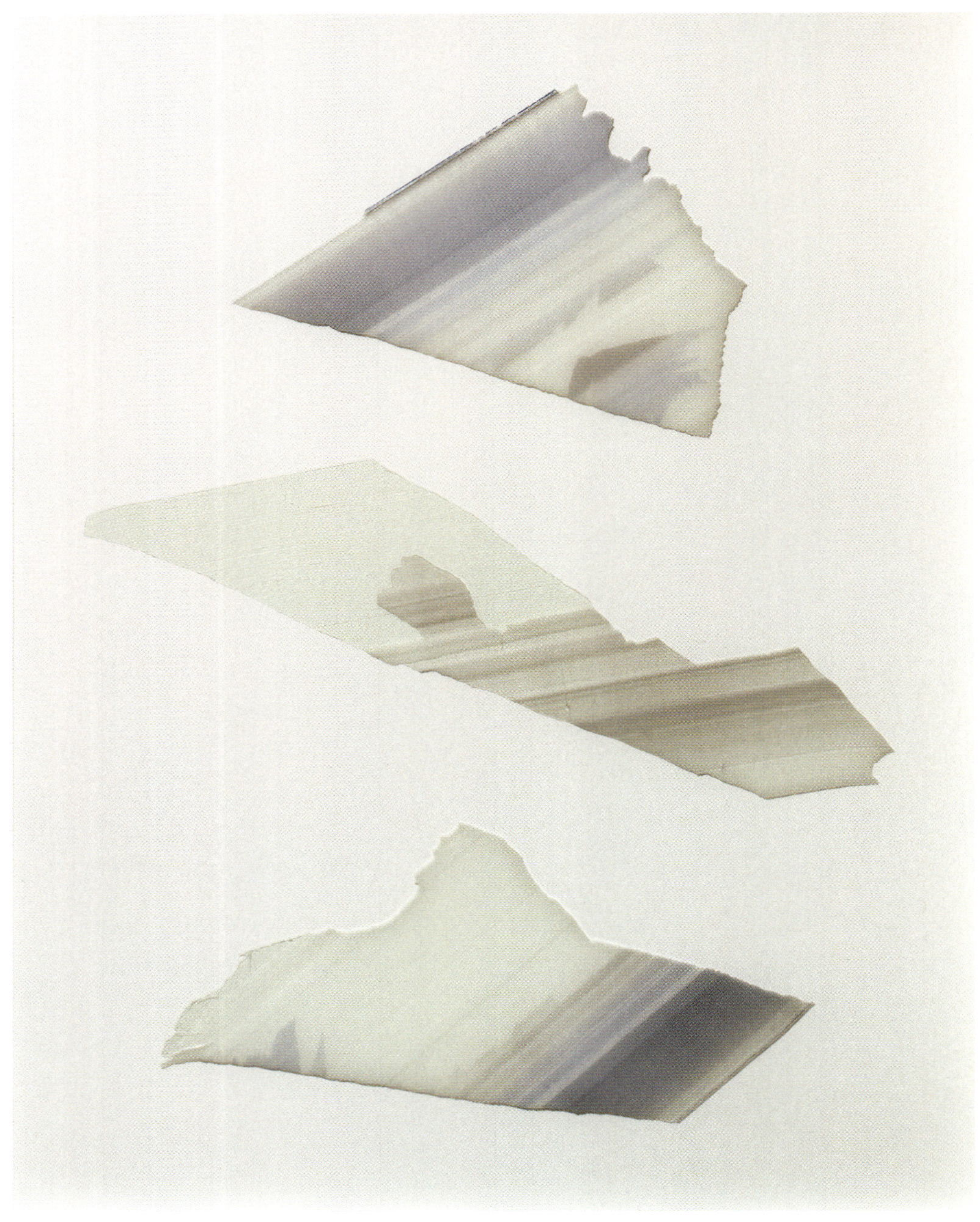

T/R.1073, Recycled Paint Fragments: Acrylic, Graphite, Tin + Acrylic Gel on Glass, 55×44 cm, 2025

T/R.1074, Recycled Paint Fragments: Acrylic, Graphite, Tin + Acrylic Gel on Glass, 55×44 cm, 2025

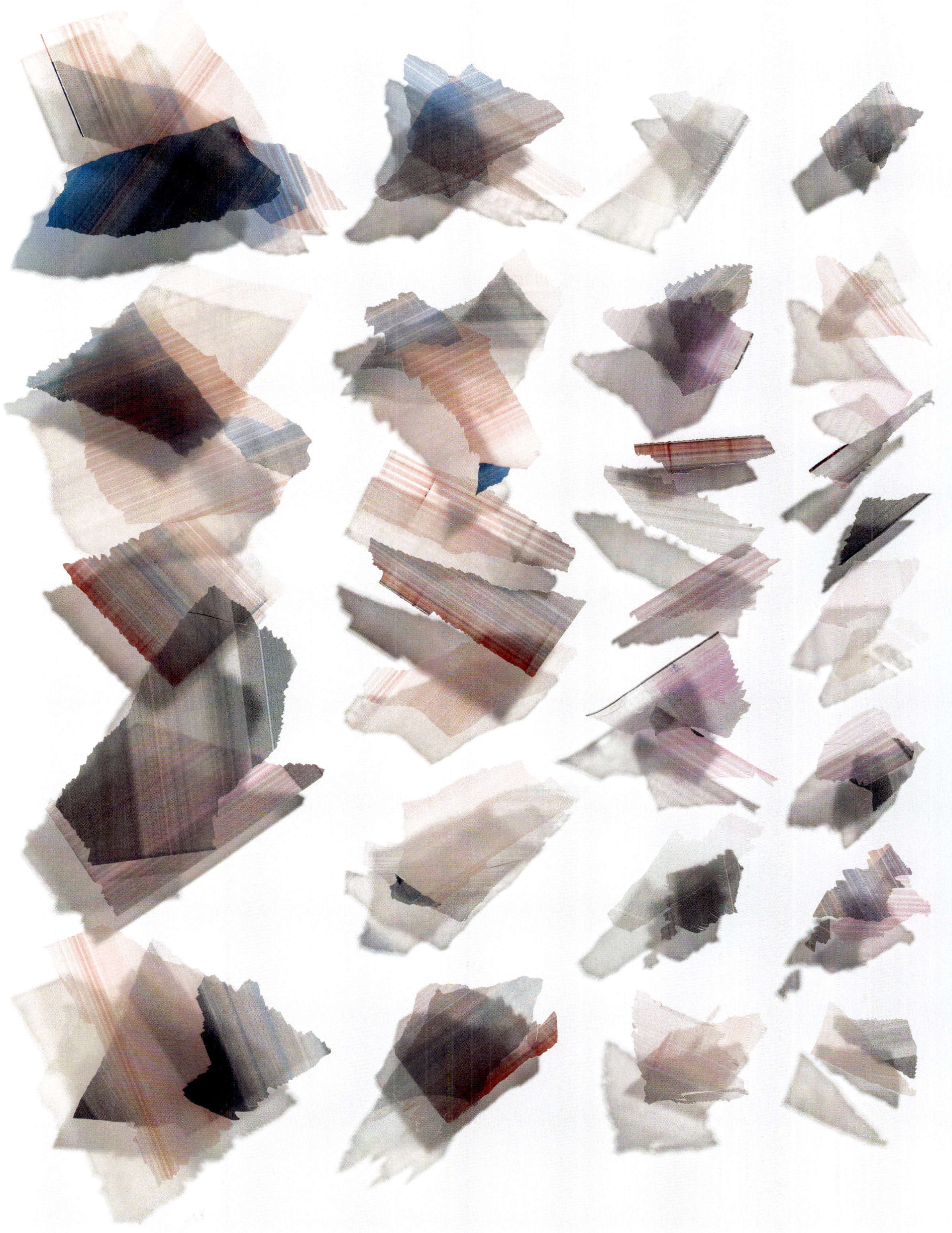

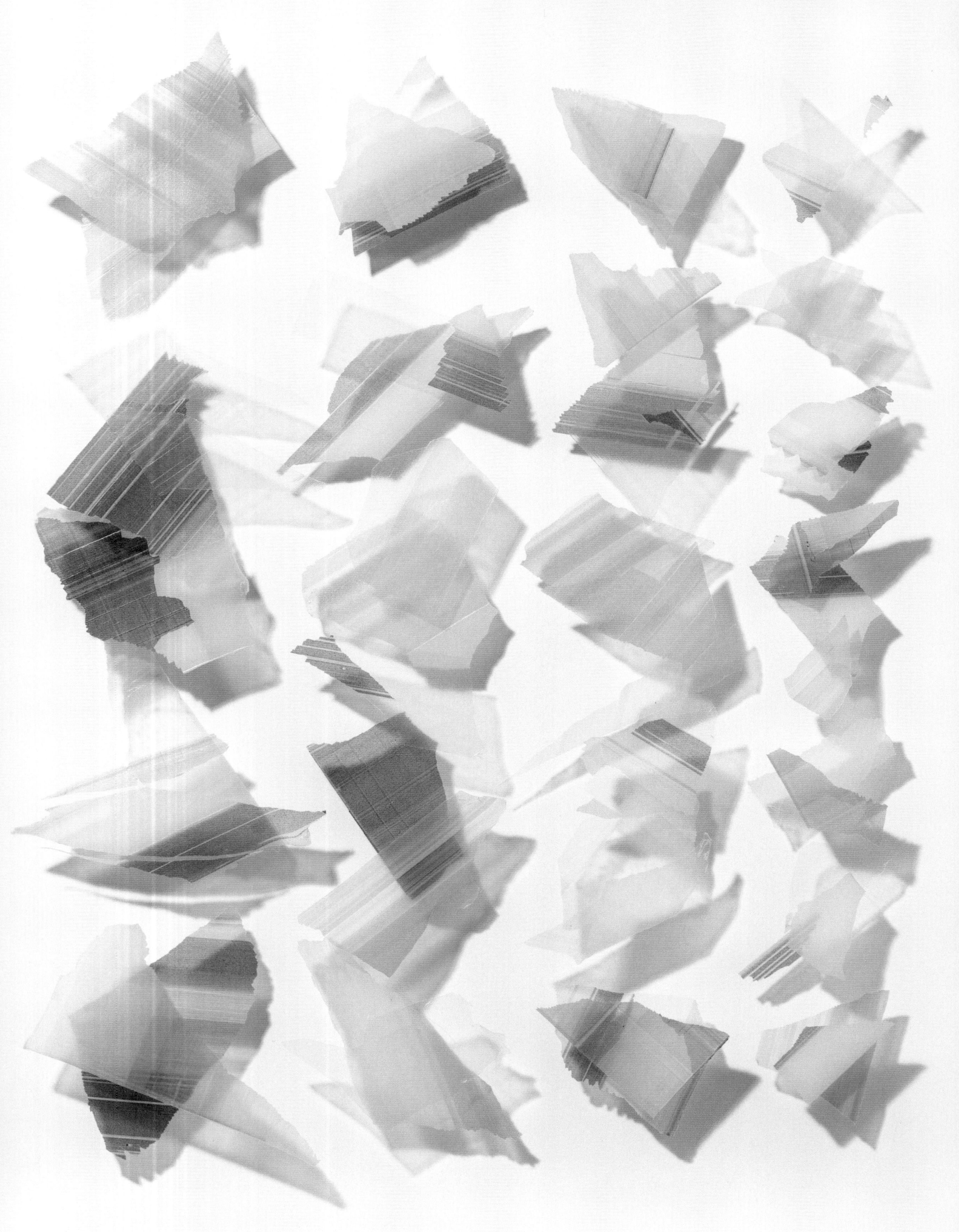

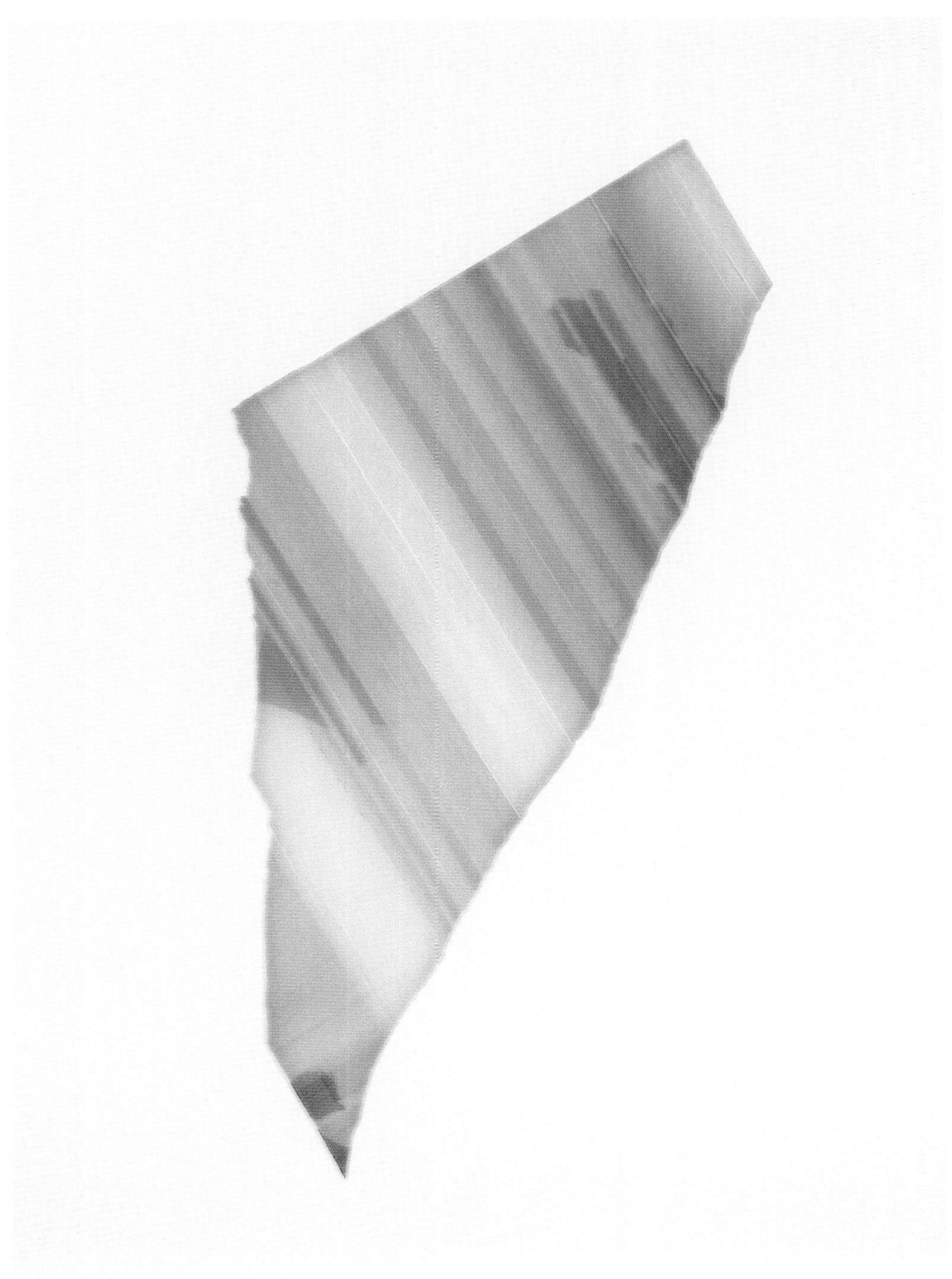

T/R.1075, Recycled Paint Fragments: Acrylic, Graphite, Tin + Acrylic Gel on Glass, 55×44 cm, 2025

T/R.1076, Recycled Paint Fragment: Acrylic, Graphite, Tin + Acrylic Gel on Glass, 55×44 cm, 2025

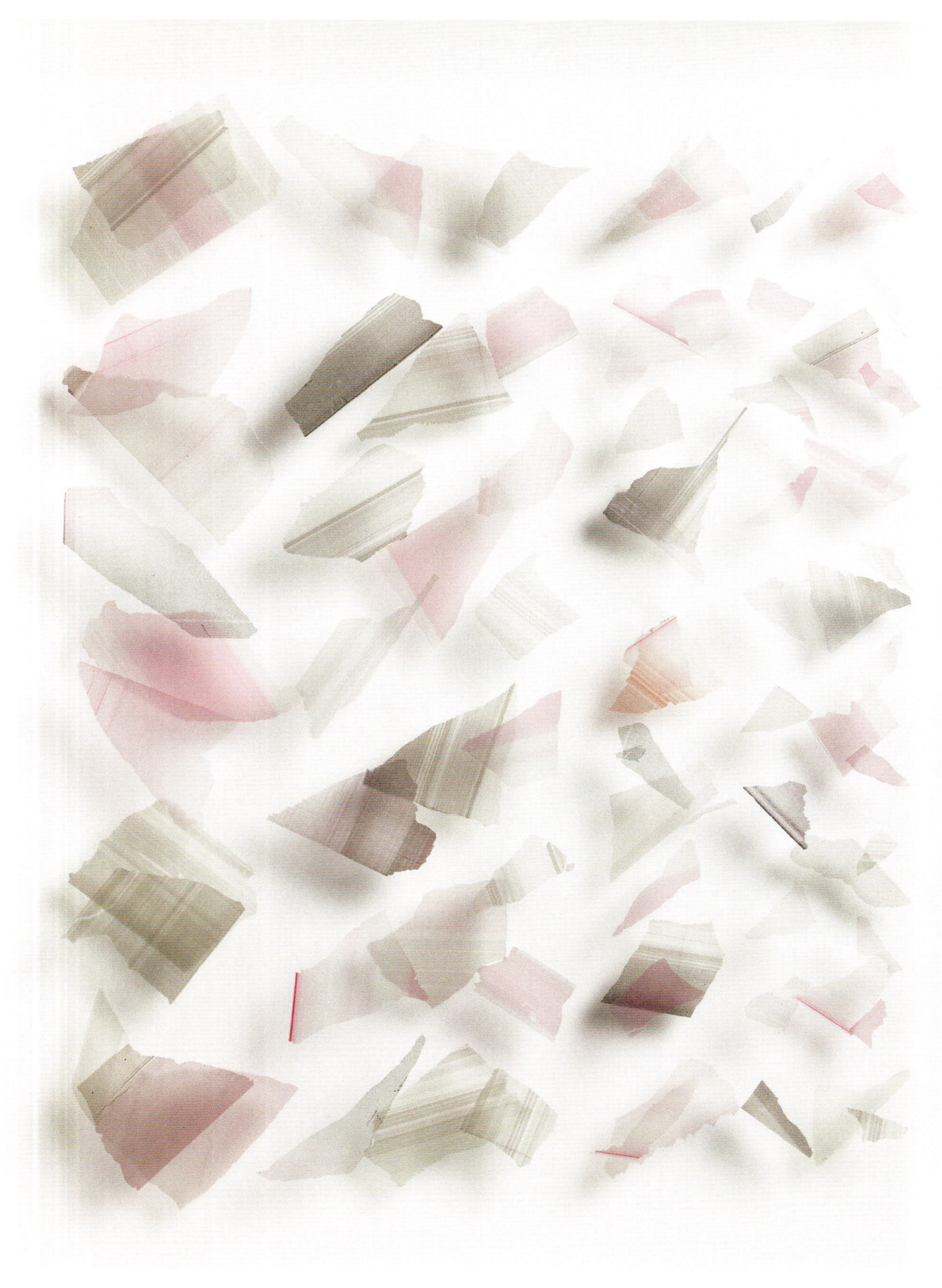

T/R.1065, Recycled Paint Fragments: Acrylic, Graphite, Tin + Acrylic Gel on Glass, 55 × 44 cm, 2025

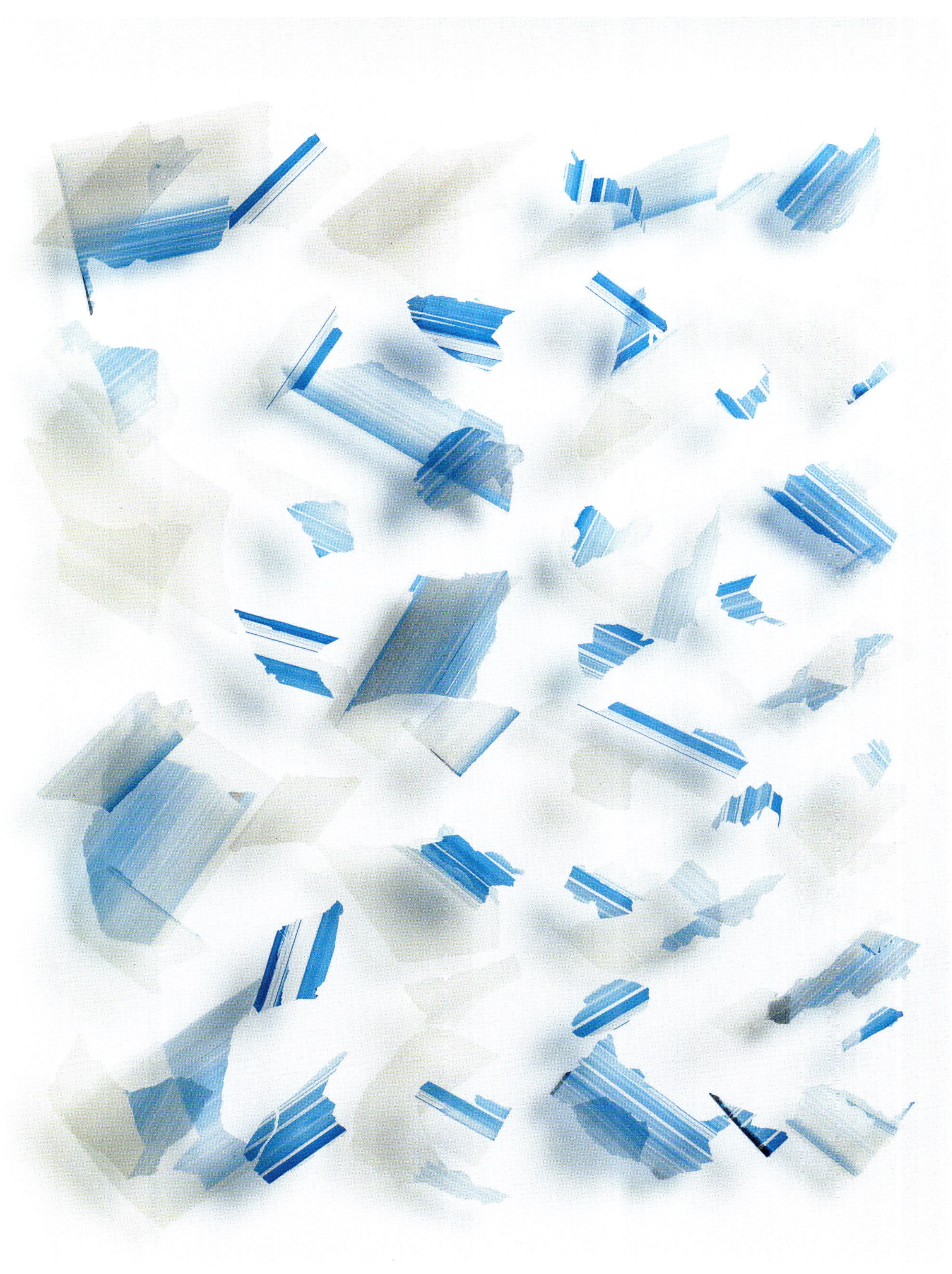

T/R.1066, Recycled Paint Fragments: Acrylic, Graphite, Tin + Acrylic Gel on Glass, 55×44 cm, 2025

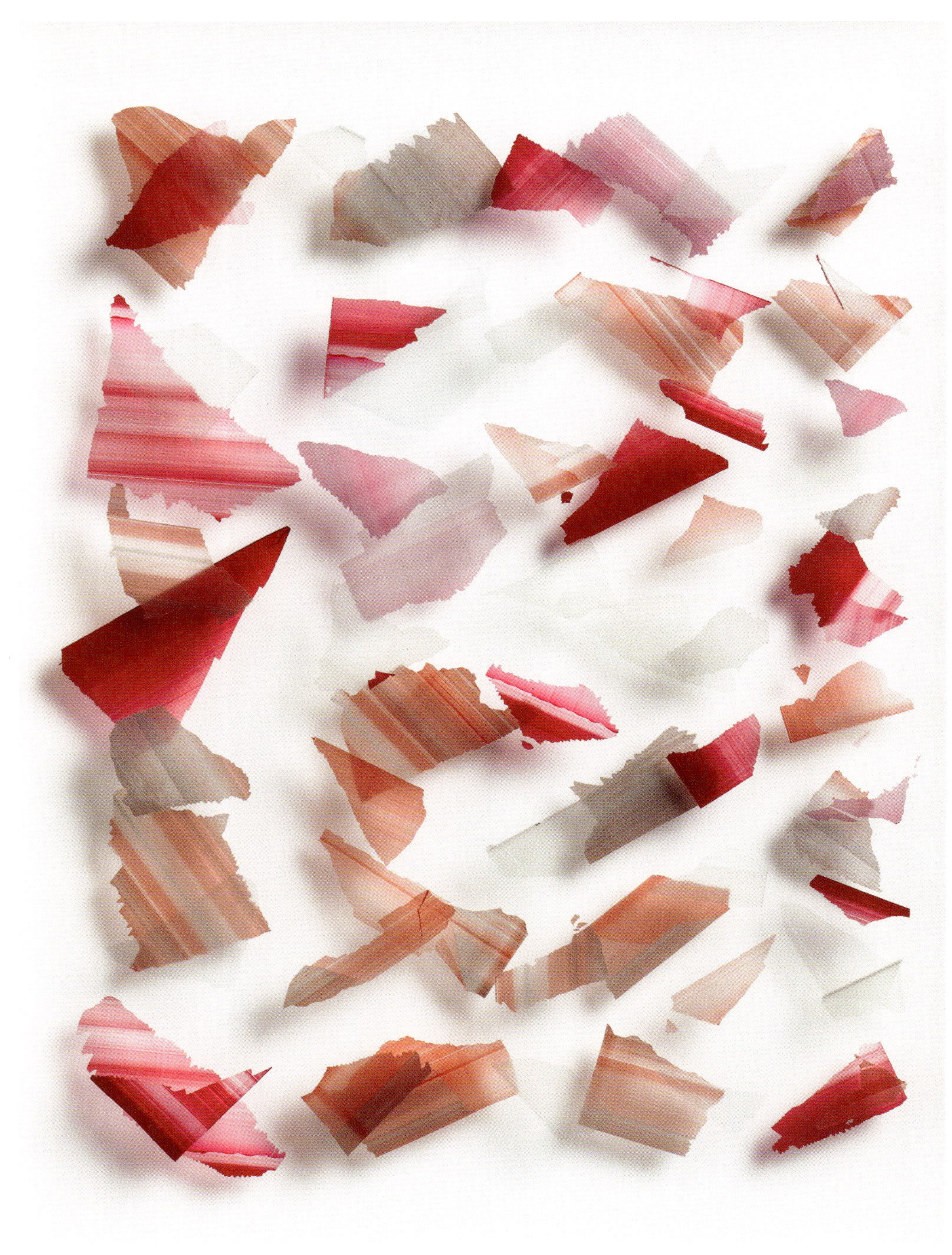

T/R.1063, Recycled Paint Fragments: Acrylic, Graphite, Tin + Acrylic Gel on Glass, 55×44 cm, 2025

T/R.1077, Recycled Paint Fragments: Acrylic, Graphite, Tin + Acrylic Gel on Glass, 55×44 cm, 2025

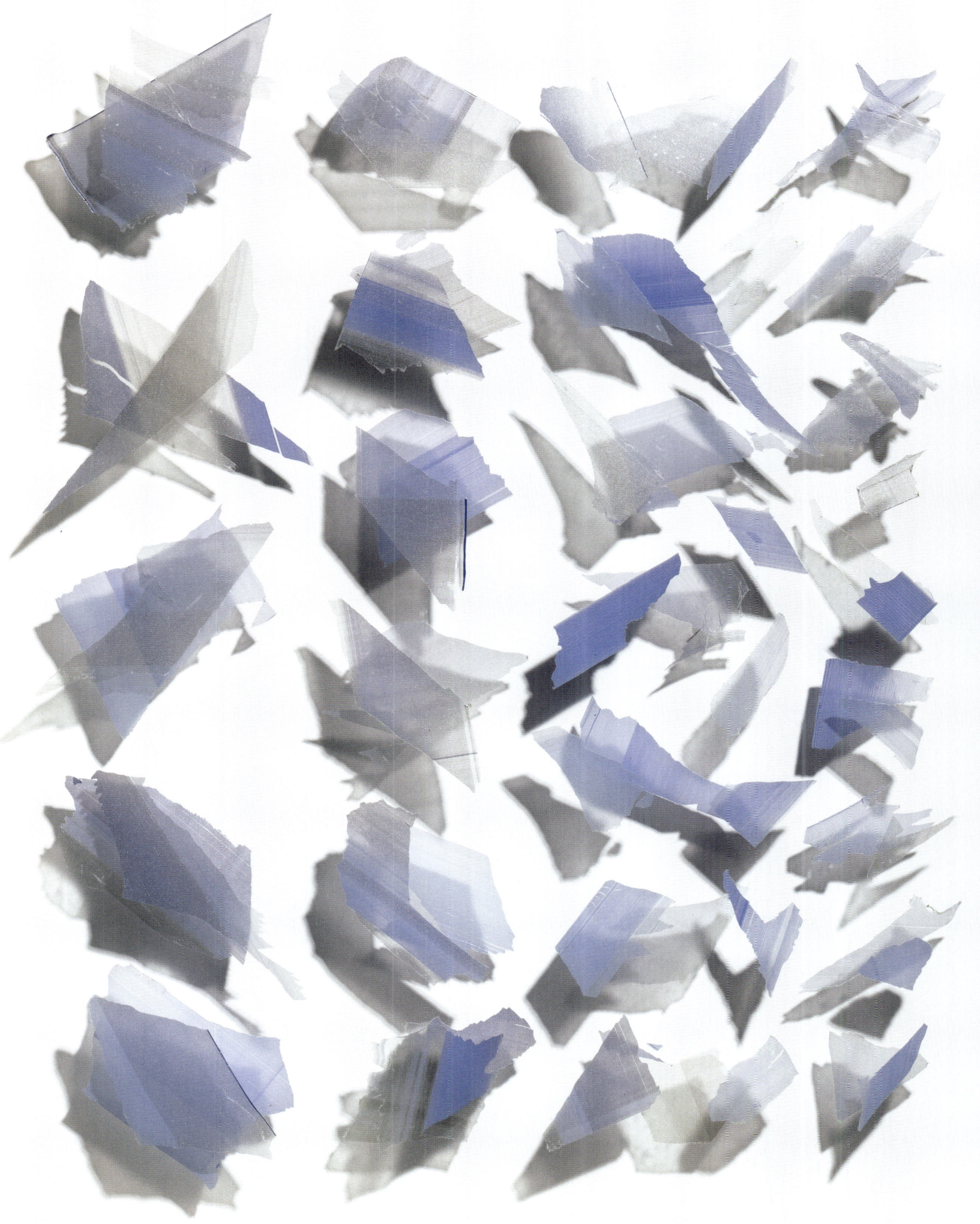

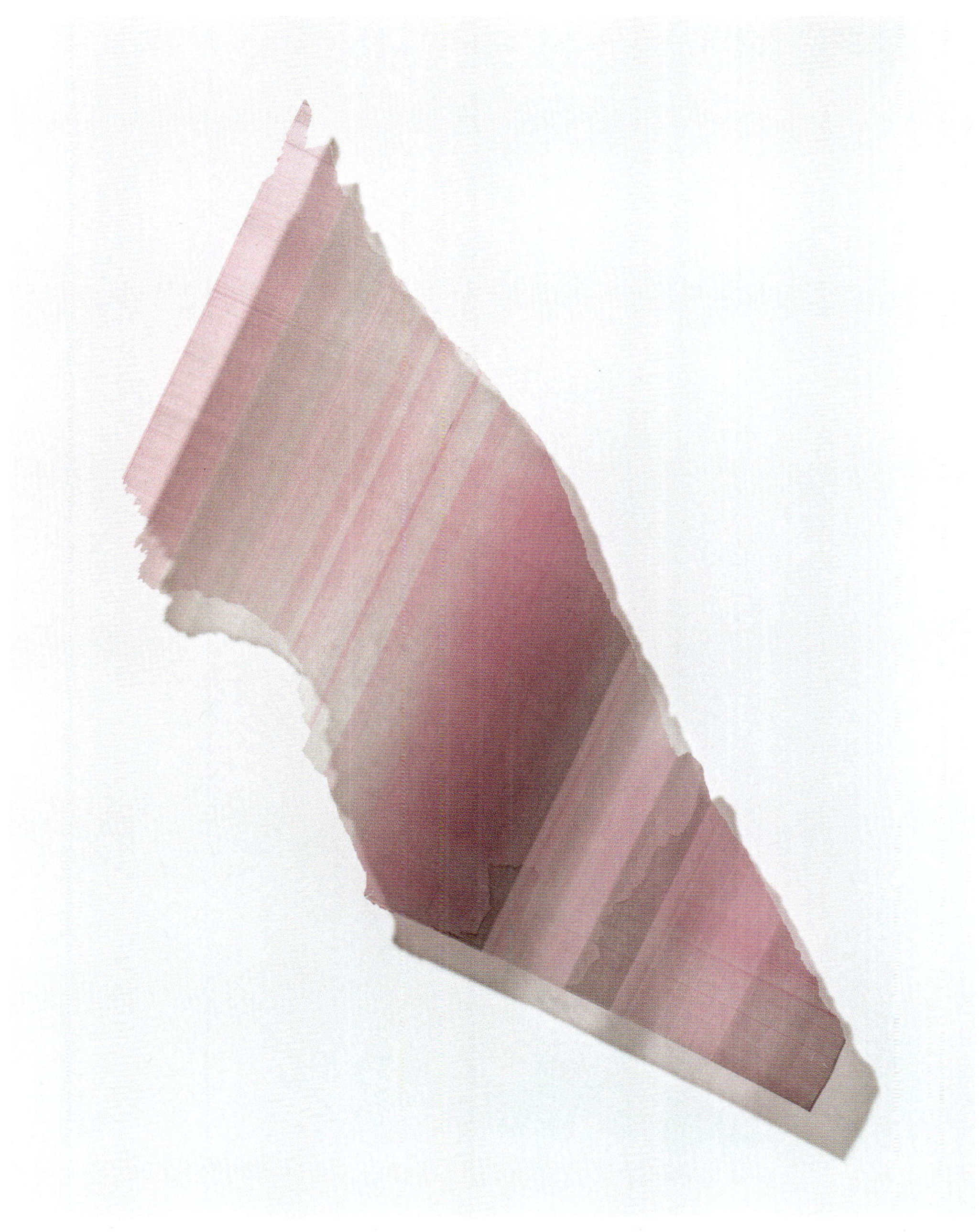

T/R.1078, Recycled Paint Fragments: Acrylic, Graphite, Tin + Acrylic Gel on Glass, 55 × 44 cm, 2025

T/P.1079, Recycled Paint Fragment: Acrylic, Graphite, Tin + Acrylic Gel on Glass, 55 × 44 cm, 2025

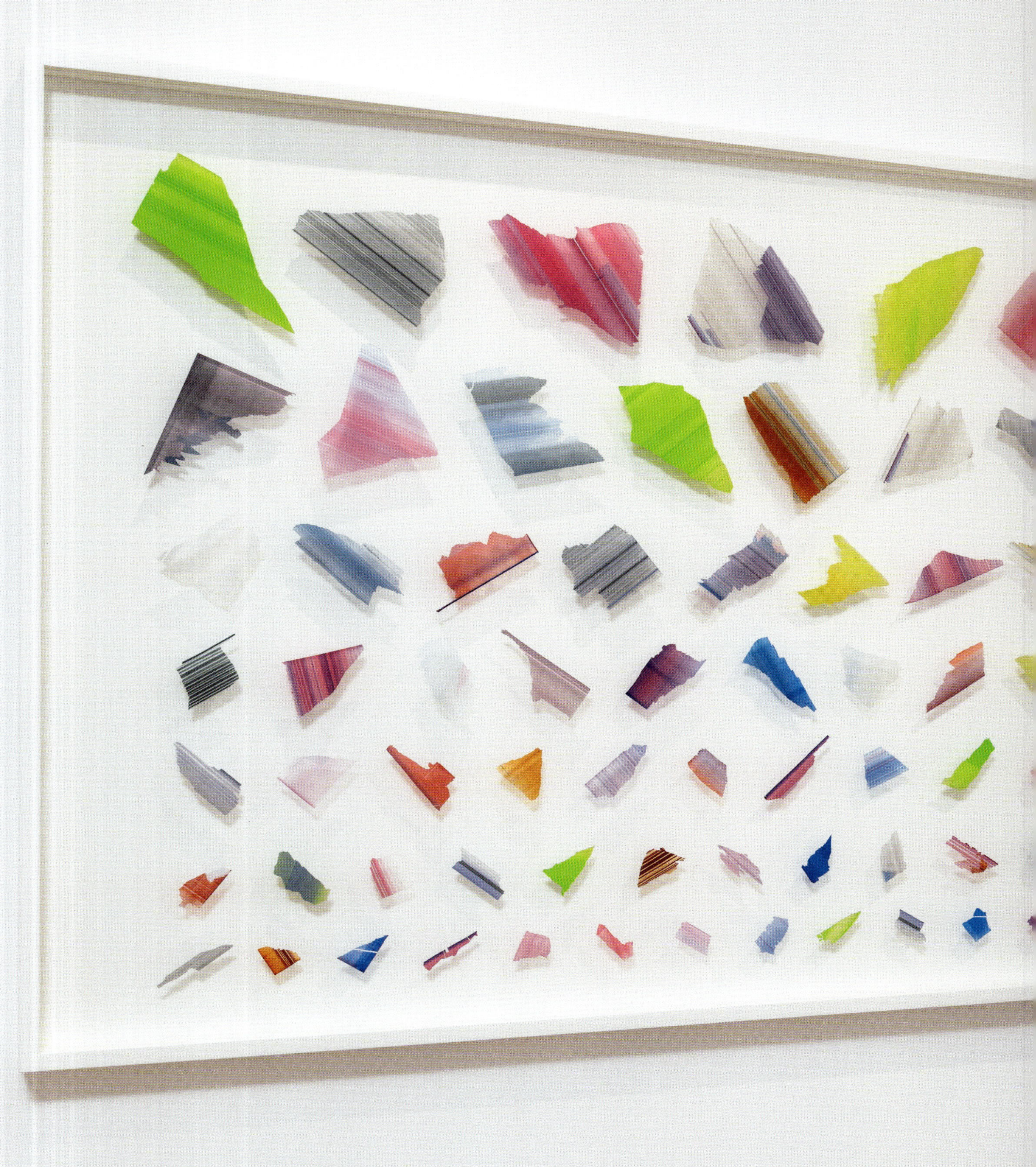

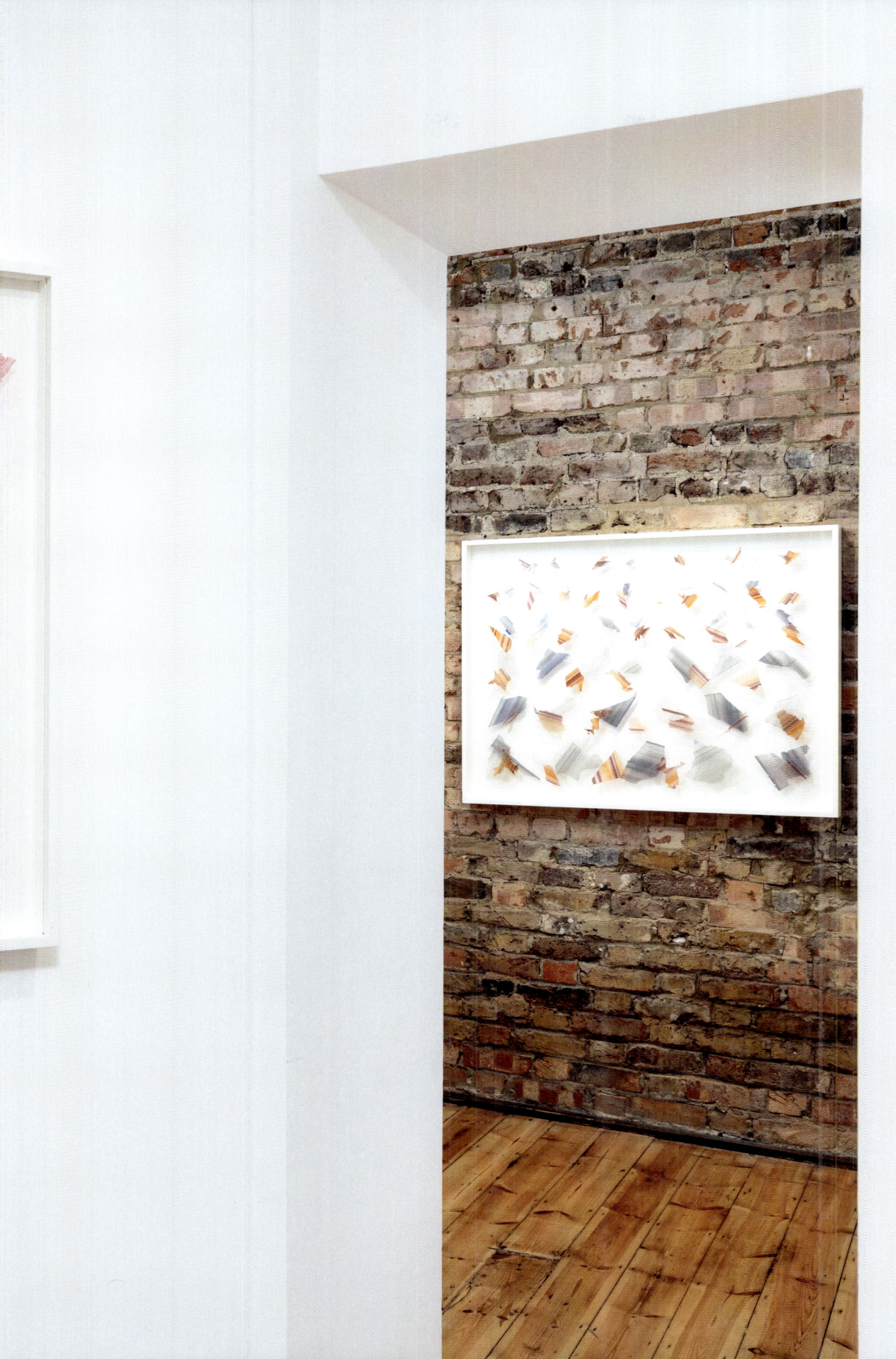

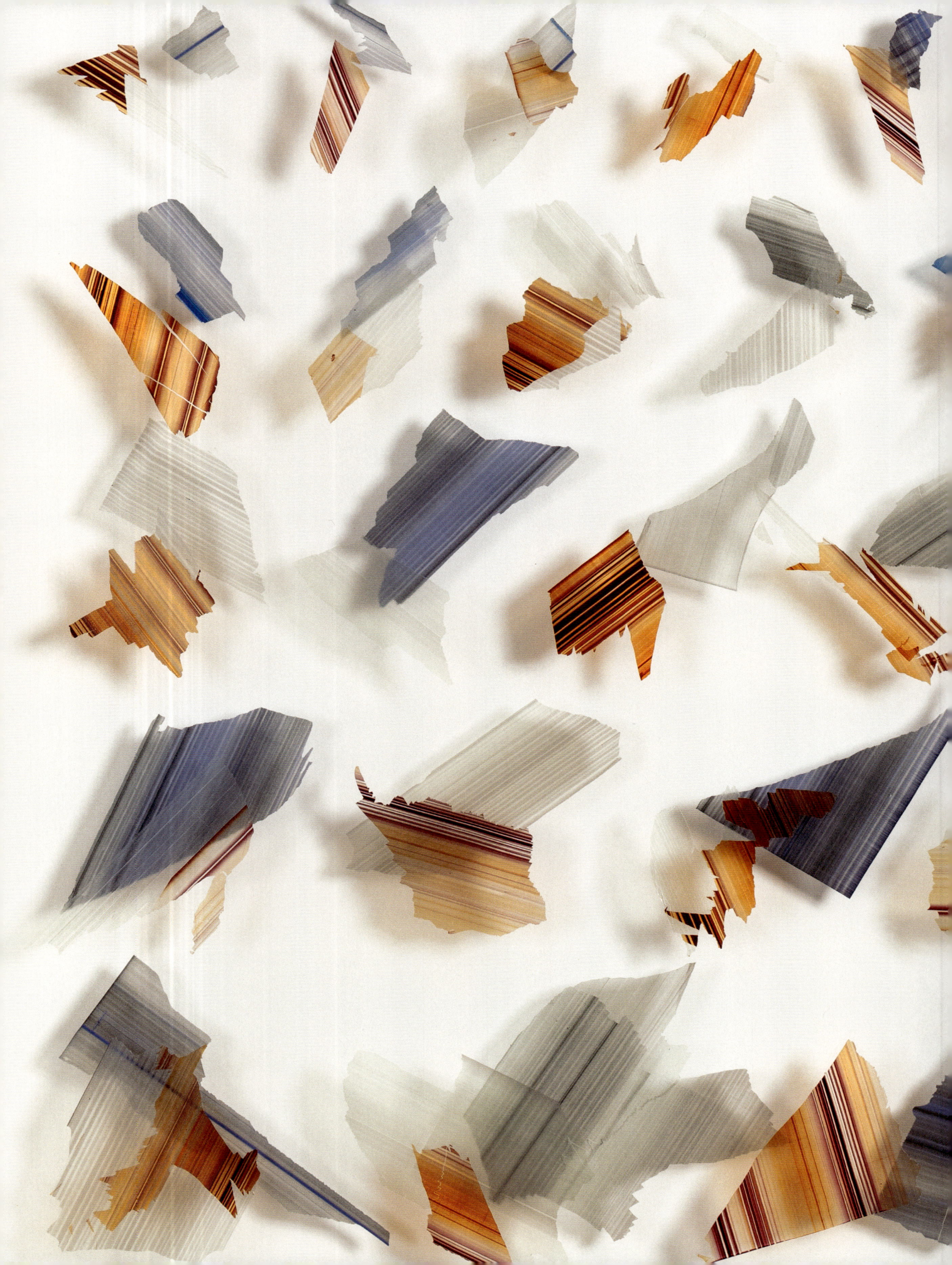

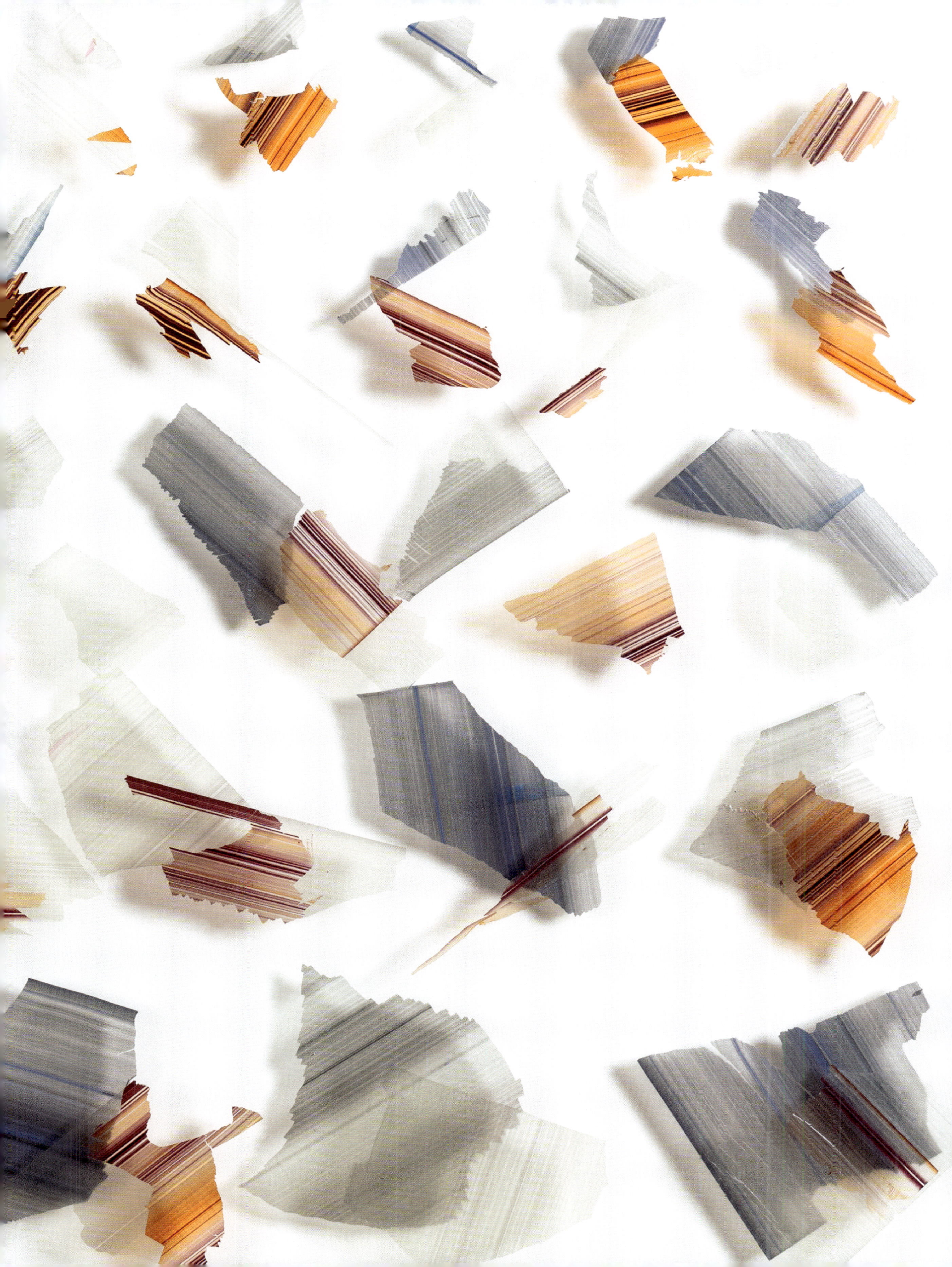

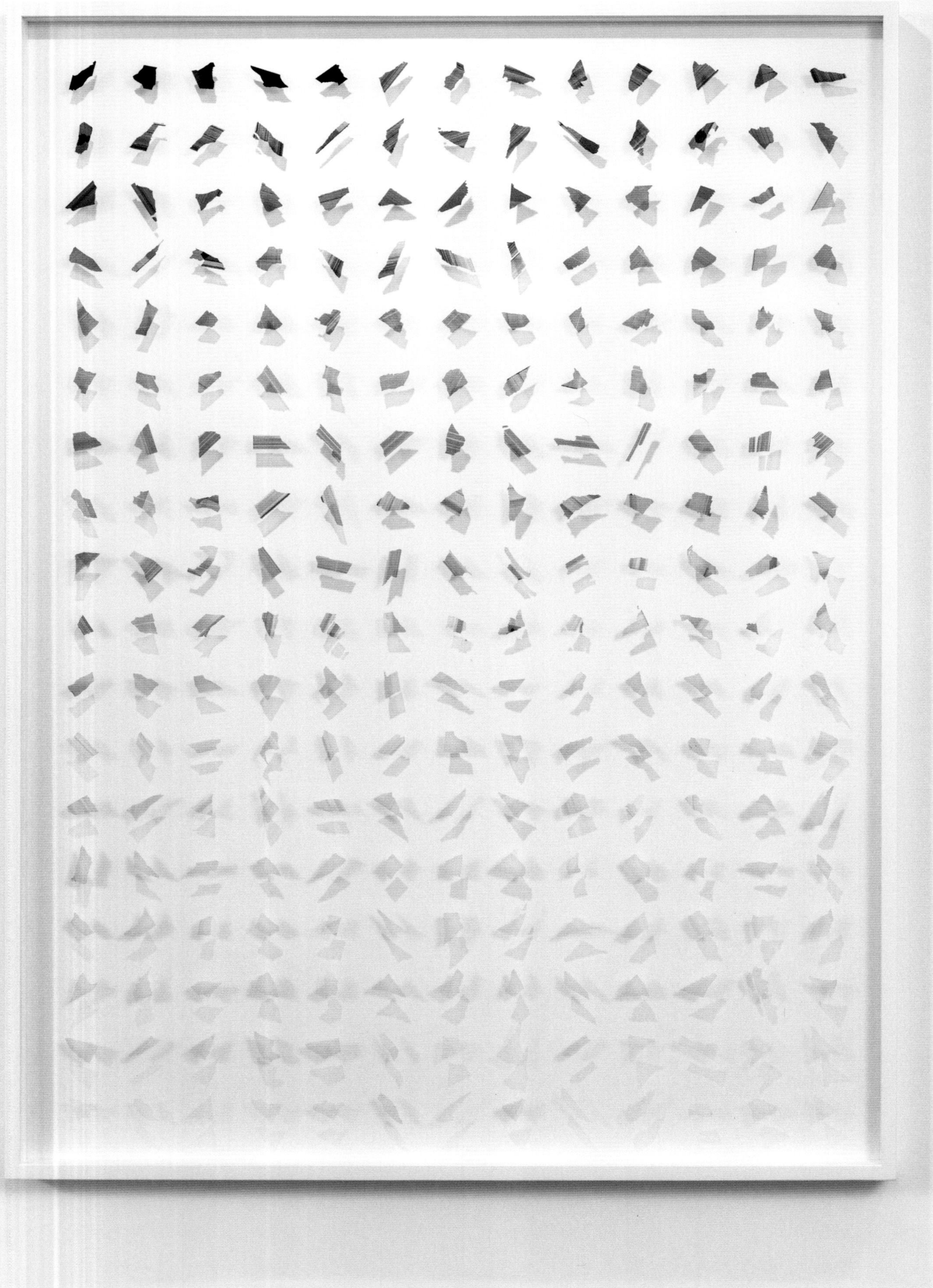

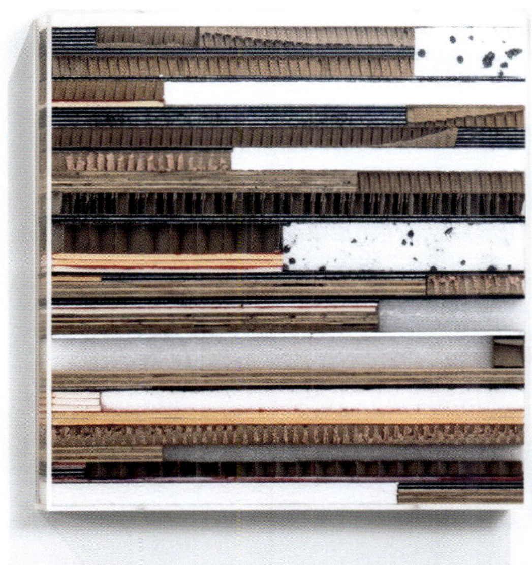

T/R.1080, Recycled Paint Fragments: Acrylic, Graphite, Tin + Acrylic Gel on Glass, 140×104 cm, 2025

P/R.1081, Studio Detritus: Aluminium, Cardboard, Packing Foam, Plywood, Foamboard, Composite Board in Plexiglas, 40×38 cm, 2025

Previous double page:
T/R.1039 (detail), Recycled Paint Fragments: Acrylic, Graphite + Acrylic Gel on Glass, 86×109 cm, 2024

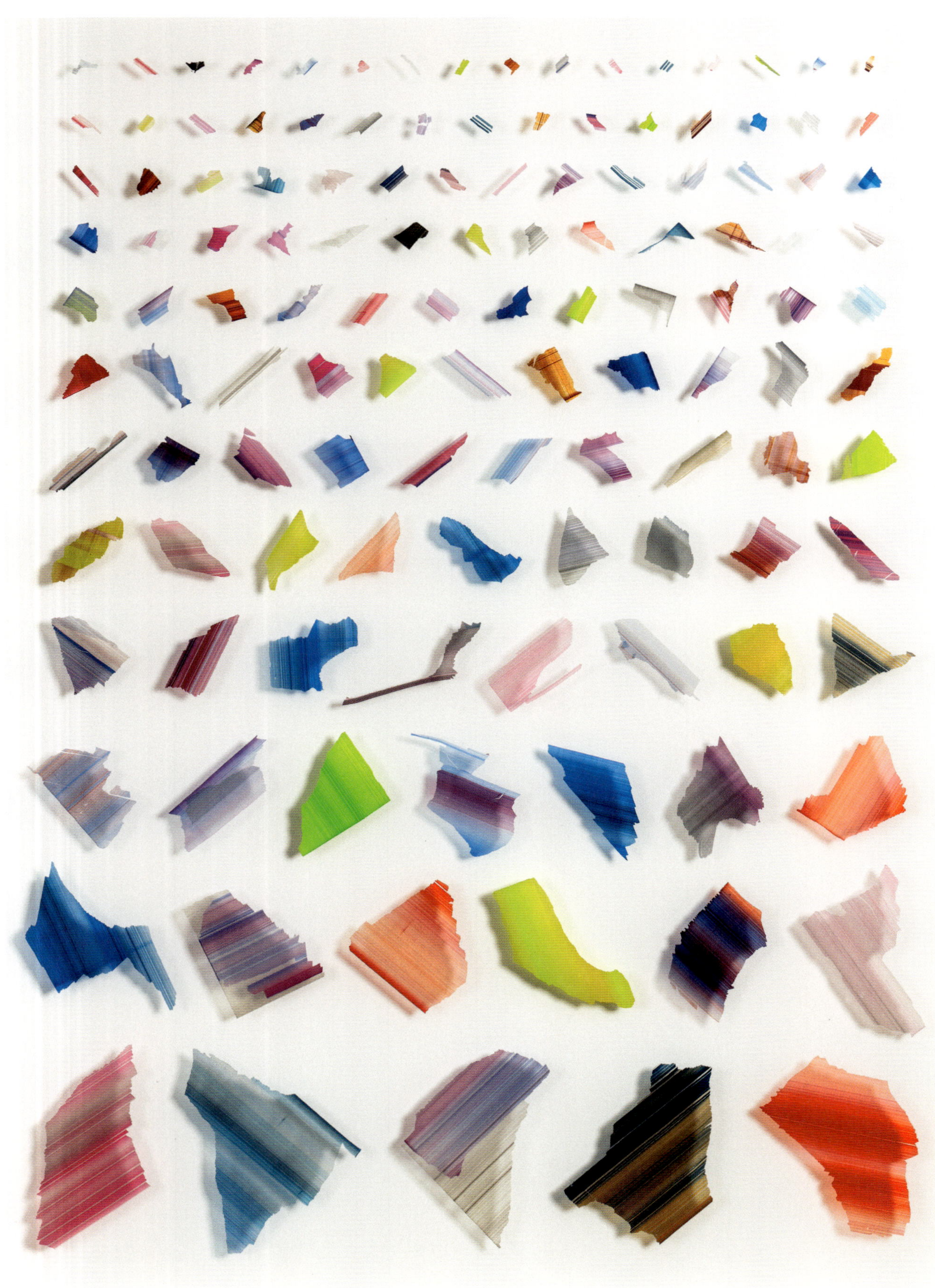

T/R.1051, Recycled Paint Fragments: Acrylic, Graphite + Acrylic Gel on Glass, 140 × 104 cm, 2024

T/R.1006, Recycled Paint Fragments: Acrylic, Graphite + Acrylic Gel on Glass, 109 × 86 cm, 2022

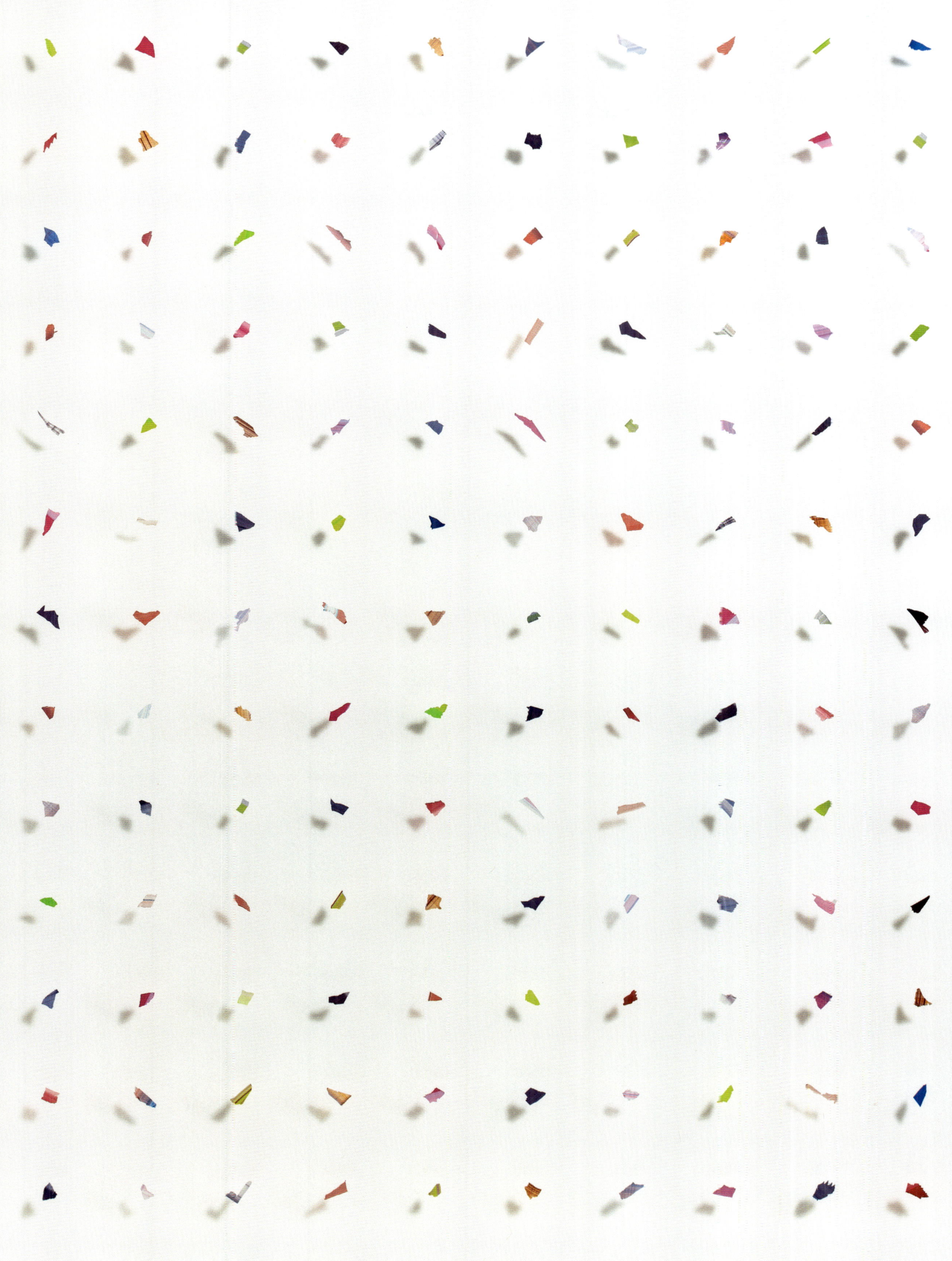

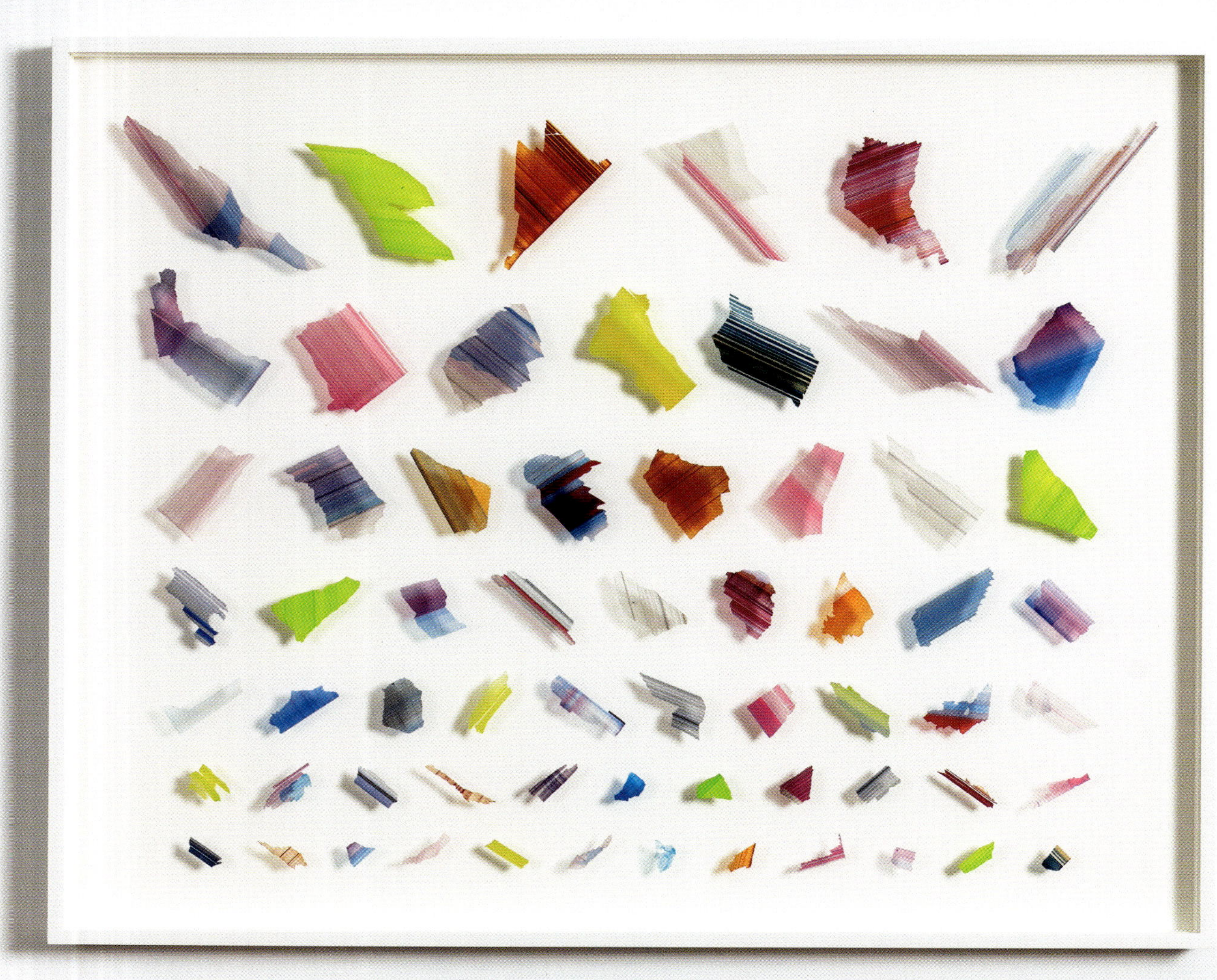

T/R.1038, Recycled Paint Fragments: Acrylic, Graphite + Acrylic Gel on Glass, 104 × 140 cm, 2024

Following double page:
T/R.1022, Recycled Paint Fragments: Acrylic, Graphite + Acrylic Gel on Glass, 44 × 55 cm, 2023

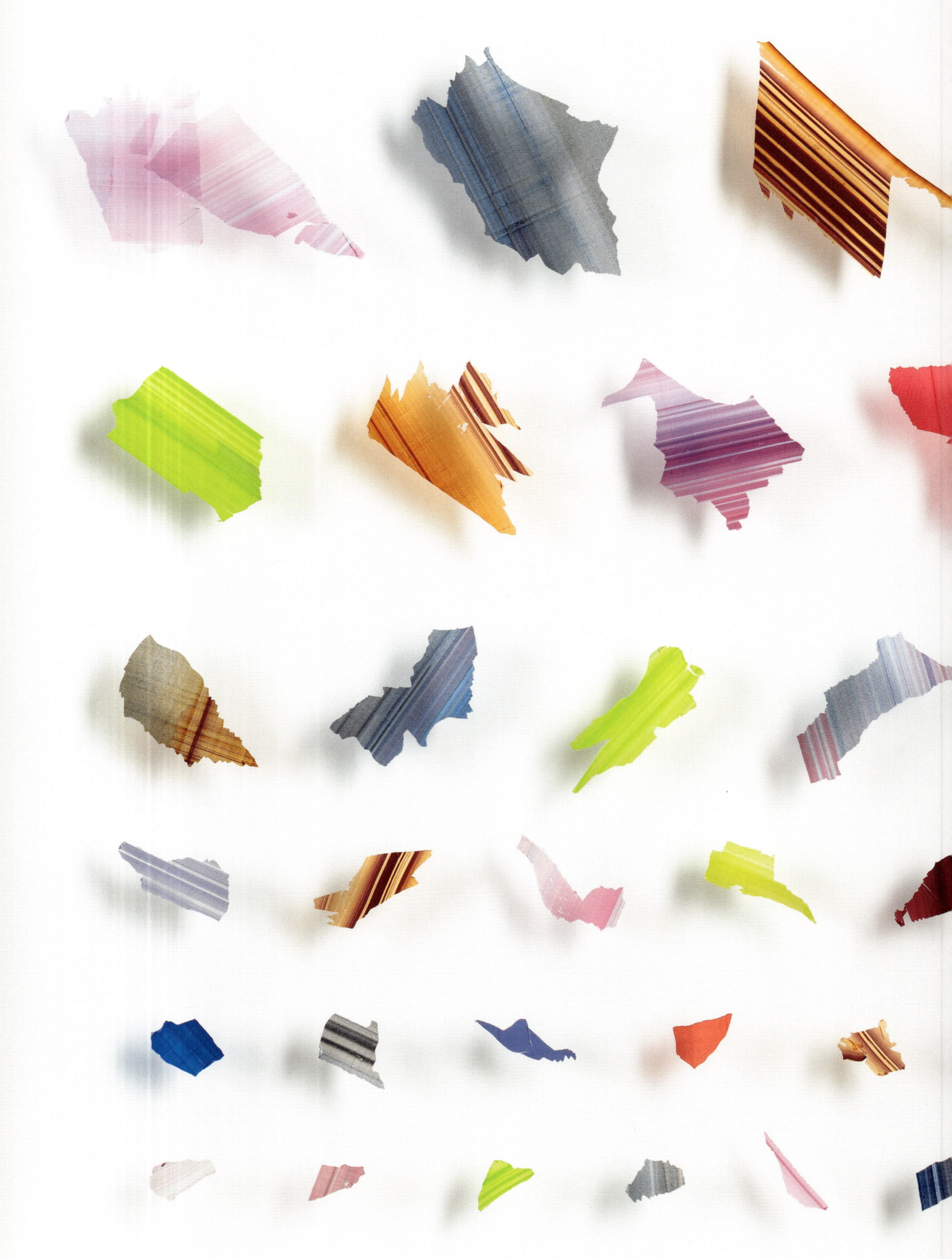

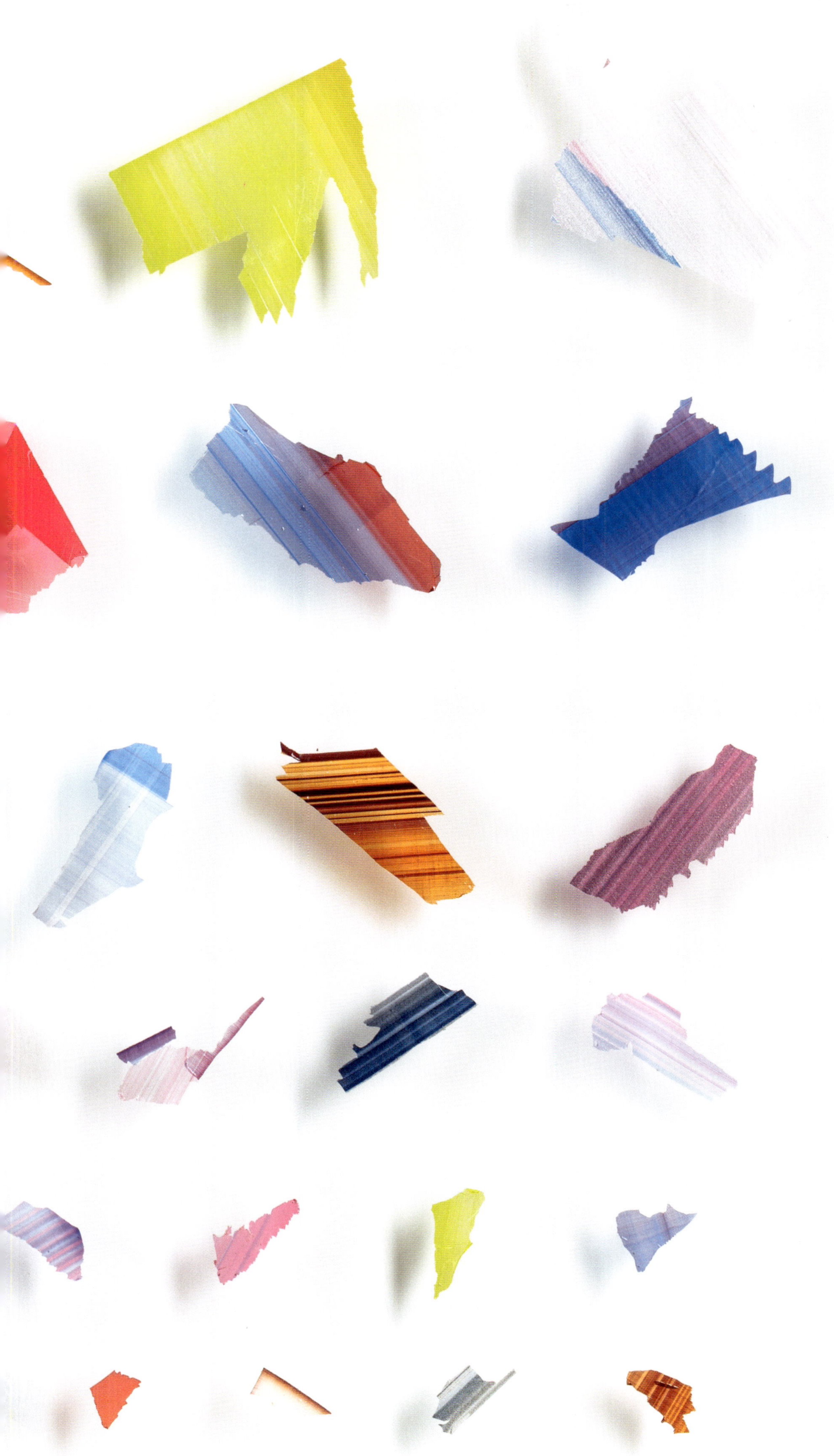

In conversation
Eric Butcher and David Batchelor

The following text is an edited and abridged transcript of a public 'in conversation', held at GPS gallery, London in October 2025, on the occasion of Eric Butcher's solo show, Shadow Archive.

DB: My name is David Batchelor. This is Eric Butcher. And this is Eric's work around you, which you probably already know. We're going to have a conversation for the next 40 minutes or so about our friendship and the work that we both do. Particularly Eric's work, I hope. Eric and I have known each other for around 10 years now. We actually met rather oddly in that I was in a hotel room in Vancouver and I got this email, not from Eric at all but from Eric's daughter Tzipi, who was about 10 years old at the time. She was working on a school project and wrote to me, sort of out of the blue, asking me some questions about my work. And because I was stuck in this bloody hotel room chasing a commission that never happened, I had a lot of time on my hands. So I actually ended up writing this very long response to Tzipi, who then responded to that, and through those exchanges I met Eric, who came to the studio and we began a conversation about work. I think we both found that it was a very easy conversation for us to have; to talk about art, obviously, but also more broadly than that; ethics perhaps (he's done philosophy, I haven't), and the place of art in the world and so on. On the occasions we've met, we always had very long and very engaging conversations. So when Eric was putting this show together, he proposed that we might try one of those conversations in public.

One of the reasons I think we've been able to have this extended conversation, is because even though our works in many respects are quite different, they have certain things in common. Maybe all artists' work have certain things in common. But I think in our case there are issues concerning the kinds of things we work with materially, but also intellectually, if that's not too big a word. The question of colour is prominent in both of our works, and I would say there's a sort of moral in the work, of doubt and uncertainty and the pleasures that come from those doubts and uncertainties, but also the worries that come with them too.

Anyway, that's my broad introduction. Now the plan was just to have a conversation about, in a way, both of our works. But Eric's work is prominently, rather brilliantly, displayed here. So I think as a starting point, particularly for those of you who don't know Eric's work so well, I'm just going to ask Eric, briefly perhaps, how did these come about?

EB: It's quite a long story which I'll try to compress because I'm sure there are other things we want to talk about. But basically, the genesis of this work dates back to early 2020 during the first lockdown when a lot of people were having doubts, or at least misgivings, or reflections on the way they lived their lives and whether they could live differently. And I was no exception in that respect. I'd had doubts about making art or about making the sort of art I had been making for a long time. I think I've always thought two things almost simultaneously: one of them is that being an artist is a brilliant job; you can pursue your own creative inclinations wherever they might lead without having someone breathing down your neck telling you 'you shouldn't do it like that, you should do it like this', and that's a privilege. But at the same time I also think that making art is a very vain, self-indulgent and selfish kind of activity.

DB: I'd say narcissistic as well.

EB: Yes, narcissistic, absolutely.

DB: Delusional?

EB: Yes, often. We could go on …

DB: Oh, we will!

EB: So during lockdown I was going in to the studio and listening on the radio to how many people had died that week. It was *that* period. For some reason I've got lots of friends who are doctors, and these friends would be going to work and literally save people's lives for a living. Whereas I would go to the studio and push funny coloured bits of mud around a two-dimensional surface. At the time it felt profoundly insufficient and beside the point, rather futile and fatuous. It precipitated a kind of crisis of confidence in my own practice, but also my *being* an artist. My solution was to subject my entire practice, to a kind of forensic analysis. I physically and intellectually deconstructed what I had been making to try and work out if there was anything of value. Was there anything here that was fruitful and I could legitimately, morally, take forward, or was it all just crap and I should, there and then, stop being an artist?

I've had various points before that of feeling the same. What was new was this investigative process which resulted in this work. I've pulled the skins of paint from their original supports and re-presented them, sandwiched them between sheets of glass like scientific specimens. I've been looking at entomological collections of bugs and butterflies from the 19th century and applied many of the same presentational devices, treating them in a quasi-scientific way. Presenting them as findings as opposed to new works of art.

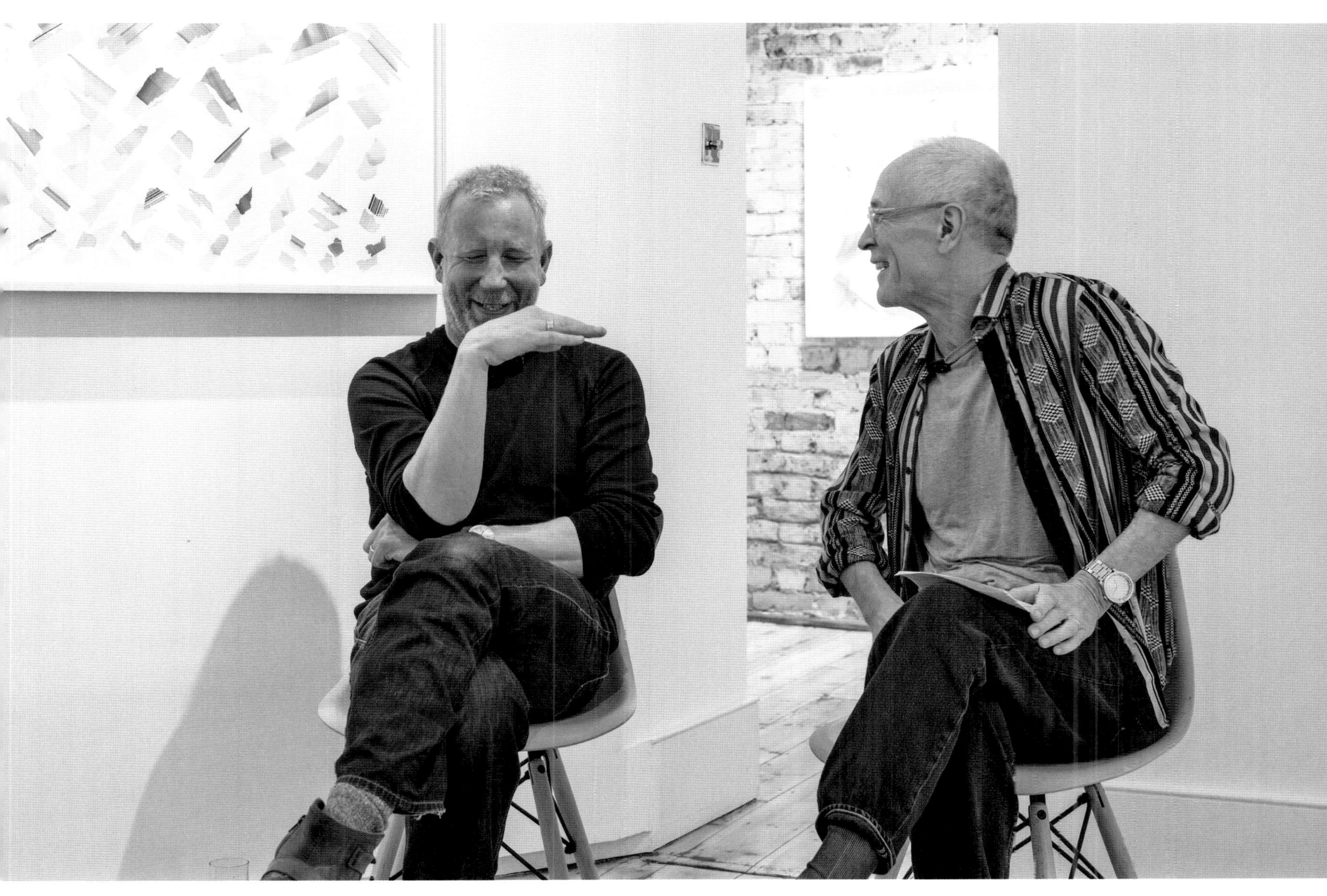

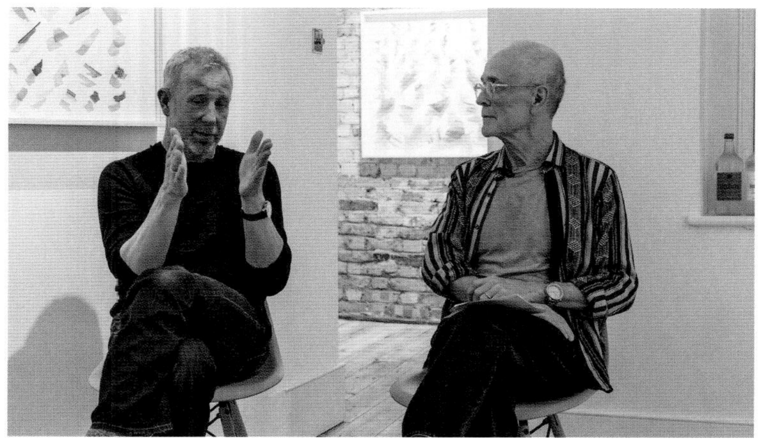

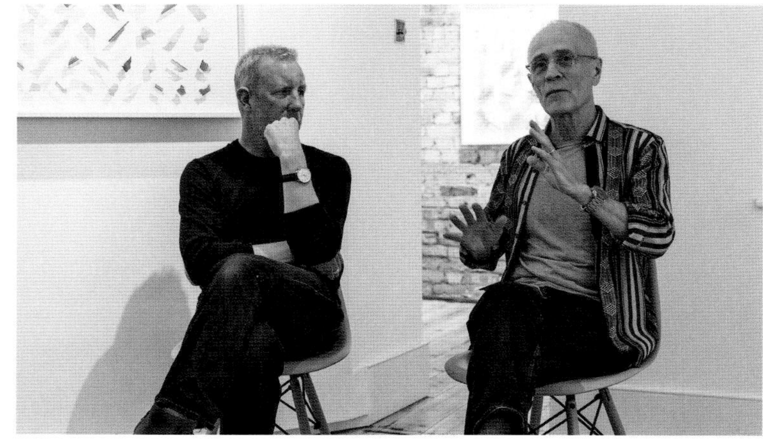

DB: I think any artist who's just listened to what you've said will recognise those anxieties and those questions; there's a lot to talk about in that. But I remember, from the very little I've read about Adorno, he says that self-doubt is actually a precondition of art in the 20th century, or *was* a precondition of art in that century. You can't do art with any degree of the sense of certainty that you might possibly have had in the mid-19th century, say, and that it's that self-doubt which gives art its character in the 20th century. And for me that makes sense.

EB: It's quite reassuring, isn't it? Making this work has utterly reinvigorated my experience in the studio. I think part of it is that I don't know where it's going to lead me. What I've decided to do is to only use the materials that I currently have and not introduce any new materials. When I've used up all the materials in my studio I will simply stop being an artist. There's something I find very engaging about that. As certain groups of materials are used up, I'll have to use other materials. And to use those materials, I'm going to have to think of creative solutions, which I haven't conceived of yet. That's exciting for me. But there's also something really exciting about the fact that there's an end point.

DB: Are you sure there's an end point?

EB: Yes, I'm absolutely sure.

DB: Because if what you're saying is that there's something unpredictable about this process, and I understand the process you're describing, maybe one of the unpredictable results could be that you change your mind.

EB: No, I can't do that because I have to have rules. In order to do this I have to have a system. I mean, I've done that throughout my career, I've always done that. I've always needed parameters, needed to set myself rules. I can't arbitrarily choose a colour. I have to have a reason for choosing it, or at least something that starts off the process. Each decision has to be within certain restrictions. And this is the ultimate restriction. I've found it utterly liberating to have this end point where – I don't like it to be described as 'retiring'. I much prefer, 'I will stop being an artist' – I'm not going to be like a premiership footballer who then plays for a championship side –

DB: Well, I'm going to say, you could drag this out a bit!

EB: – Or who does a bit of management before ending up at LA Galaxy. I will just stop because there's something intellectually satisfying about that, you know. People have said, 'Could you use somebody else's work and destroy their work or –'

DB: Hey, back off!

EB: – 'or could you use materials that you found in skip?' Yeah, I know, I could do all these things, but I'm not going to.

DB: Do you know when that end point is? Do you have a timetable?

EB: Depends how fast I am.

DB: Well, again, you could slow it down.

EB: I could, I can slow it down. It's a very frugal process and I'm trying to make as much of as little as I can, to be as frugal as possible with these materials.

DB: But I also do understand the whole question of the anxiety about waste because that's, in a way, one of the great human catastrophes. It's not the materials we use that are the problem, it's how we use the materials. And the problem with plastic, for example, is not the material itself, which is a rather astonishingly valuable material. It's how we use it and how we waste it. I have a rule in the studio. It's one of the few rules I have – well, maybe not – which is that any plastic that comes into the studio does not leave the studio as waste. It has to enter the work. And that's a rather weak response, probably, to the whole issue.

EB: But you're already using materials, plastics, that were waste. I remember that piece you put in the show I curated in Hanover, that was sheets of orange plastic with holes cut out which you got that from a skip somewhere.

DB: Oh yes. Well, not just *somewhere*, actually it's the skip at the back of the acrylic production place near my studio.

EB: Even better. So, plenty more where that came from!

DB: Down in Canning Town, as it happens. But that wasn't done for decent environmental reasons. It was done because I often think the things that get thrown away are more interesting than the things you keep. And that's a studio experience I think a lot of artists have. I remember vividly – this was maybe 30 years ago – I was working on this rather elaborate wannabe sculpture which involved cutting bits of plastic off and sticking them over there, and working on this, but then I kept looking to my side thinking the bits I was throwing away were clearly more interesting than the bits I was keeping. That logic is quite demanding, because on the one hand, first of all, you have to admit it; your brilliant idea is less interesting than what you're chucking out. But then, once you do admit it, it is quite liberating too. When you think, okay it's not what I'm planning that's interesting, it's the spillage and the noise that it generates.

EB: I think that's a familiar experience, isn't it? Part of the trick is to work out which mistakes are fruitful, profitable ones, and which ones are just, you know, crap. I think artistic maturity resides, in part, in being able to decipher, or being able to work out, what's a useful mistake or a good outcome or chance occurrence, from one that isn't a useful, fruitful, profitable one.

DB: I think that some of these are inadvertent effects, and you think, 'Well, can I use that'? Can I even see that? And if so, what does that do to the rest of it? But again, that's part of the doubt in the studio. It can be a real pleasure. It could be an absolute pain as well. But that's the nature of the beast. So, what are your rules of colour?

EB: Well, I've had various rules at various times. I think one of the things I've always struggled with is the potential whimsicality of it, the fact that you can choose any one you like. So what I tried to do was to impose reasons. For example, at one point I was making myself use – and this was perhaps an early 'recycling thing' – I made myself use, as a starting point when I first started painting in the morning, the colour that I finished with the previous night. So the starting point would be set and then it became a kind of formal game; one colour would then respond to the next colour and so on. But the first colour was in a sense like a tuning fork. That was determined. I wanted to get away from painting in miserable colours because I was fed up or painting in bright colours because I was happy. That kind of thing, that seemed rather whimsical.

DB: I mean, again, Adorno said that you should only use black because it's a bad world. I mean, *oh come on*!

EB: Miserable bastard!

DB: And there's a much better Johnny Cash song about the man in black which says "I'd like to wear a rainbow on my back, but for now I'm going to carry this blackness for you". Johnny Cash is much funnier than Adorno about the mood of colours. I think my only rule of colour is that if I put two colours together that look obvious then that's no good. If it goes red, yellow, blue, you think, uh-uh, primaries, uh-uh, Bauhaus circa 1920 get rid of that. So I think, for me, the rule is just that it's got to hold your attention and take you by surprise, or take you somewhere where you think 'I didn't know that would work or I could do that'.

EB: But you have a much more deliberate approach to colour, I think. It's much more obviously central to your practice. You are always, it seems to me, drawn to highly saturated colours. I mean you want a lot of it, don't you?

DB: Oh yes.

EB: Whereas I quite often find I'm trying to rein it in. I use a lot of graphite, powdered tin and aluminium in the paint, and part of that is because I think, for me, it's less about colours per se and more about the relationship between transparency and opacity, or absorption and reflection, and so on. And I quite often find myself, perhaps unintentionally, kind of pulling it back, which I don't ever sense in your work. Is that fair?

DB: Oh, probably! But actually the minute you say that, I'm looking at the work in the room and I'm thinking, there's a lot of transparency in these works, but there's a lot of opacity in some of them, too. And I hadn't thought of those relationships quite before. I just try to max out the colour every time! That's not actually entirely true, because I've used a lot of grey and I think grey is a very complex and very interesting colour and almost all of my works have an element of black or white in them even if that's just the ground on which they're painted or made. I think black, white and grey are as valuable as colours as anything else. And you often need them as counterpoints perhaps. When I started using colour, which is now over 30 years ago, I was always looking to max it out, or rather to try to make the colour the subject and the centre of the work. So rather than it just be a colourful work, that it would be a work-of-colour somehow. That's quite difficult. I mean that's what I've been trying to do ever since.

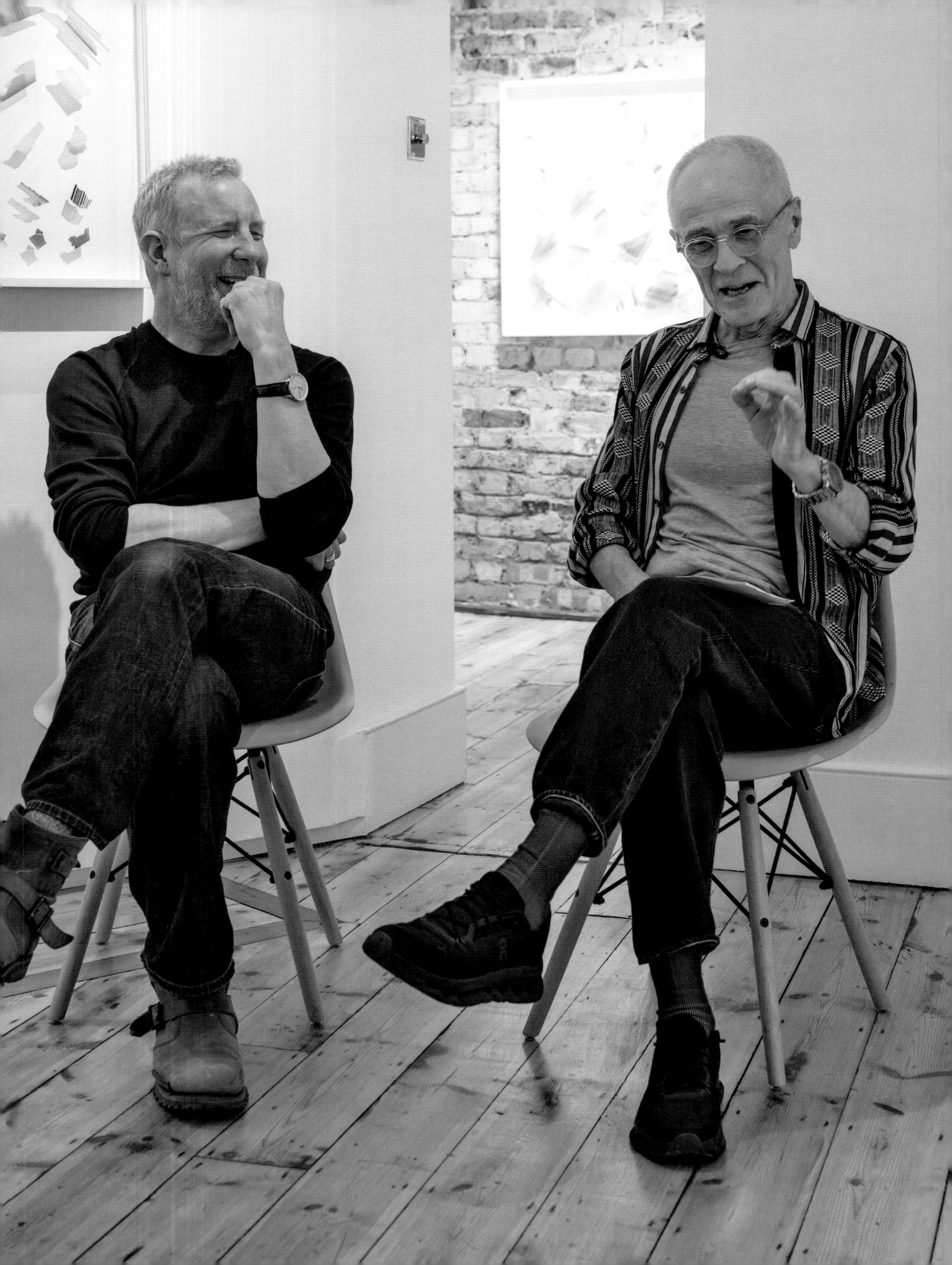

EB: You've been trying to get away from colour being a vehicle, but an end in itself.

DB: It should be that it's the noun rather than the adjective, as it were. Quite how you make that happen is what has sustained me.

EB: How much is projected colour significant in your work? I'm thinking again about that piece we showed in Hanover, one of your Concretos. A big one with the orange drilled plastic sheets. I placed it in the window.

DB: Oh, I know. I was very happy about that.

EB: And it was all about the pool of coloured light that was on the floor. That was the star of the show, that experience and the way it moved across the floor.

DB: Unfortunately I didn't see the show but I was so delighted with those photographs. So the sunlight came through the transparent orange plastic and produced these reflections on the floor. I mean that for me, that's pure colour. It's unbounded by anything material and it's also fugitive and ephemeral; it's always moving, it's never one thing. I think I first experienced that when I made works using illuminated light boxes with panels of solid colour which would just throw the light out. And those stacks of light boxes, if I did them in any space that had reflective or shiny surfaces, you'd get these bounces of colour, none of which you could predict or plan.

EB: And that's part of the beauty of it.

DB: That is, in a way, the – I don't use the word 'essence' very often, but what the hell – that was for me the essence of them. Because that's when colour is really its own thing. But at the same time it's also the most fragile version of colour because you know it's like those reflections; the minute you move by six inches, they can go. But then that is, for me, the nature of colour; that fragility.

EB: One of the things I find fascinating about *this* work is the pools of coloured light that you get when you've got a coloured transparent skin of paint and how – with a with a dynamic light source such as daylight – those coloured shadows move across the work and they're different every time you see them.

DB: To what extent were those shadows planned in the production of the work and to what extent were they an effect that you enjoyed?

EB: They're largely an effect.

DB: So they're a happenstance that you could then exploit.

EB: Yes. So for example in this one, this has been a complete revelation to me. Seeing it in this light, you get at the top opaque dark skins of paint which throw a shadow, but it's very clear what the object is and what the shadow is. By the time you get down to the bottom, the shadow is completely dominant because the skin of paint is so transparent, and at some point there's an inversion between the object and the shadow. I only really saw that putting it up here and I thought, 'Oh, that works. I'm going to do more of those'!

DB: Is there more to say about rules?

EB: I've always struggled to make art without rules. Over time they've changed and some have been more prescriptive than others, but I've always needed to find ways of limiting the possibilities, because I find limitless possibilities really – counterintuitively perhaps – crippling.

DB: No, I think every artist has rules of some description. Whether you call them rules or not, I don't know. But if you don't have some sense of what you're limiting yourself to, then if you can do anything, then you'll do nothing.

EB: Yes, absolutely.

DB: So, I think sometimes those limits are established by the work you've just made; it will suggest what you might do next or what you might not do next.

EB: Do you enjoy breaking them? I mean, is there a pleasure in that? You set yourself rules and then is it about the rule or is it about what the rule allows you to do?

DB: I think the rule, so to speak, that sets those limits, allows you to focus and to develop the possibilities within those constraints. At a certain point those constraints become hindrances. Sometimes for me that happens a year later and I'll work on them again. Because I don't care about them anymore, I'm much more relaxed about risking ruining them. And that risk of ruining them sometimes – but only sometimes – actually makes the works become much better or richer.

EB: It's that sense of jeopardy within the piece. I think that's also part of why I've always either worked in pairs or in series because of exactly that. So you never feel too precious about any one piece. You think, 'okay, well that works; I'm now going to take more risks in this next one' and you can then transfer the learning back to the previous one.

DB: Yes, I describe the way I work as in 'clusters' – you've seen my studio. 'Series' sounds a bit strict for me. Perhaps less so for you. So clusters of Concretos, clusters of collages. And then at some point that cluster will become boring or repetitive which is the worst thing in the world. Isn't it?

So tell me, do you go to the studio every day, five days a week, seven days a week?

EB: I go to the studio seven days a week, but it's not all day. It used to be much more like that when I was making paintings. Now there are several different stages in the process. For example, the skins of paint are put onto this – I found a fantastic product which is basically a 50 metre-long roll of release paper, which is sprayed in the factory with an adhesive. Each skin of paint is put onto that, carefully expelling the air, then cut around with a scalpel, it's very fiddly and takes a long time. But I really enjoy that, it's utterly mindless. In the winter I just sit at the kitchen table, where it's warm, listening to podcasts about history, cutting out, for days on end. It's great, I love it. I love the uncreative nature of that as an activity, it's such a relief. So there are these distinct stages to this; the stripping off the original support is one stage – the destruction. Then there's the applying it to the adhesive paper, there's the cutting out, then there's the arranging and composing, which is entirely separate and very much a creative activity. So some of these activities are much more creative than others and some are relatively mindless. It's not as if I'm going into the studio seven days a week 9-to-5.

But you have the same; one day you're mixing up a load of concrete and another day you're rummaging around with the rats in that skip in Canning Town.

DB: Then I'm feeding the cats. Yes, it's true. I love mixing concrete. And may I say it requires a certain skill. I think one of the pleasures of a studio is that there's a strange combination of mental and manual activity. You know in most of our lives, traditionally the idea is that mental work and manual work are separated out in our industrial societies. But there's a curious moment of always having to negotiate that relationship between doing something seemingly dumb and physical and the highfalutin ideas that relate to it.

EB: I think that's one of the draws of specifically visual art and making visual art as opposed to being a writer or something else. It's that tension, in a way, between the thinking and the doing. I often think it's a bit like a kind of 'Jeckyll and Hyde' experience. You immerse yourself in making and you're sort of playing, you're not really thinking about means-ends related activity because you don't know what the end is going to be. And then you have to stop doing that, step back and say, 'okay, well what happened here'? Then it's almost like a forensic experience; you're trying to work out what happened and whether *this* is any good or *that's* good. Intellectually it's a completely different kind of activity.

DB: I'm going to open up to questions in a moment. I just wanted to refer back to your very important point at the beginning, about why do we make work? Is it sustainable? Is it justifiable in you the world we live in, the world we've always lived in, which is always awful and beautiful at the same time. There was a wonderful comment by Philip Guston, written in the mid '70s – this is to paraphrase entirely – 'the world has gone to shit; Nixon's in power, there're riots on the streets, people are being killed, people are sleeping on streets, we're doing horrors in Vietnam, everything is awful, and what do I do? I go to the studio and I change a blue to a red'.

EB: That's exactly how I felt.

DB: And that is fantastic because it seems to me to be incredibly honest. On one hand it seems to be saying, 'All I do is go and change a blue to a red', but maybe he's also saying, 'All I *can* do is change a blue to a red'; and maybe it's both. In a way that ambivalence about the studio; on the one hand you love what you do, on the other hand you kind of hate it, maybe that ambivalence, that coexistence of opposite thoughts, opposite feelings, is perhaps the condition we live in.

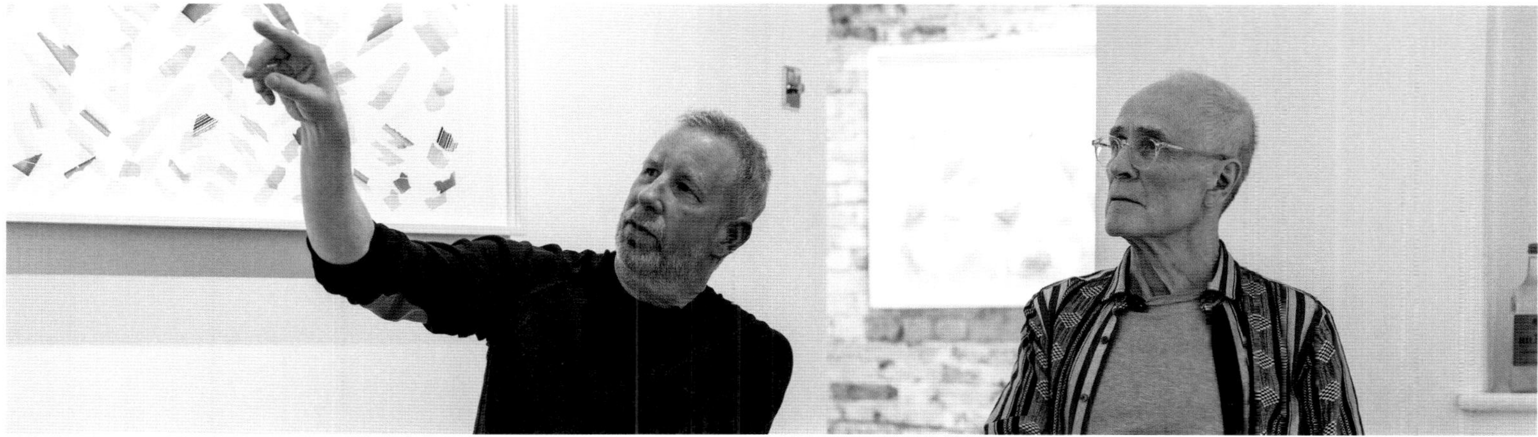

ATTENDEE 1: But maybe that's a validation of what it means to be alive? To change a blue to a red is potentially a political act because it's a validation of what it is to be alive, to have agency.

DB: Yes, I think it's a rich and open statement and yes, it's like saying I have some agency but then... how much? As individuals, what power do we have? Very little. But at the same time – I think someone said to me: 'you know art doesn't change the world but it does change people, and what's the world made up of apart from people'.

ATTENDEE 1: I think it does change the world.

DB: I want to go back to the first question. I was reminded of something that Terry Eagleton wrote about Marx. He said Marx didn't want artists to make work about communism, he wanted artists to be a model of how you might live. Marx thought that of Milton – the great poet – not because of what he told people about the world directly, but about how he lived, how his poetry lived at least, I don't know. I'm struggling with that one a bit!

ATTENDEE 1: Do you think that relates to the idea that nowadays we have forgotten about beauty? We are not seeing it anymore. We are disconnected from the idea that beauty can actually help us be better humans, to be in a better world. Do you think it's related to the concept of beauty?

EB: I'd like to answer a slightly different but related question, if I may? Something I find problematic is the way in which visual pleasure in art is somehow considered superficial or irrelevant, as though somehow it's a bad thing. I don't think visual pleasure is a bad thing at all. I think these things are very seductive objects, but there's more to it than that. I don't have a problem with seducing the viewer into lingering, spending more time finding out more about these objects. It's a starting point. Whereas I think for a long time the arts have been dominated by a view where that's considered necessarily superficial, and that we should have deliberately ugly, ungenerous work because only that work is serious and worthwhile and so on, which I don't agree with.

ATTENDEE 1: You've talked about colour, you've talked about rules. I was wondering whether there was something to be said about the shape of the marks that you made.

EB: What, you mean the shape of these skins of paint? They are literally as they've been ripped off the previous painting.

ATTENDEE 1: It strikes me very much that there's a great deal about floating; things floating above other things. They're almost like a shallow stream in the sunlight, that's perfectly clear, and you're getting things floating in it, which is a real delight in life and is a real delight in these works. They have an extraordinary quality like this, whether it's colour or whether it's more tonal. They have an extraordinary beauty and I think it's an extremely valuable thing.

DB: A floating world.

EB: I'm very pleased, flattered, that you've described them like that, but it's also important to remember they come from quite a dark place. The thoughts that generated these things are quite difficult. There does seem to be a kind of a disjuncture between why I make them and the objects themselves. And I actually rather like that. I think there's a tension between those two things.

ATTENDEE 2: Just to go to that question of why you make them, as you described it during COVID. It wasn't a rule you set yourself. You took a vow. You took a vow that you were going to – and you presupposed – that it would have an end. I think you may find it doesn't. You found a new way of making art that came out of that vow that had certain kinds of ethical characteristics. You made that sort of vow, and I think there's an interesting question about whether vows can ever be broken or not.

EB: It's an interesting word and I think it's very appropriate. Yes, I suppose it did have that kind of characteristic for me.

ATTENDEE 2: There's a certain narcissism about making vows. In the first Cantos of Dante's Paradiso, this is much discussed, and there are some appalling examples given of people who made vows and the results were terrible. like a particular general in the ancient world who made a vow that if he won a battle, he would sacrifice the first thing he saw after the battle. The first thing he saw was his daughter and he killed her. So, there's a big discussion between Dante and Beatrice as to whether vows can ever be broken and under what conditions they can be broken. The answer from Beatrice is that vows can be broken as long as the breaking of them continues the conditions, the reasons, for making the vow in the first place. As long as those ethical conditions are still met by the breaking of the vow.

ATTENDEE 3: Are you reprocessing all the work you've made to date in your studio through this practice; like you said: it's existing work.

EB: There are two things going on. One is the destruction of previously made work. The second thing is using up the materials that I have in the studio. So, I'm also making new surfaces. Those surfaces are then being destroyed. So, there is an element of harvesting but it's still about the using up of the materials.

ATTENDEE 3: So, you're not getting rid of paintings that you made that you loved.

EB: I haven't got rid of those *yet*. I'm holding those back till the end! I'm not going to be able to help myself, am I?

ATTENDEE 3: But it feels like there was something relevant to do with the fact of the pandemic, and mortality. And then you set up this process. So it was contemplating your own disappearance.

EB: One thing I haven't talked about which I probably should have, is that there's an environmental imperative going on here as well. I am extremely anxious about the kind of world my children will get old in. I find it jaw-dropping, breathtaking, that people aren't more scared than they appear to be. The thing I find extraordinary is people's complete unwillingness to sacrifice anything or change their lifestyles in any way, shape or form in order to live sustainably. I don't know what the answer is, I'm not a climate scientist. I'm just an anxious and worried parent. But I don't think we're doing anywhere near enough. And in a sense, part of what this is, is a testament of my desire to change the way I live. It's not a manifesto. I'm not suggesting that all artists stop making art – you'll be relieved to hear – but this is right for me.

DB: I'm afraid, we've run out of time. So the anxious parent has had the last word, which I think is entirely appropriate. We have to stop there, so I just want to thank you all very much for coming. Thank you.

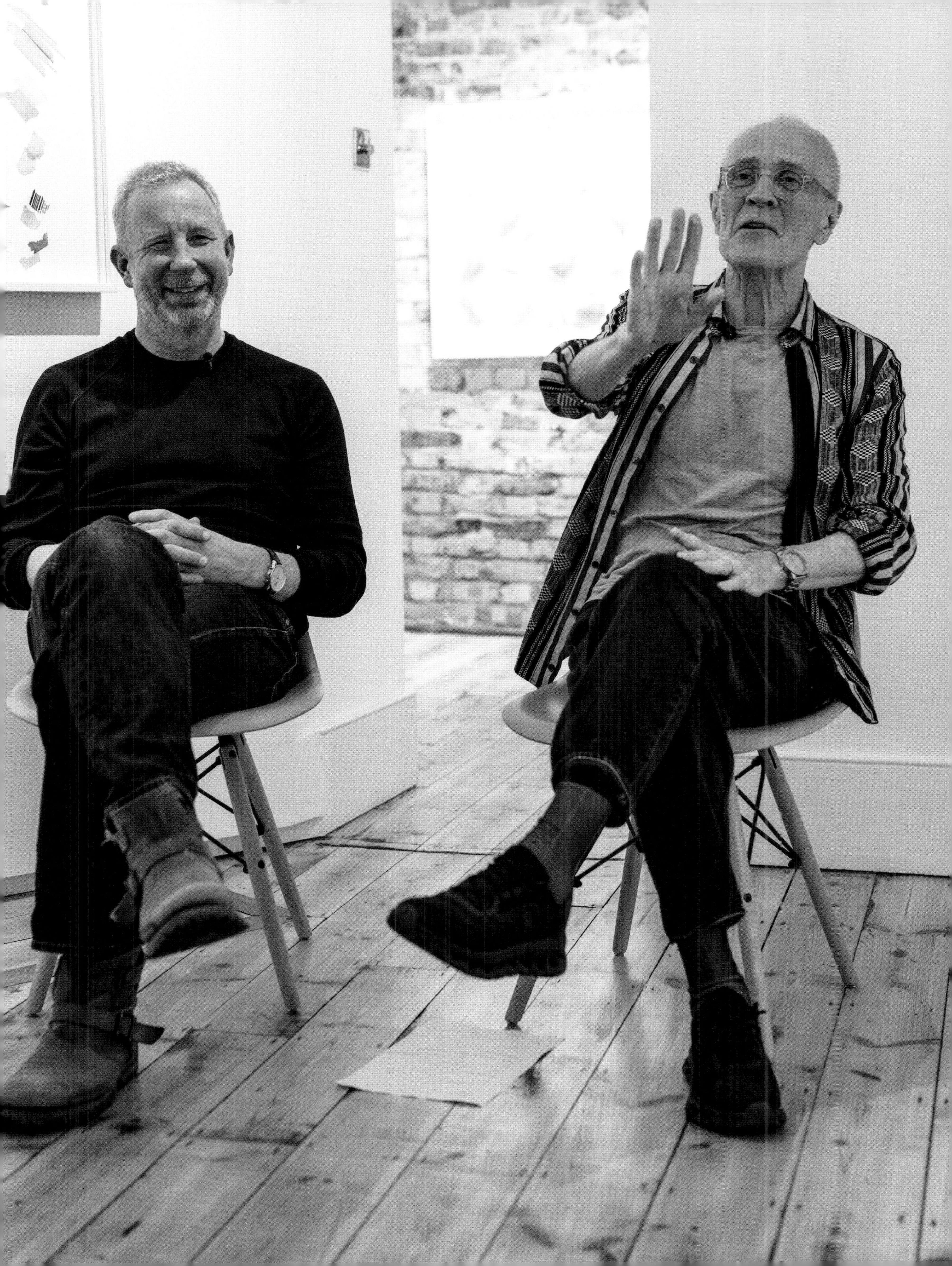

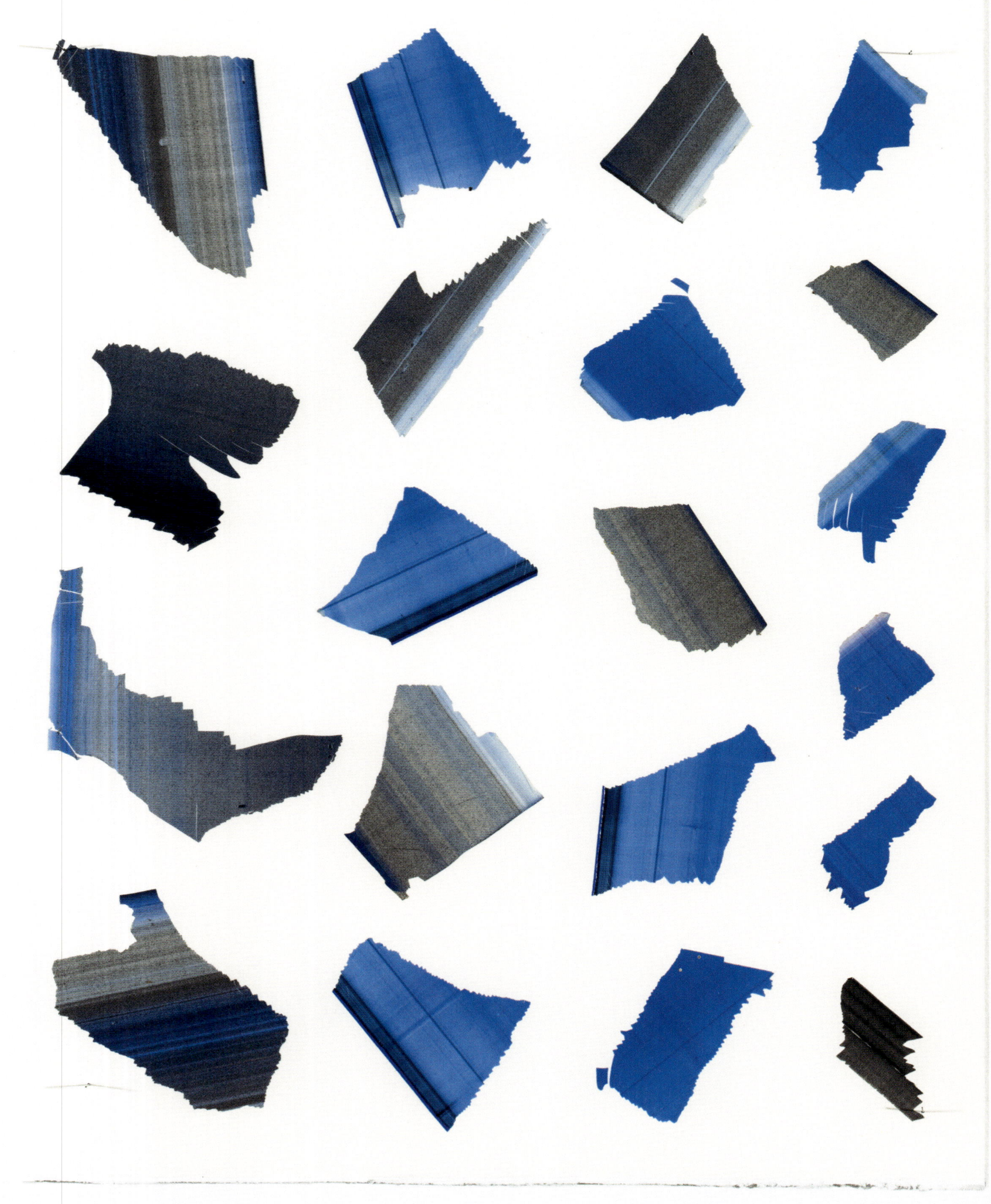

G/R.1083, Recycled Paint Fragments: Acrylic, Graphite, Acrylic Gel + Pencil on Paper, 32×54 cm, 2025

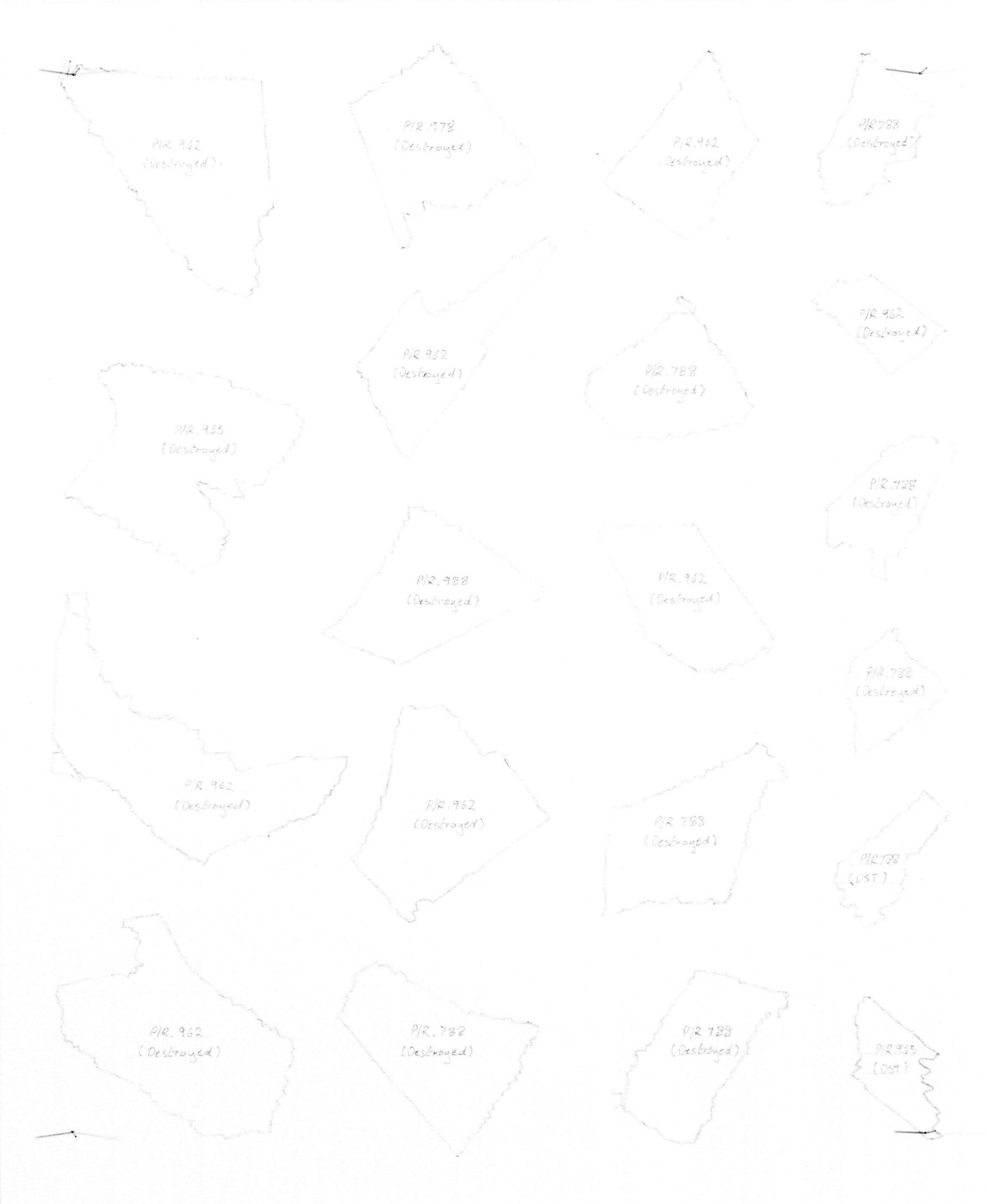

P/R. 962
(Destroyed)
P/R. 978
(Destroyed)
P/R. 962
(Destroyed)
P/R 788
(Destroyed)
P/R 962
(Destroyed)
P/R. 788
(Destroyed)
P/R 962
(Destroyed)
P/R. 935
(Destroyed)
P/R. 728
(Destroyed)
P/R. 988
(Destroyed)
P/R. 962
(Destroyed)
P/R. 788
(Destroyed)
P/R. 962
(Destroyed)
P/R. 962
(Destroyed)
P/R. 788
(Destroyed)
P/R 788
(DST)
P/R. 962
(Destroyed)
P/R. 788
(Destroyed)
P/R 788
(Destroyed)
P/R 935
(DST)

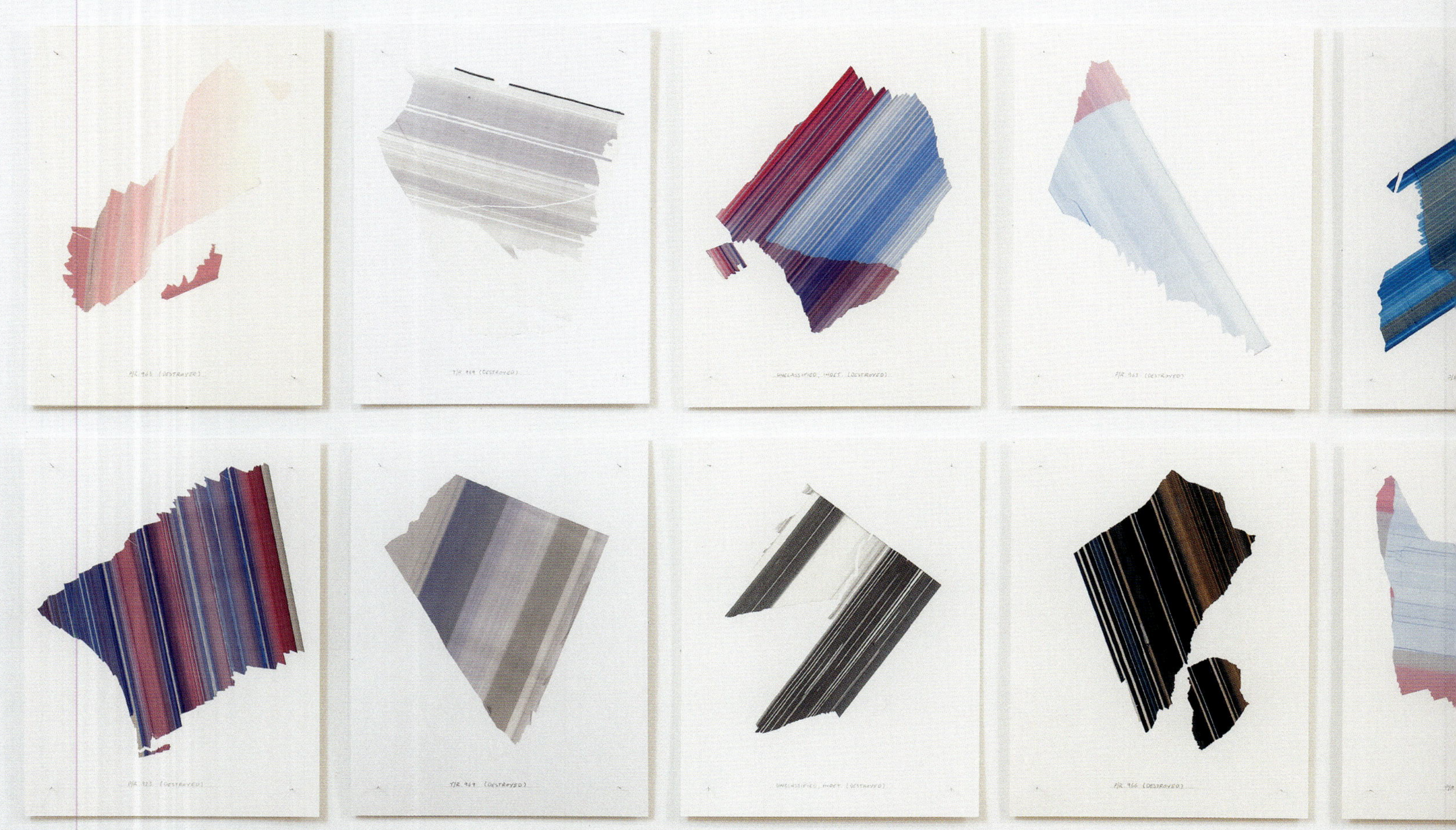

G/R.1086-1103, Recycled Paint Fragments: Acrylic, Graphite, Tin, Acrylic Gel + Pencil on Paper, 26×20 cm (each), 2025

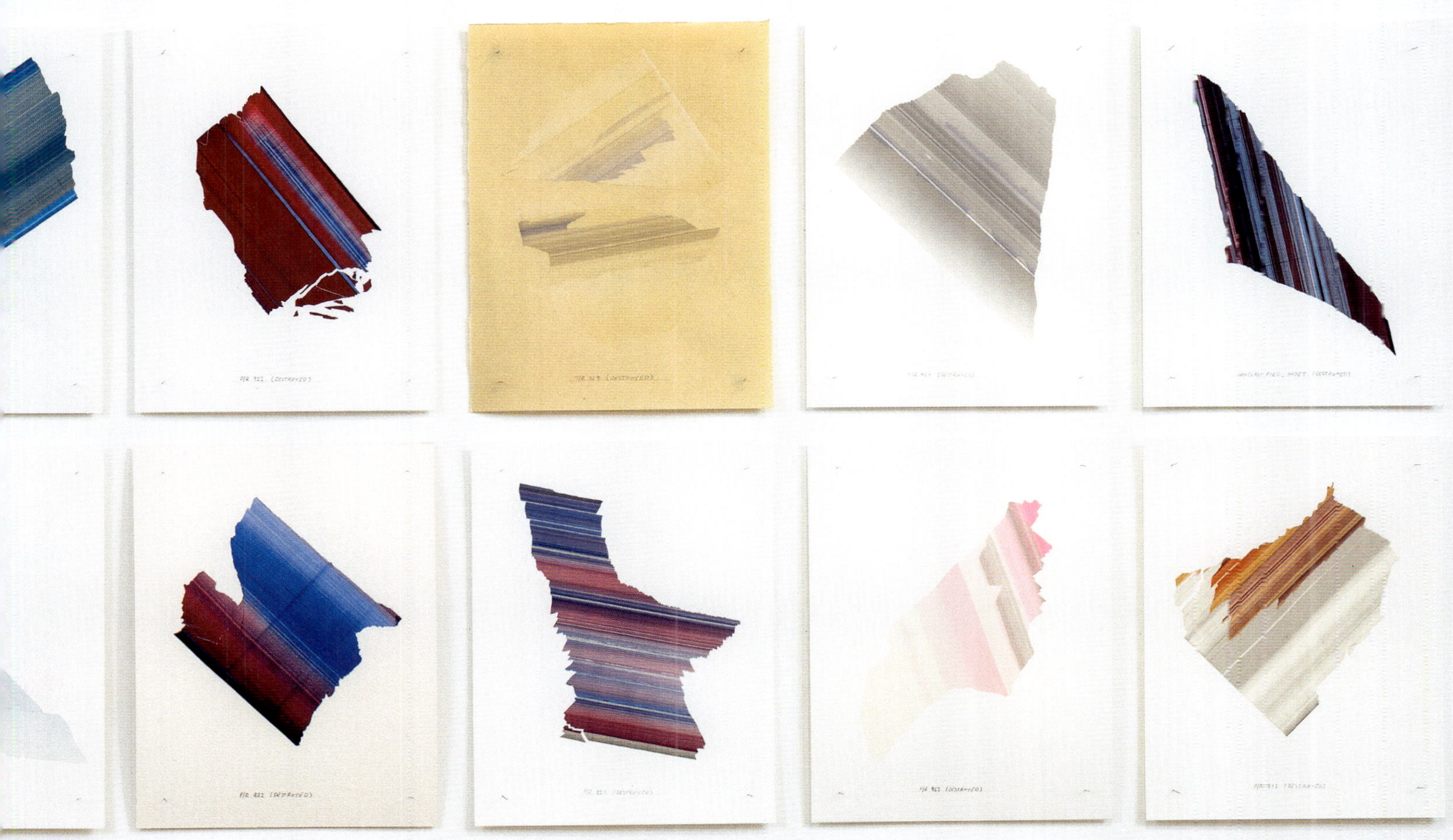

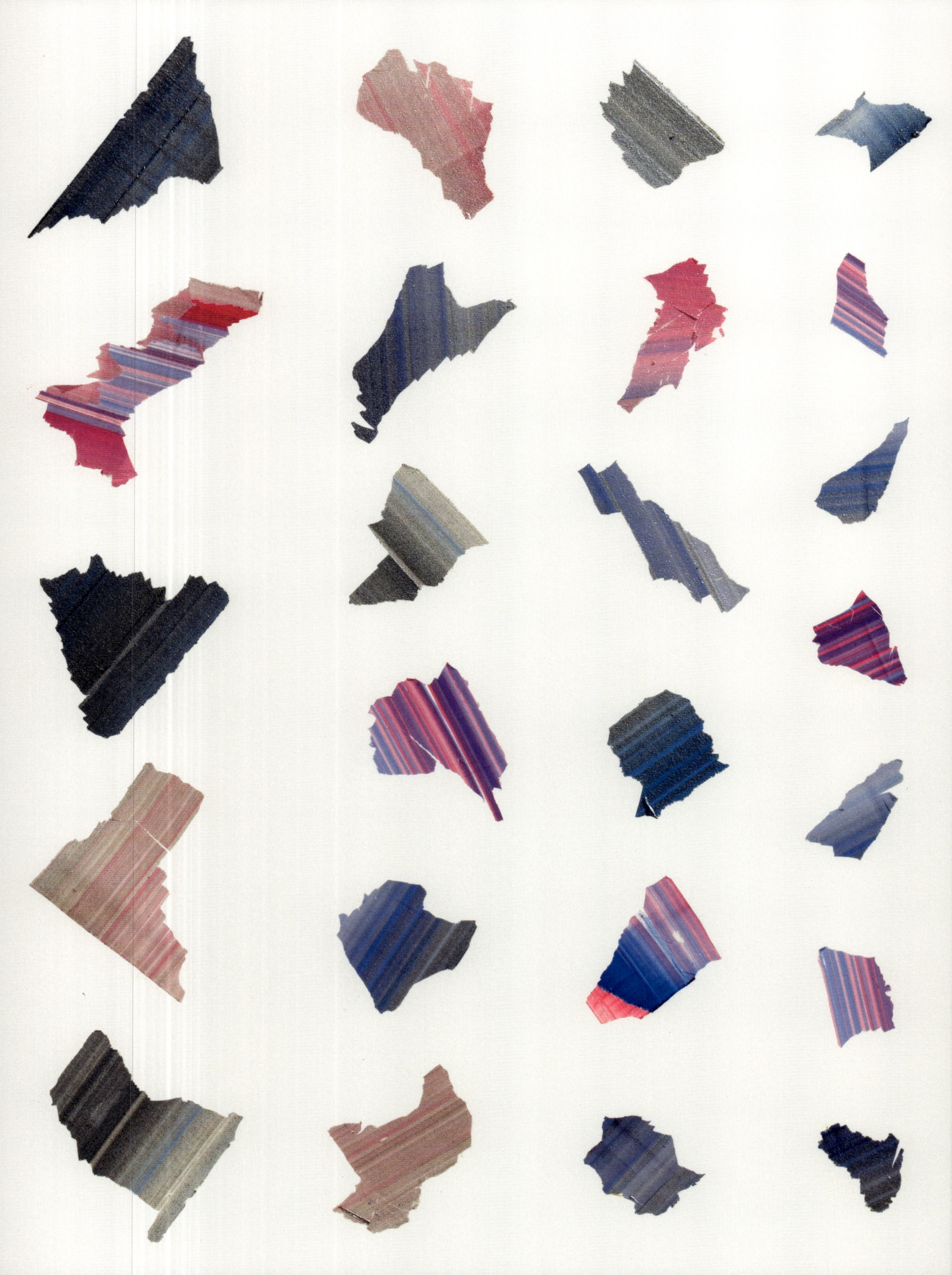

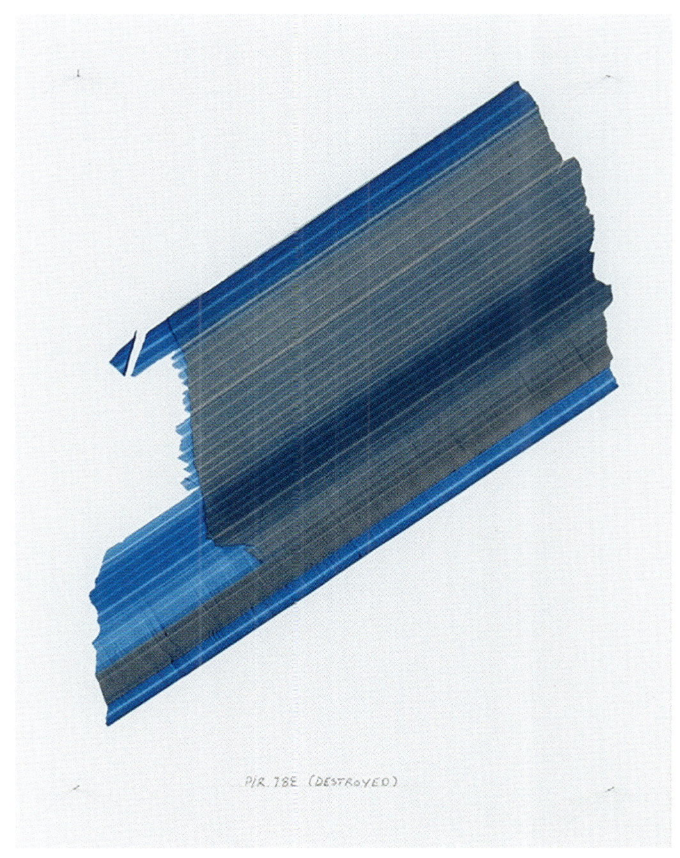

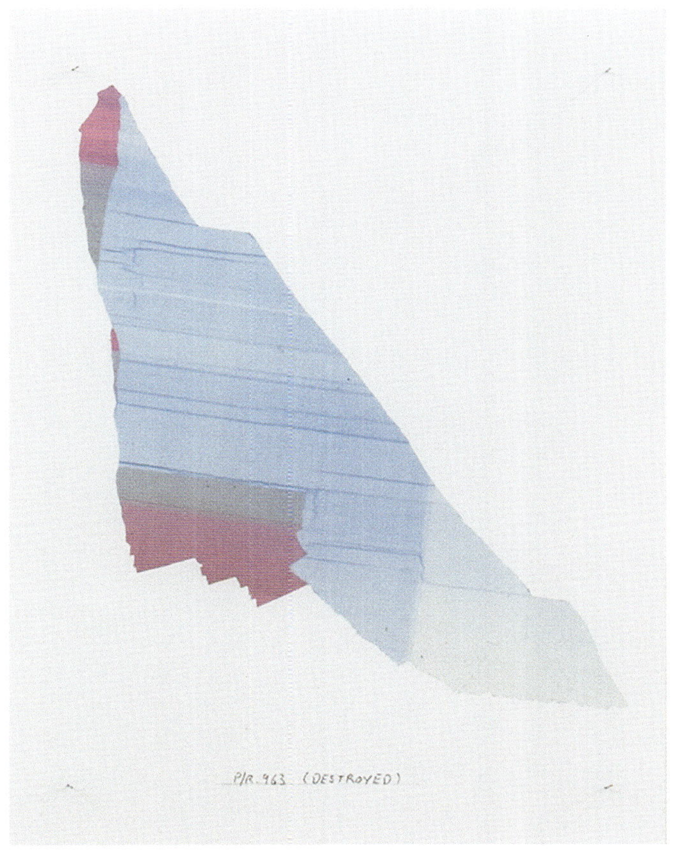

G/R.999, Recycled Paint Fragments: Acrylic, Graphite + Acrylic Gel on Paper, 39×33 cm, 2022

G/R.1090, Recycled Paint Fragment: Acrylic, Graphite, Tin, Acrylic Gel + Pencil on Paper, 26×20 cm, 2025,

G/R.1099, Recycled Paint Fragment: Acrylic, Graphite, Tin, Acrylic Gel + Pencil on Paper, 26×20 cm, 2025

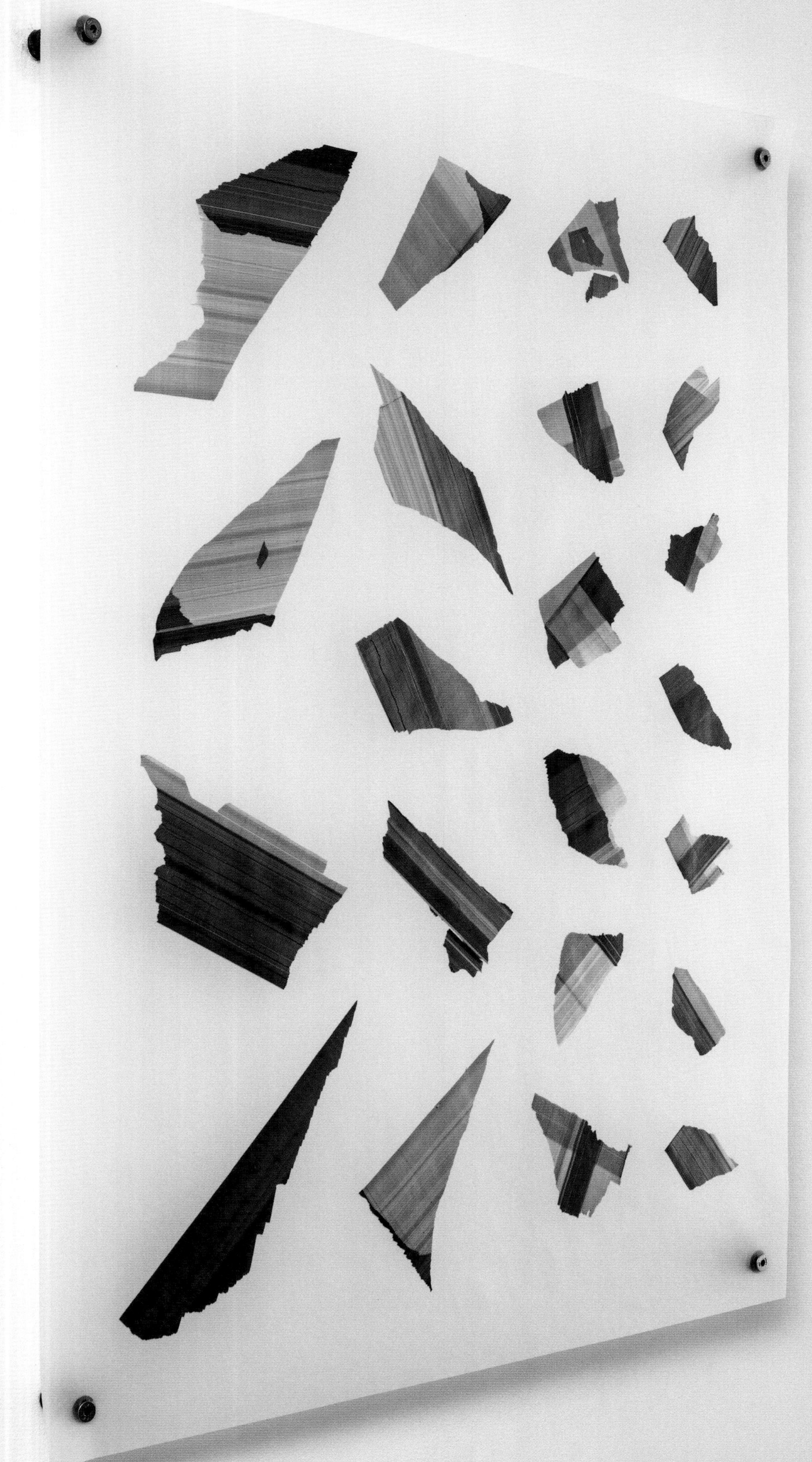

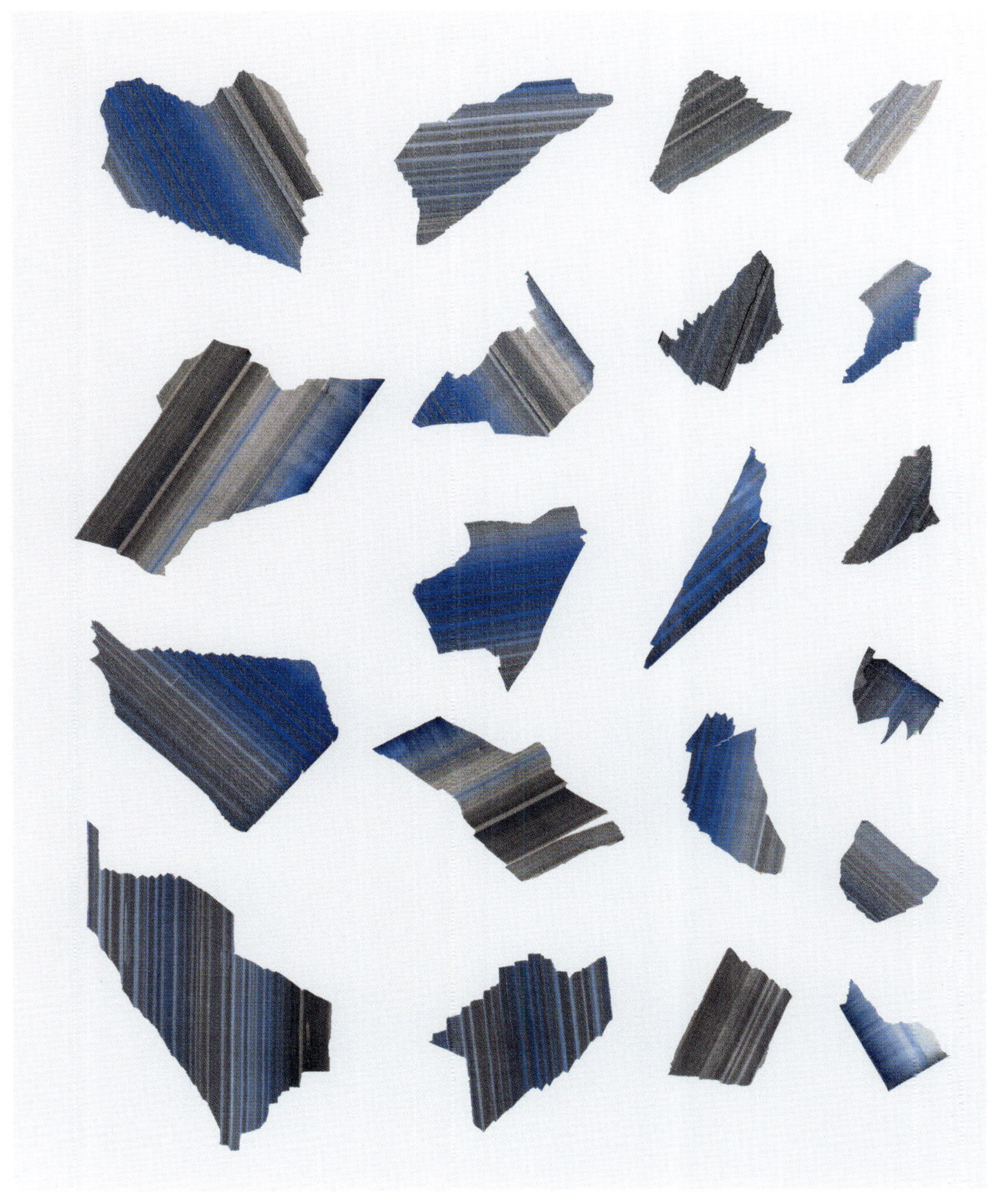

G/R.1055, Recycled Paint Fragments: Graphite, Tin + Acrylic Gel on Transparent Drafting Paper, 80 × 60 cm, 2024

G/R.994, Recycled Paint Fragments: Acrylic, Graphite + Acrylic Gel on Paper, 39 × 33 cm, 2022

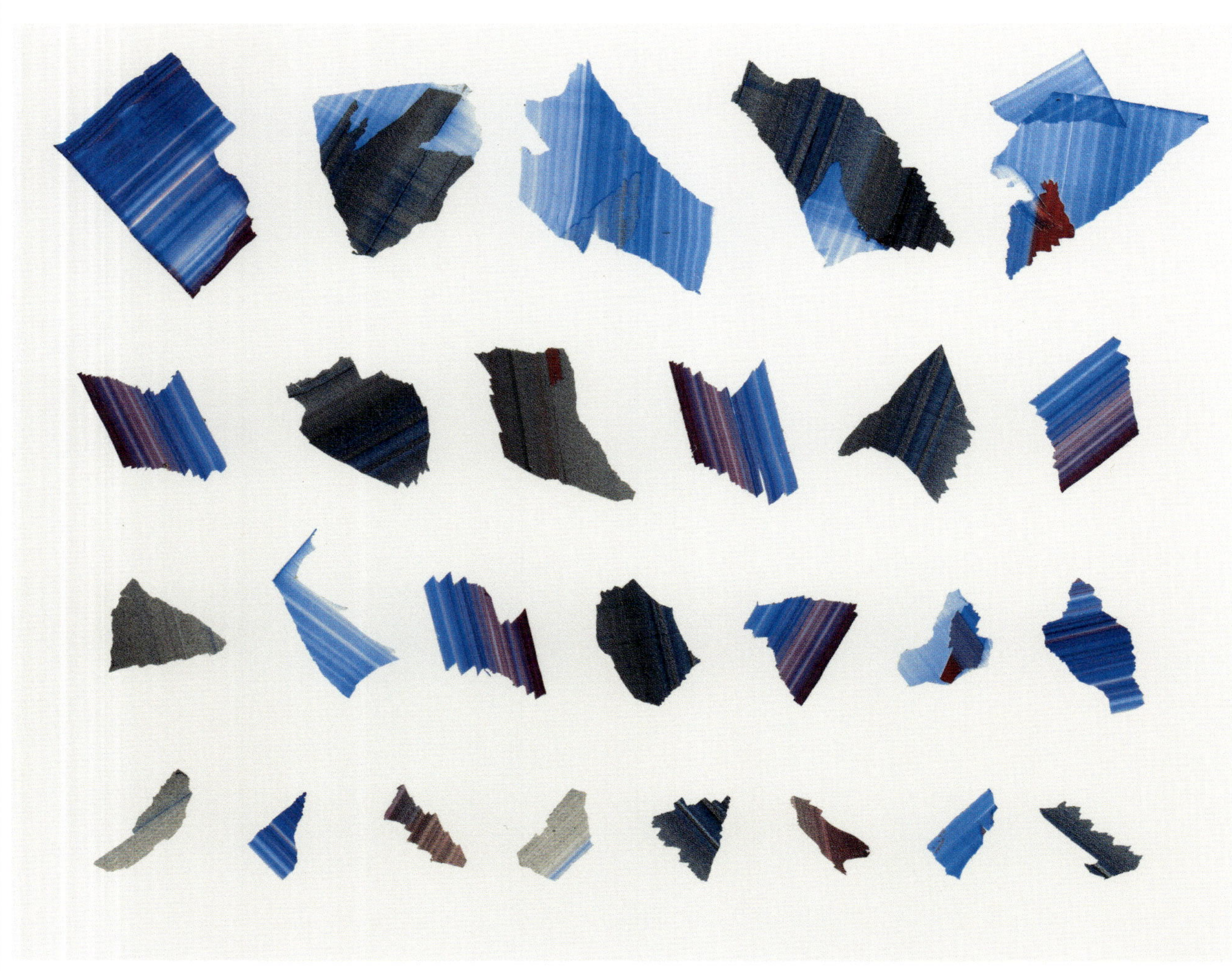

G/R.995, Recycled Paint Fragments: Acrylic, Graphite + Acrylic Gel on Paper, 33×39 cm, 2022

G/R.1104-1112, Recycled Paint Fragments: Acrylic, Graphite, Tin, Acrylic Gel + Pencil on Paper, 38×28 cm (each), 2025

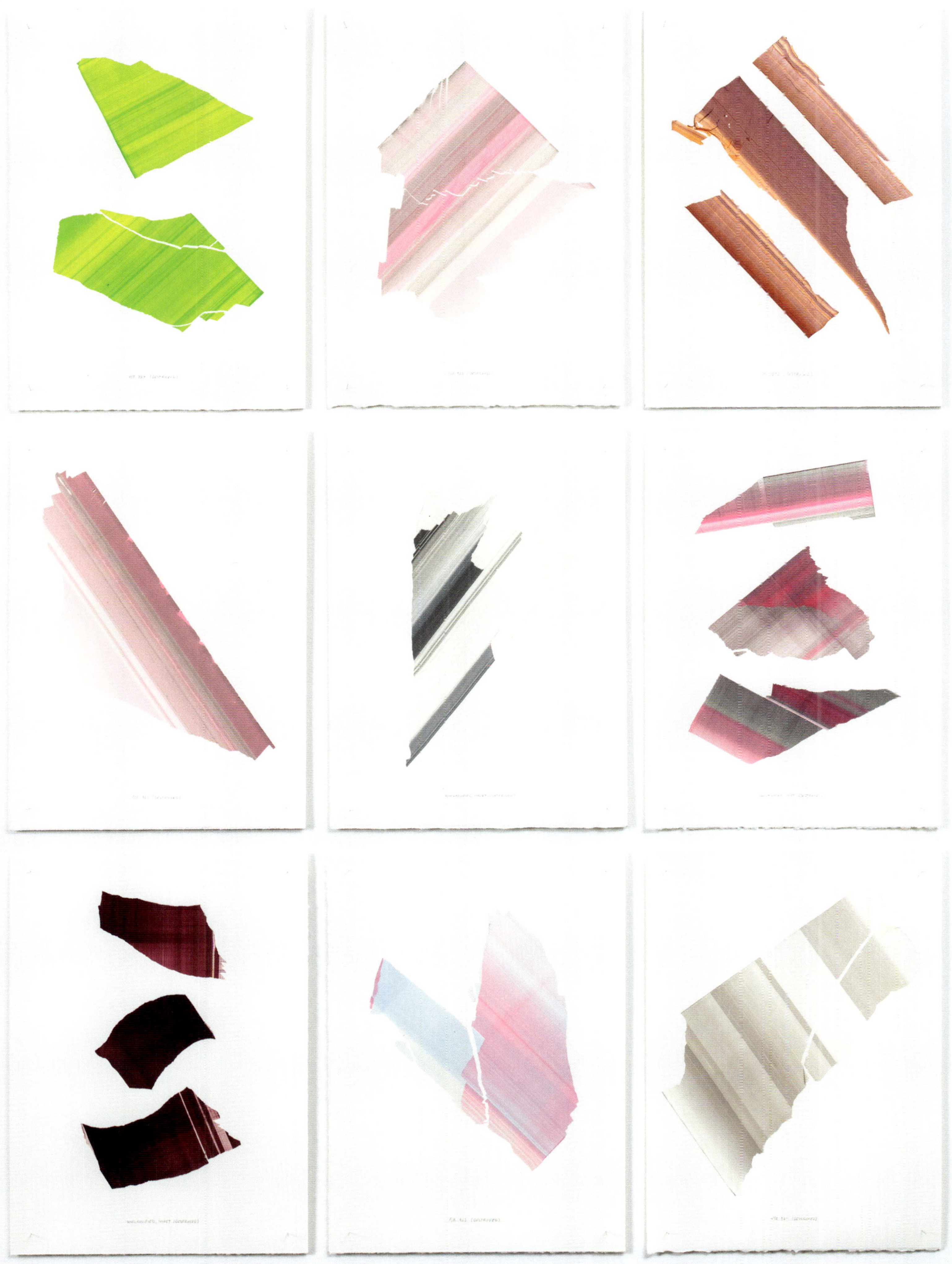

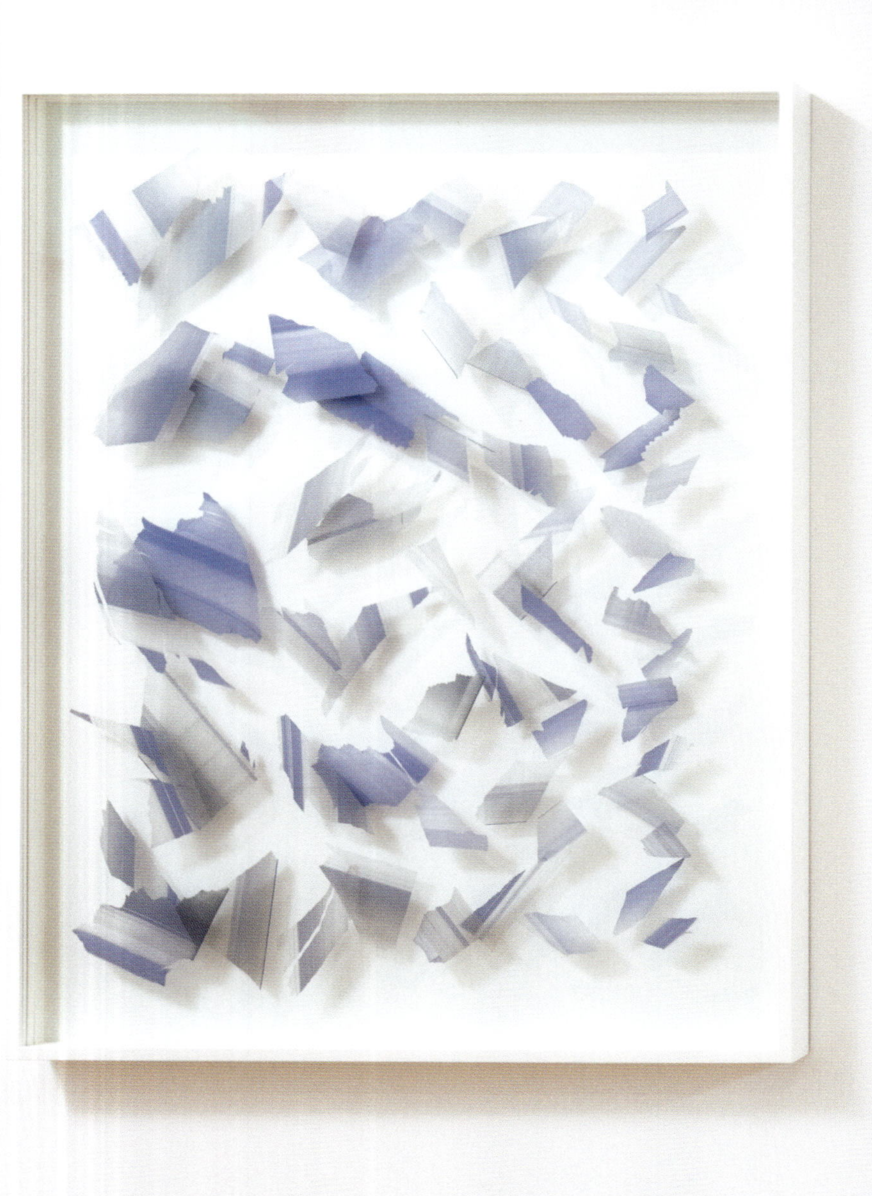

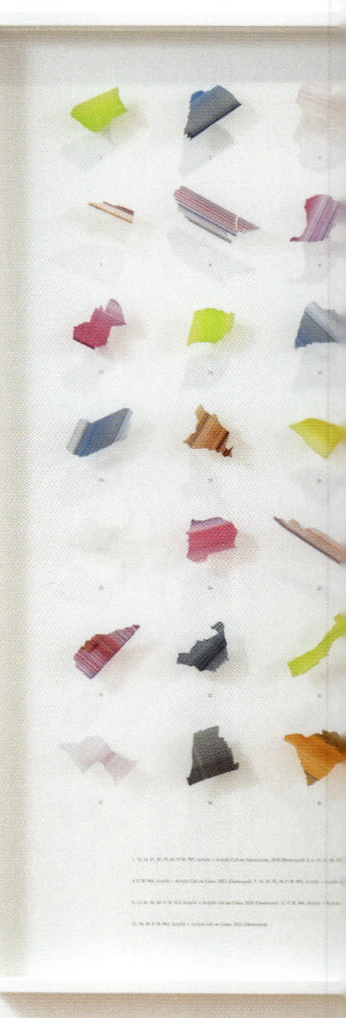

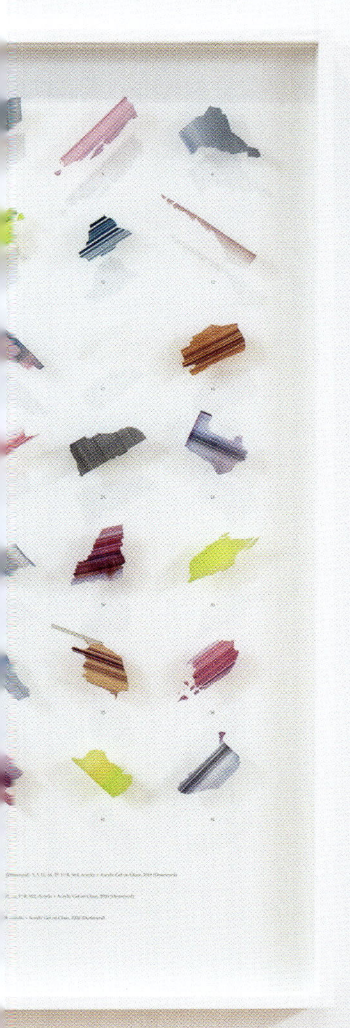
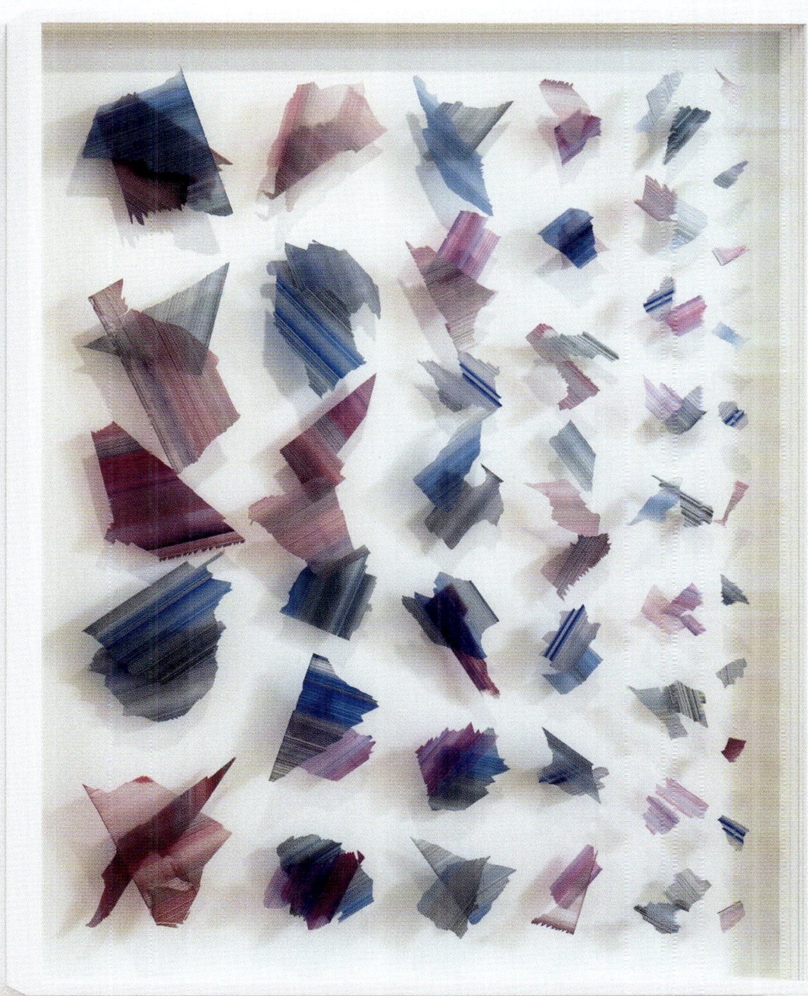

T/R.1044, Recycled Paint Fragments: Acrylic, Graphite, Acrylic Gel + Text on Glass, 109 × 86 cm, 2024

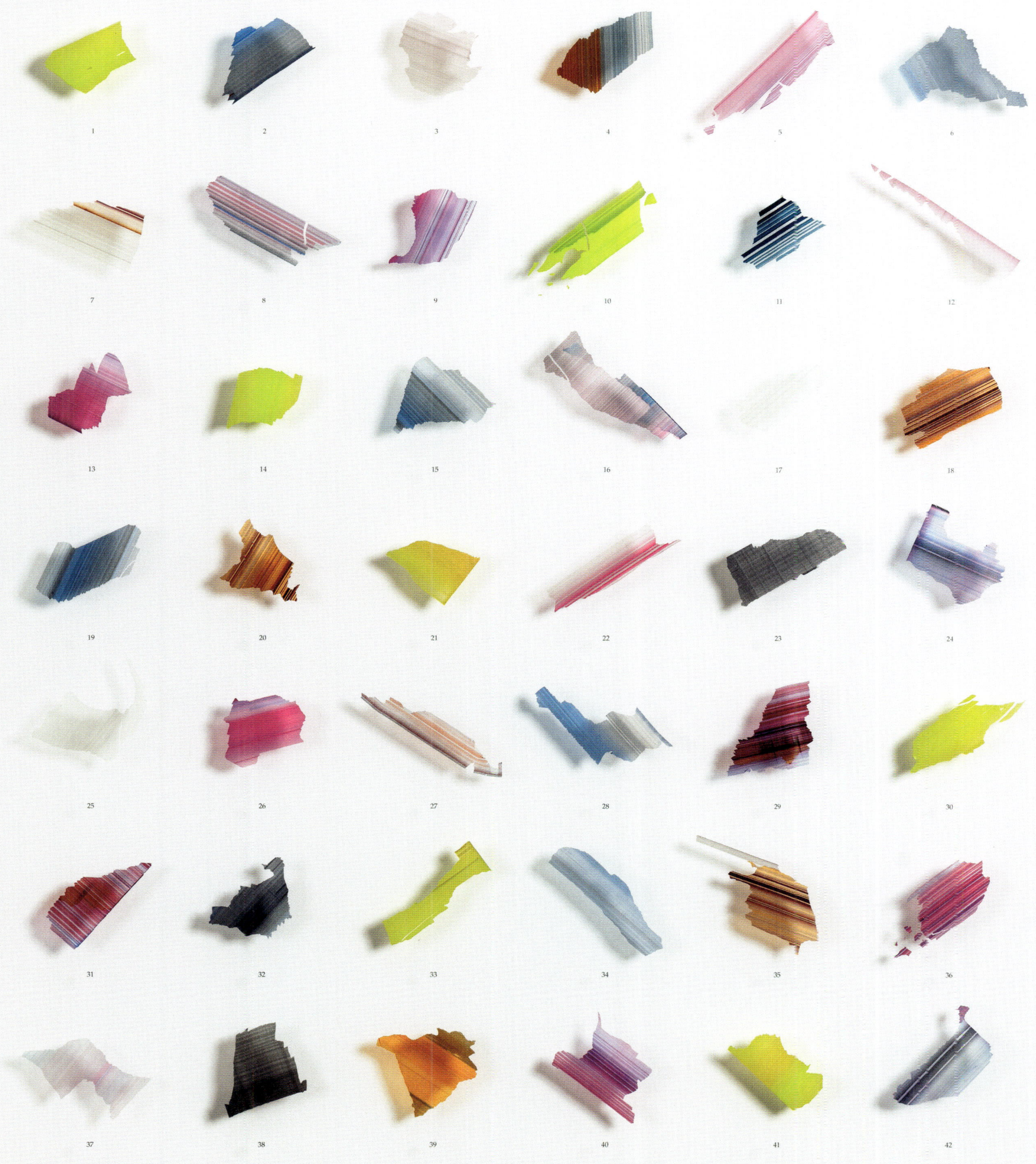

1, 10, 14, 21, 30, 33, 41: P/R. 787, Acrylic + Acrylic Gel on Aluminium, 2018 (Destroyed) 2, 6, 15, 19, 28, 32, 34: P/R. 962, Acrylic + Acrylic Gel on Glass, 2021 (Destroyed) 3, 5, 12, 16, 37: P/R. 963, Acrylic + Acrylic Gel on Glass, 2019 (Destroyed)

4: P/R. 964, Acrylic + Acrylic Gel on Glass, 2021 (Destroyed) 7, 18, 20, 35, 39: P/R. 892, Acrylic + Acrylic Gel on Aluminium, 2019 (Destroyed) 8, 24, 27, 29, 31, 42: P/R. 922, Acrylic + Acrylic Gel on Glass, 2020 (Destroyed)

9, 13, 26, 36, 40: P/R. 923, Acrylic + Acrylic Gel on Glass, 2020 (Destroyed) 11: P/R. 966, Acrylic + Acrylic Gel on Glass, 2020 (Destroyed) 17, 22, 25: P/R. 969, Acrylic + Acrylic Gel on Glass, 2020 (Destroyed)

23, 34, 38: P/R. 962, Acrylic + Acrylic Gel on Glass, 2021 (Destroyed)

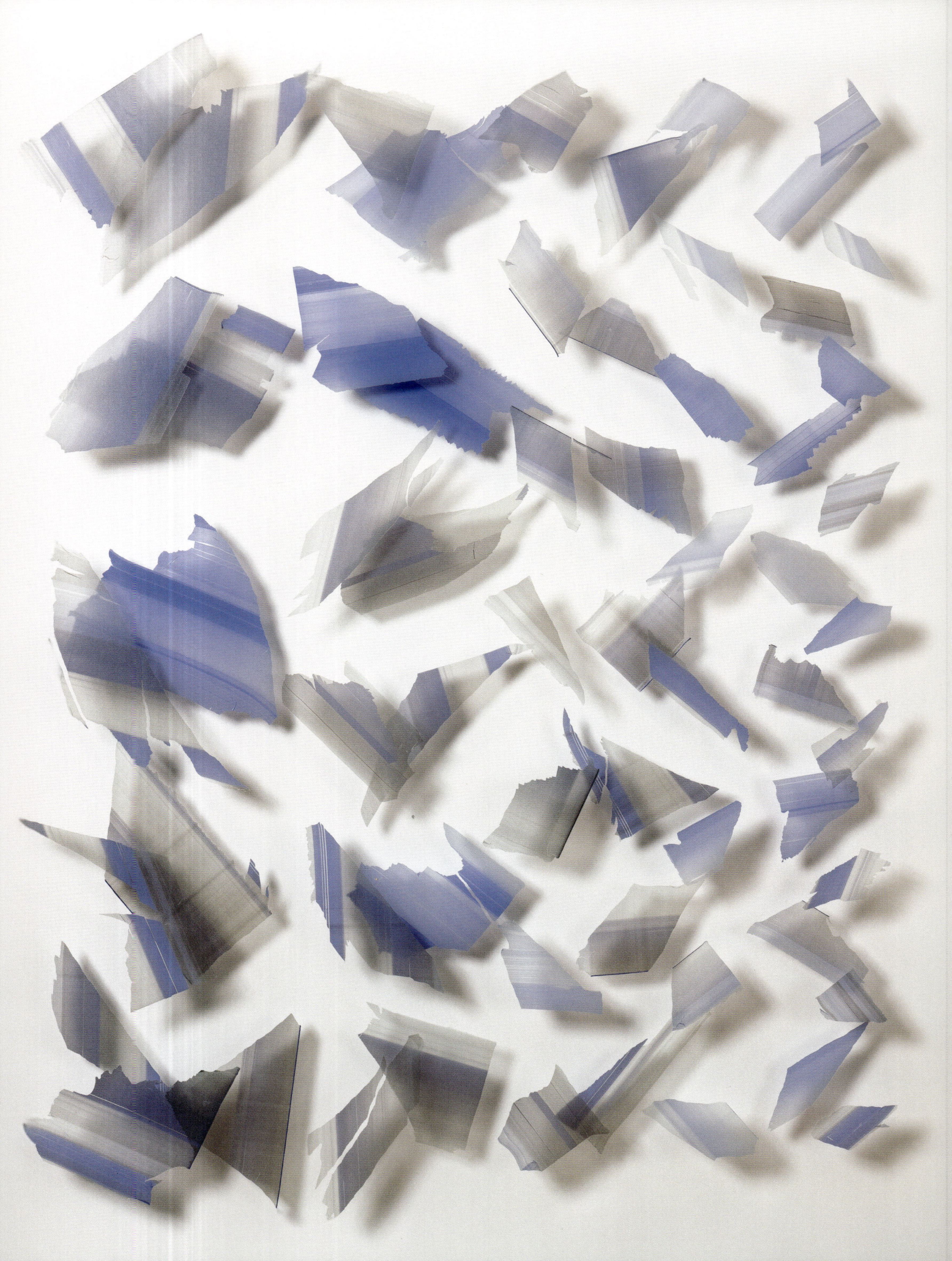

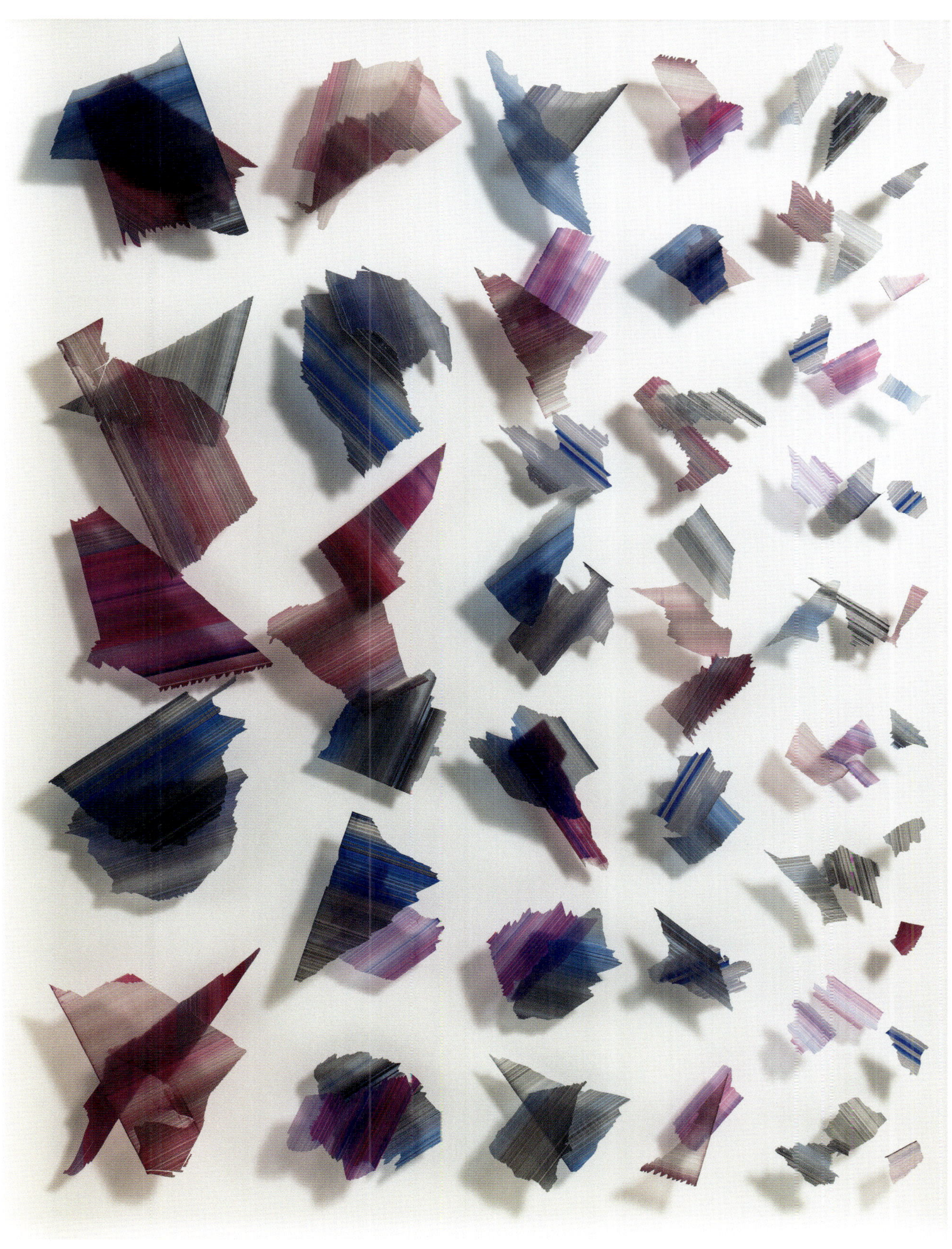

T/R.1084, Recycled Paint Fragments: Acrylic, Graphite, Tin + Acrylic Gel on Glass, 109 × 86 cm, 2025

T/R.1014, Recycled Paint Fragments: Acrylic, Graphite + Acrylic Gel on Glass, 109 × 86 cm, 2022

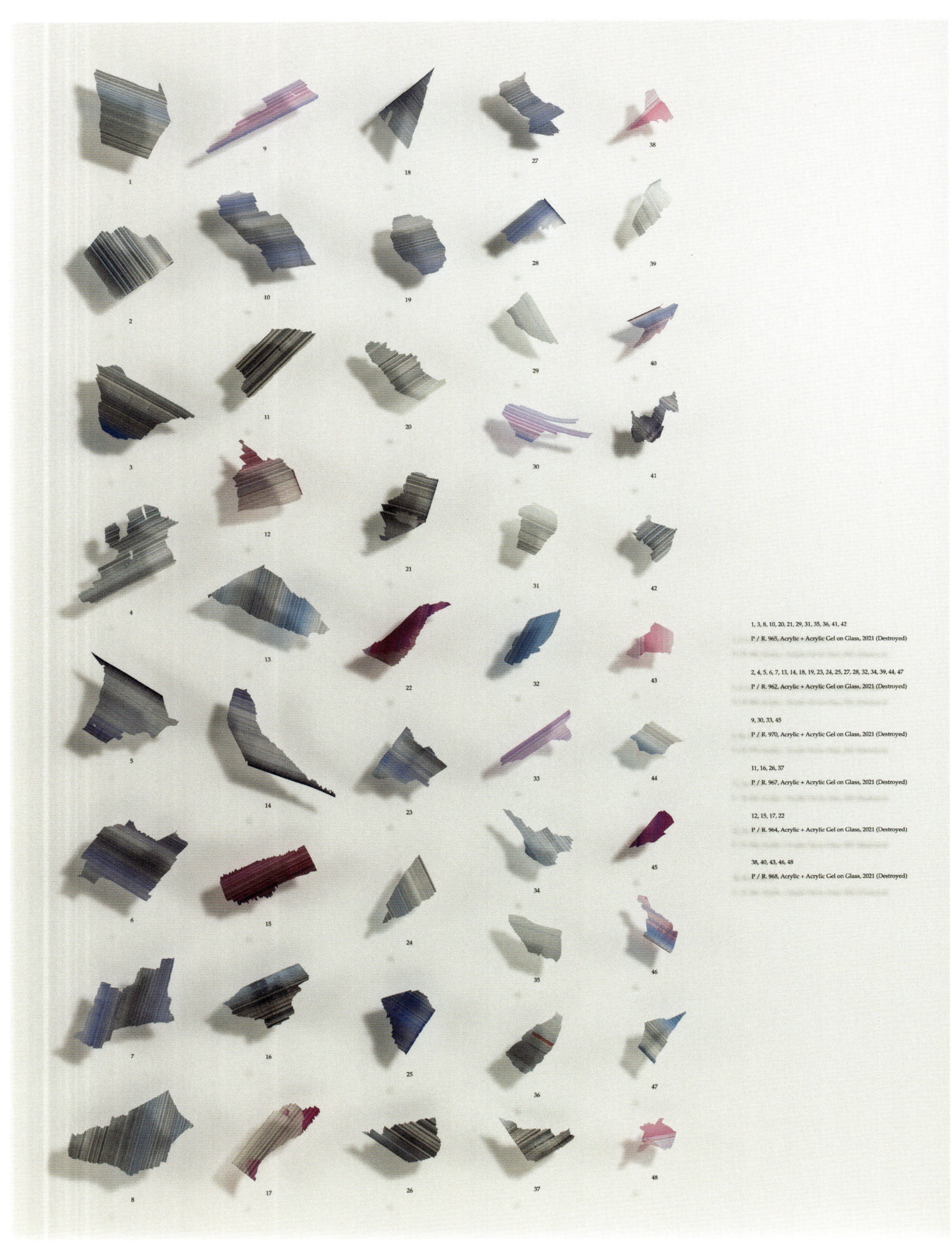

T/R.1008, Recycled Paint Fragments: Acrylic, Graphite, Acrylic Gel + Text on Glass, 109 × 86 cm, 2022

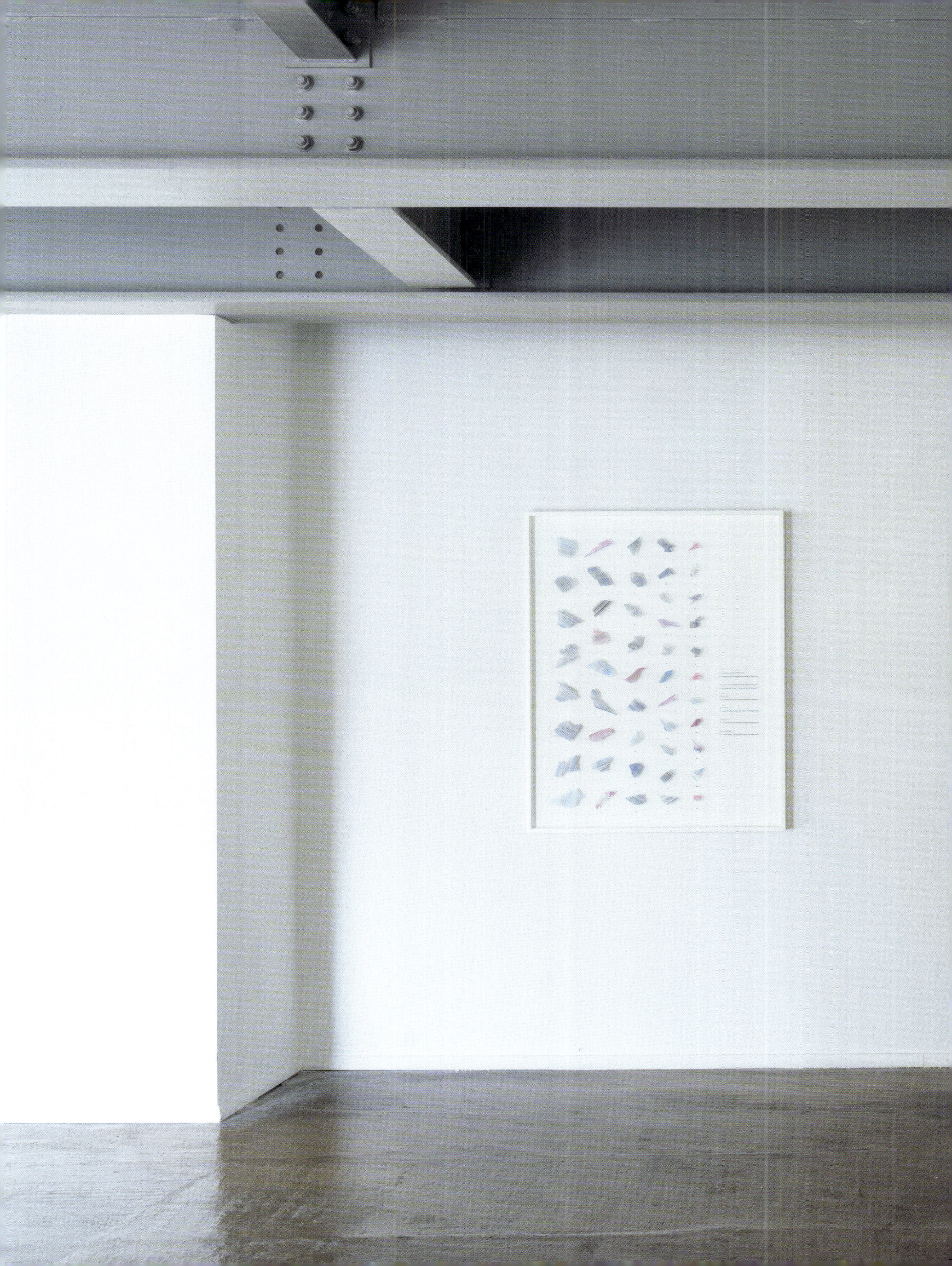

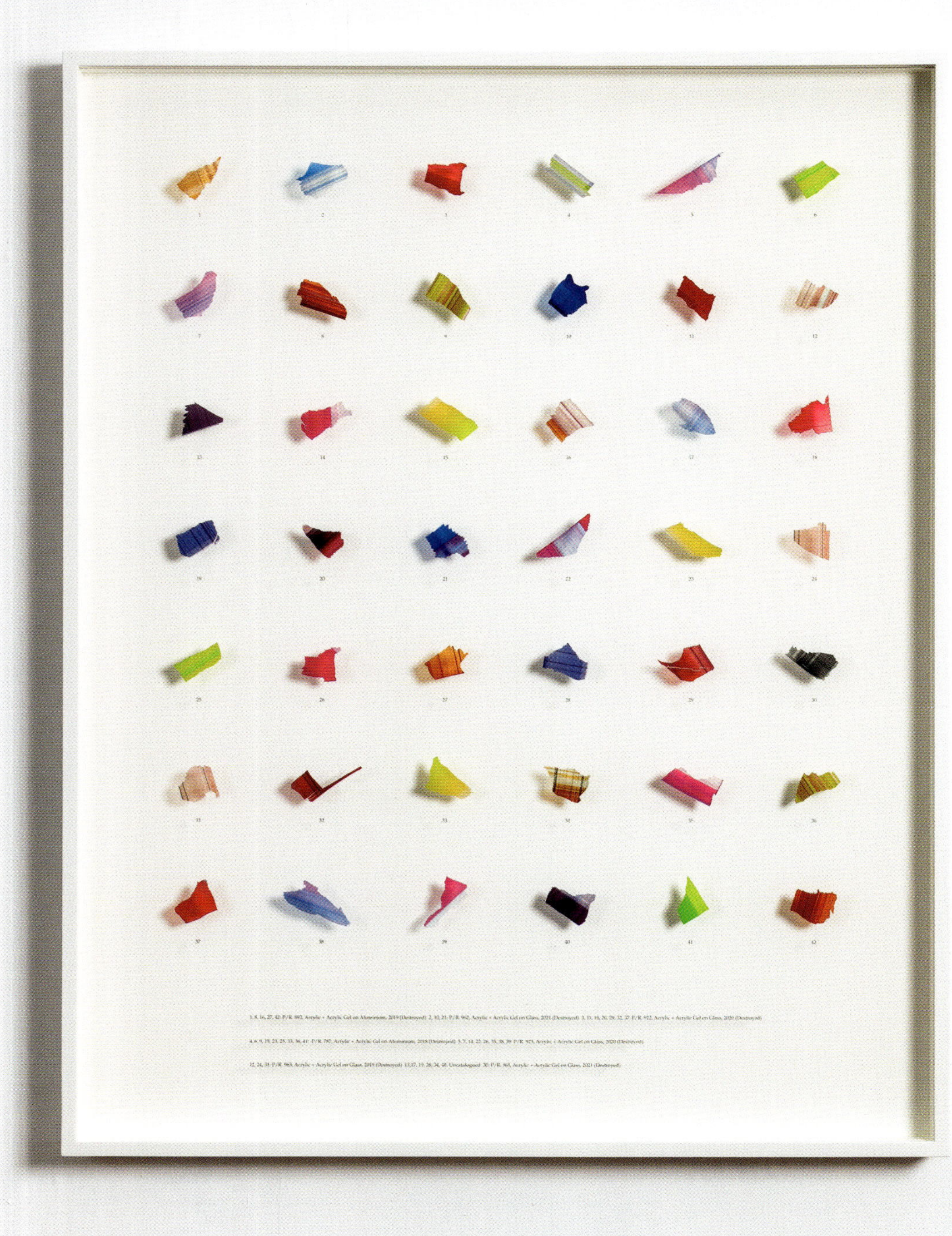

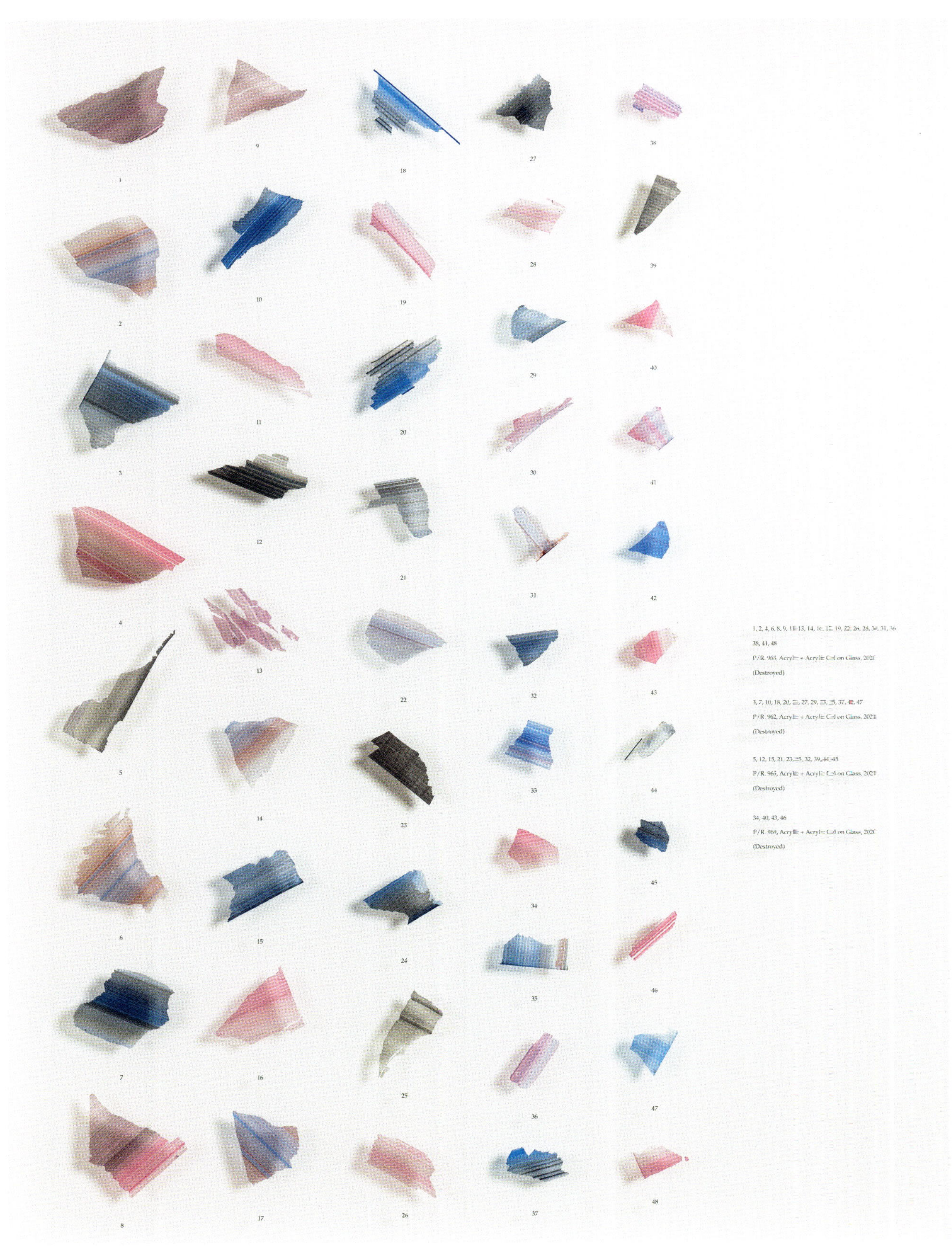

T/R.1053, Recycled Paint Fragments: Acrylic, Graphite, Acrylic Gel + Text on Glass, 109×86 cm, 2024

T/R.1047, Recycled Paint Fragments: Acrylic, Graphite, Acrylic Gel + Text on Glass, 109×86 cm, 2024

Following double page
T/R 973, Recycled Paint Fragments: Acrylic, Graphite + Acrylic Gel on Glass, 44×55 cm, 2022

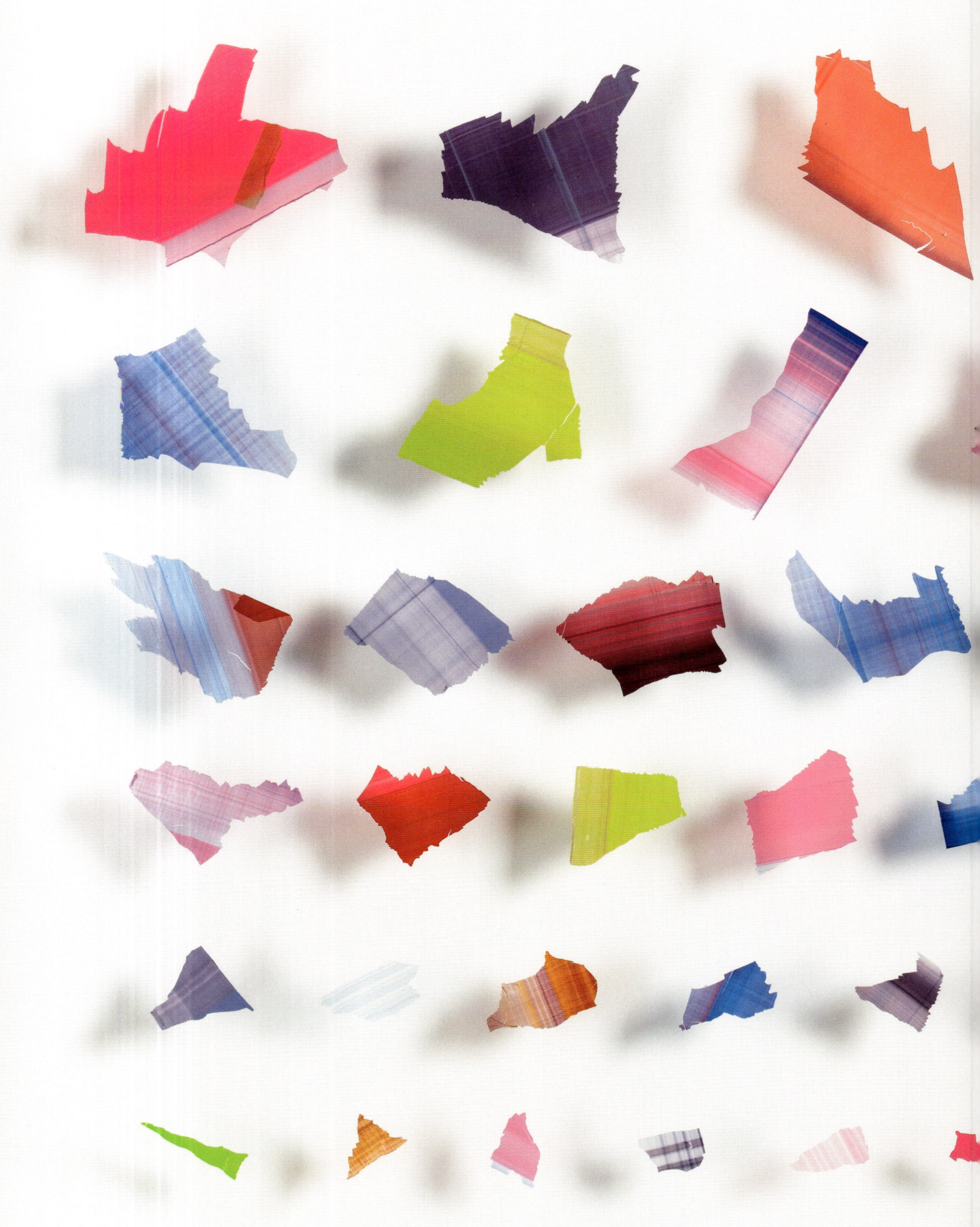

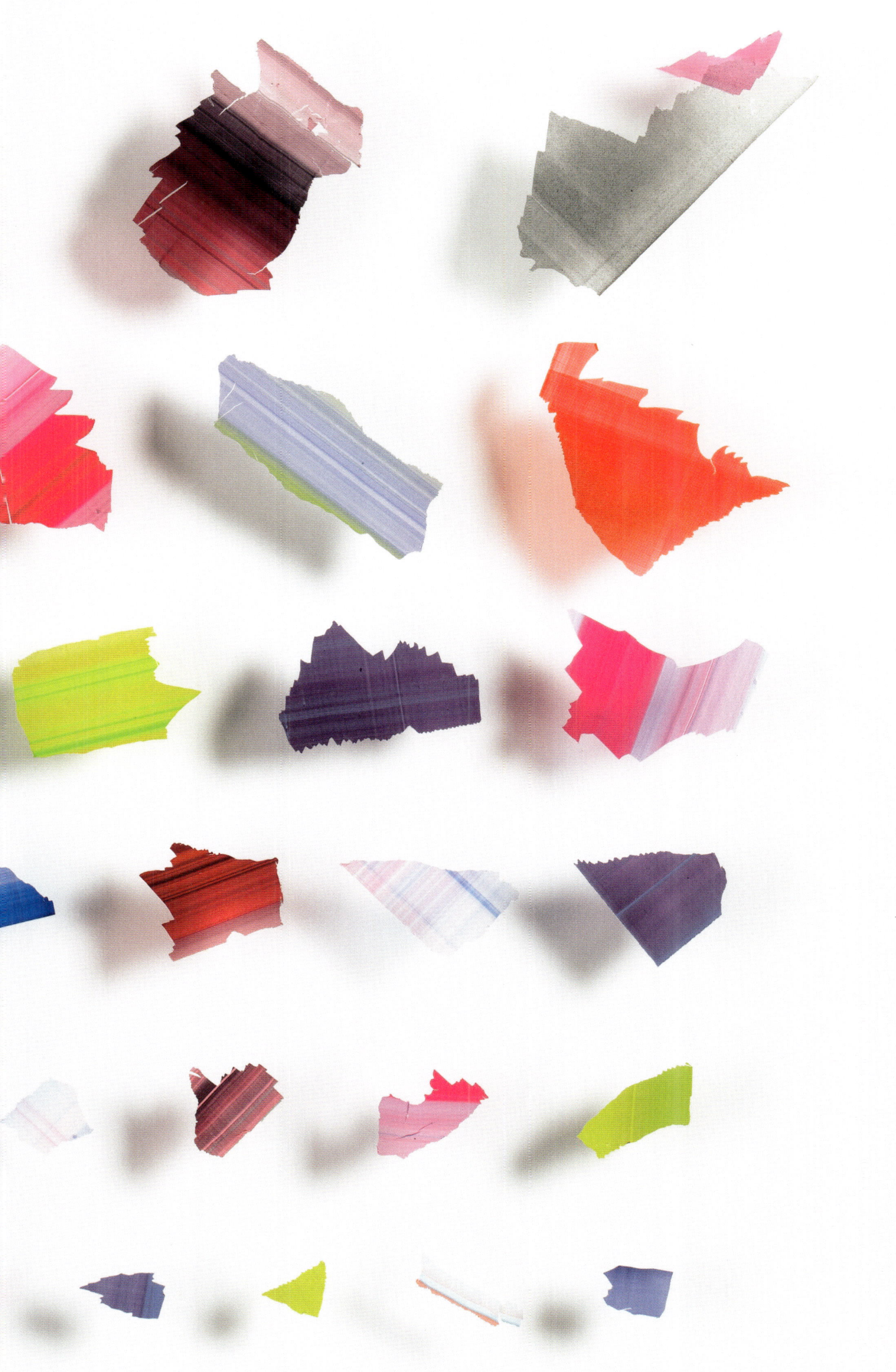

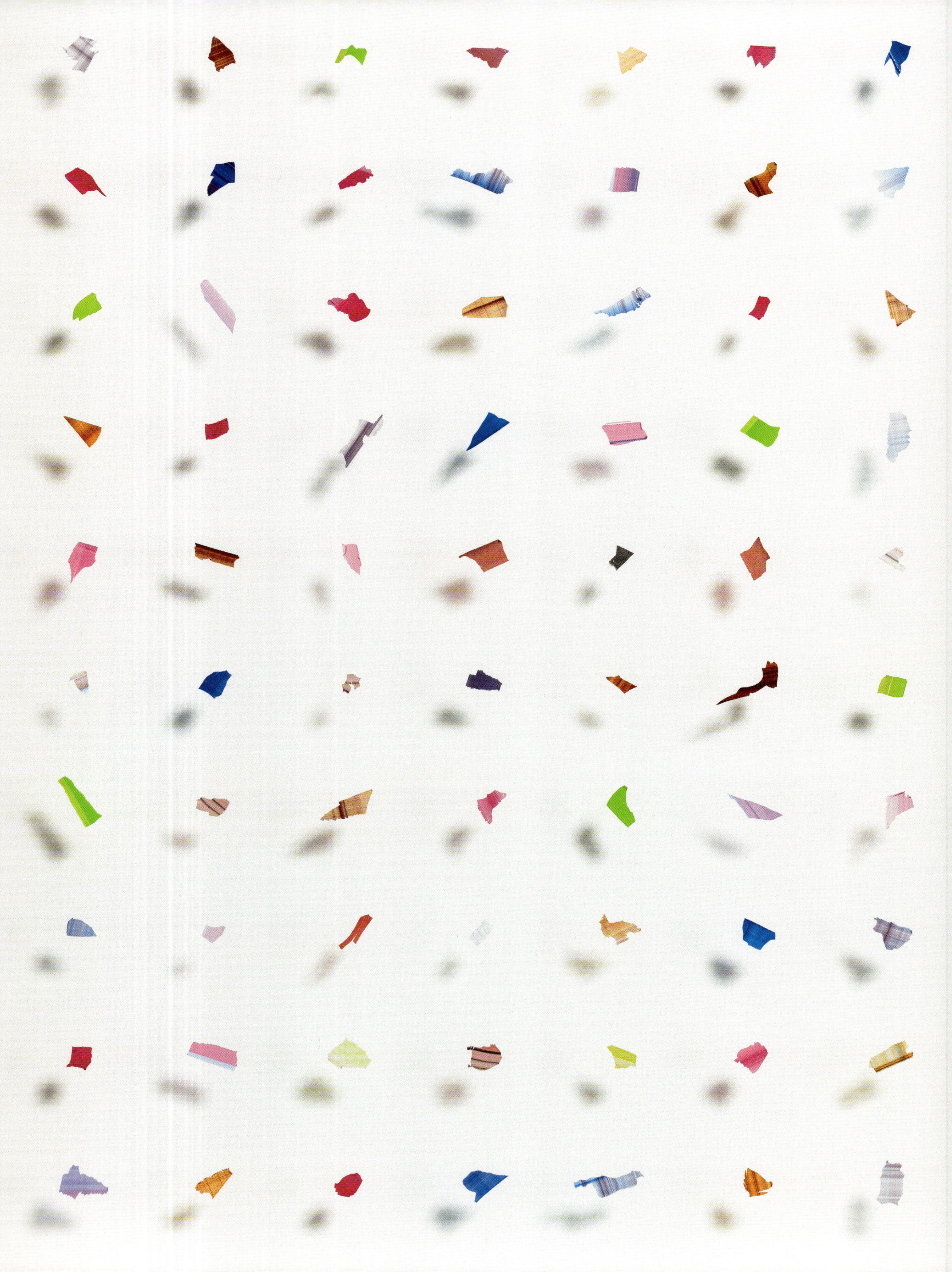

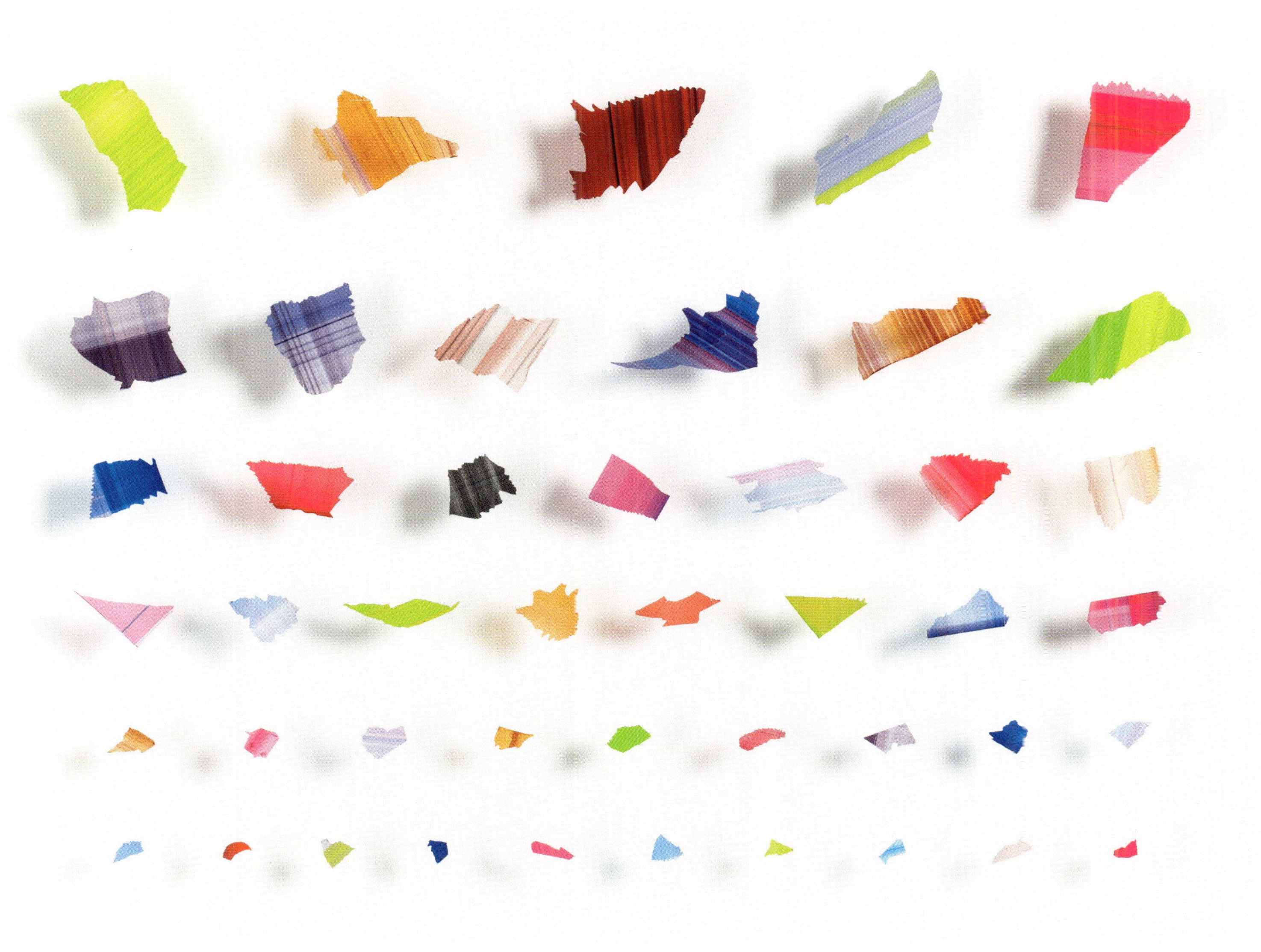

T/R.952, Recycled Paint Fragments: Acrylic, Graphite + Acrylic Gel on Glass, 55×44 cm, 2021

T/R.971, Recycled Paint Fragments: Acrylic, Graphite + Acrylic Gel on Glass, 44×55 cm, 2022

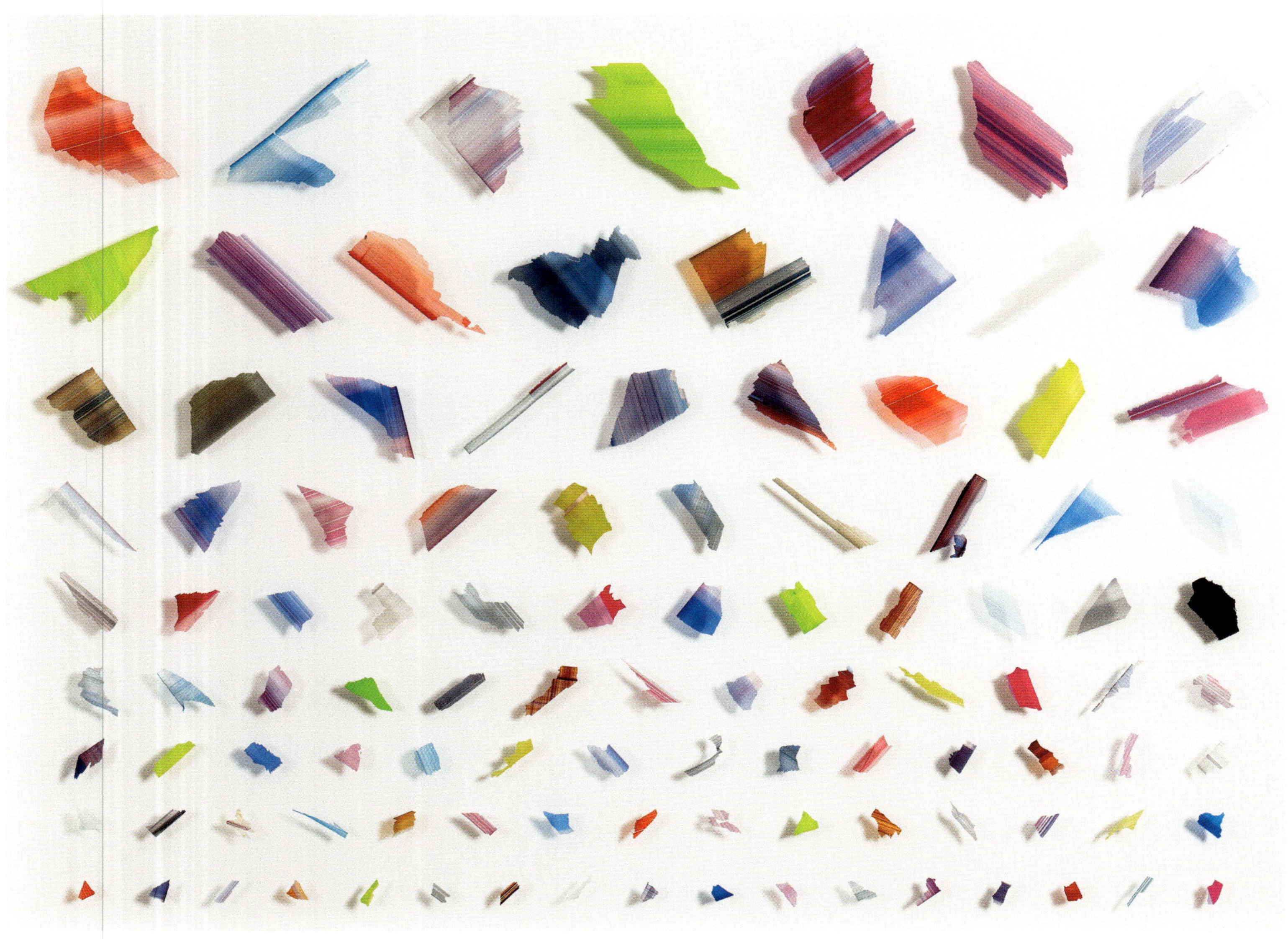

T/R.1052, Recycled Paint Fragments: Acrylic, Graphite + Acrylic Gel on Glass, 104 × 140 cm, 2024

T/R.955, Recycled Paint Fragments: Acrylic, Graphite + Acrylic Gel on Glass, 85 × 71 cm, 2021

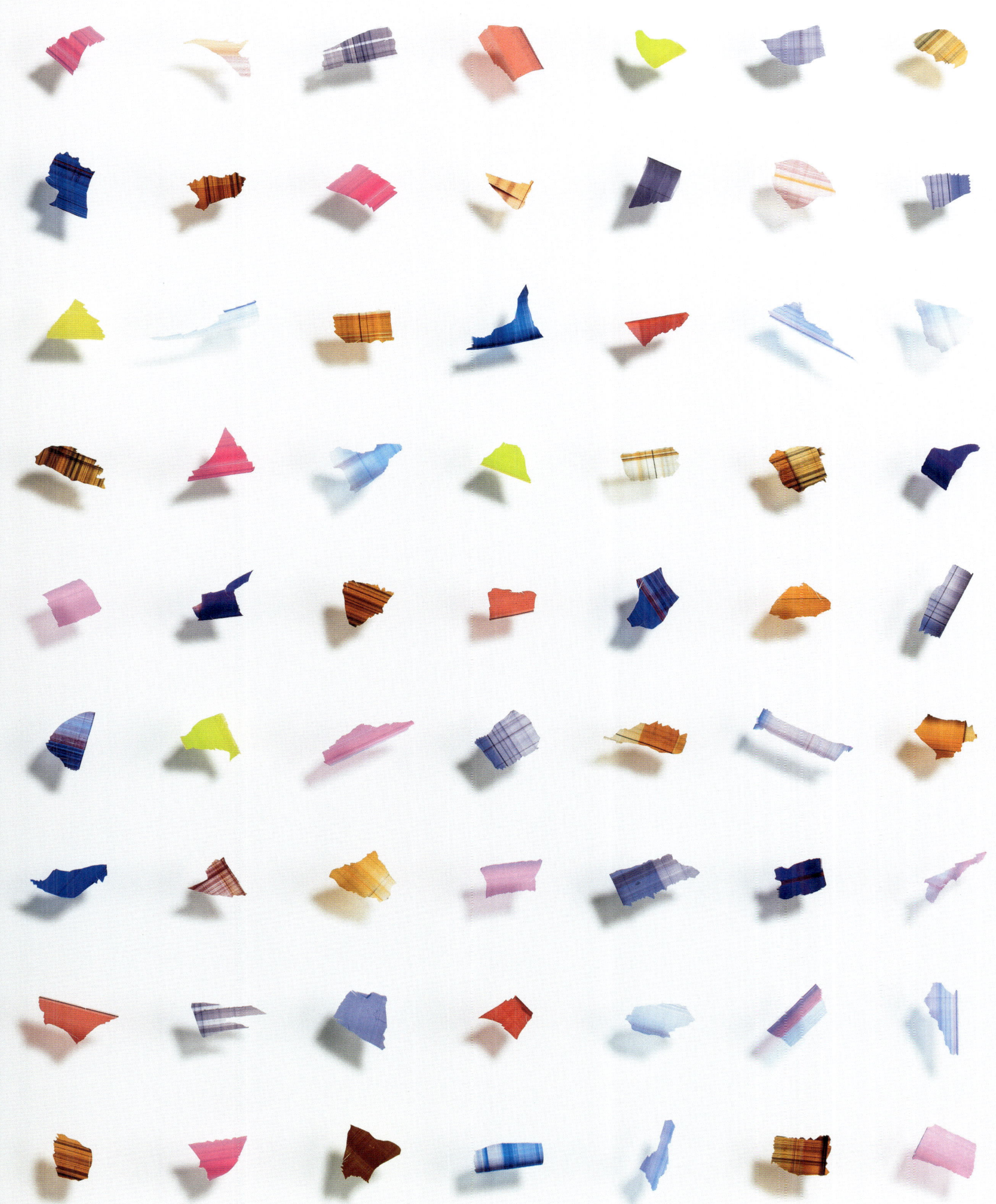

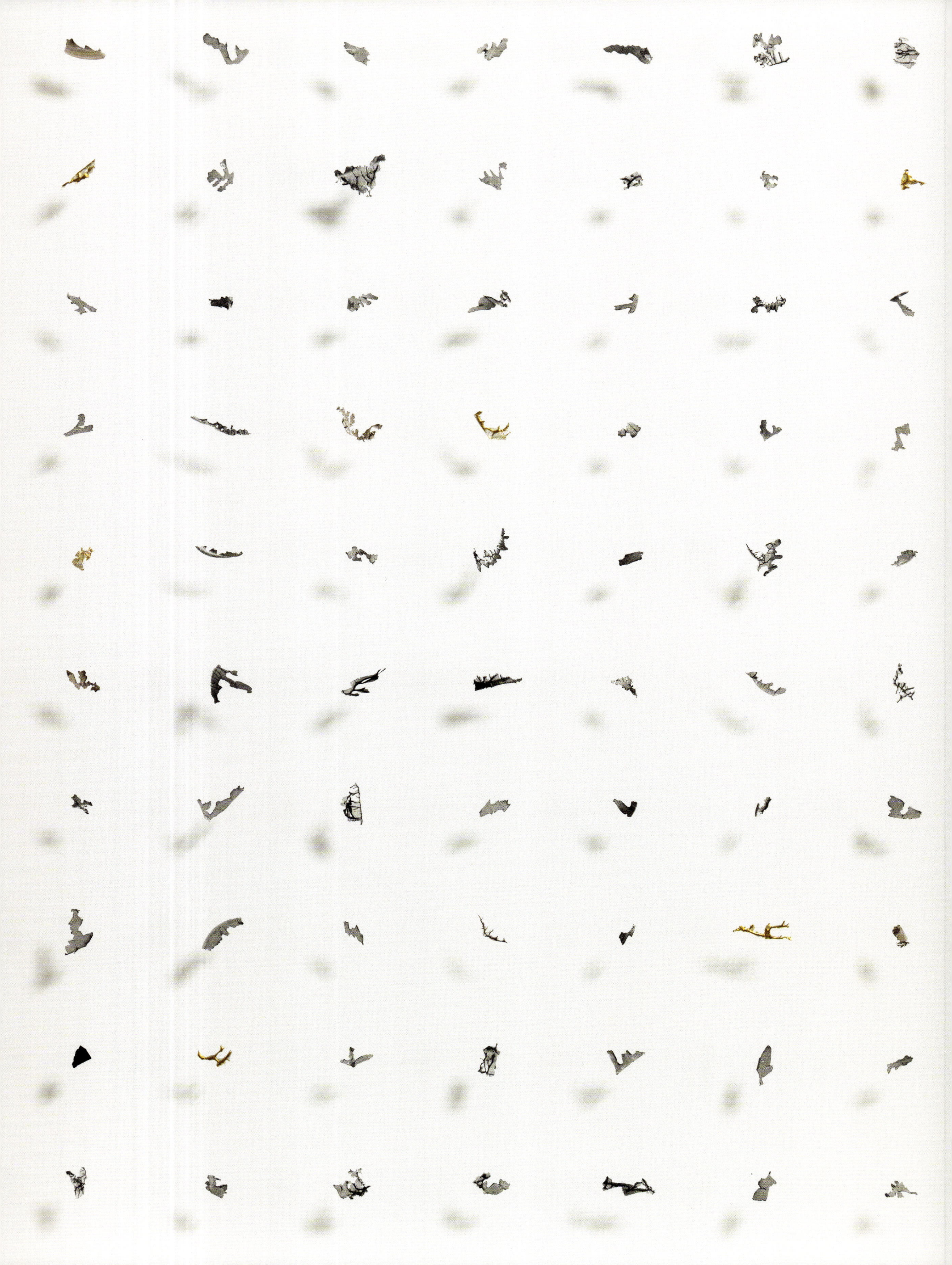

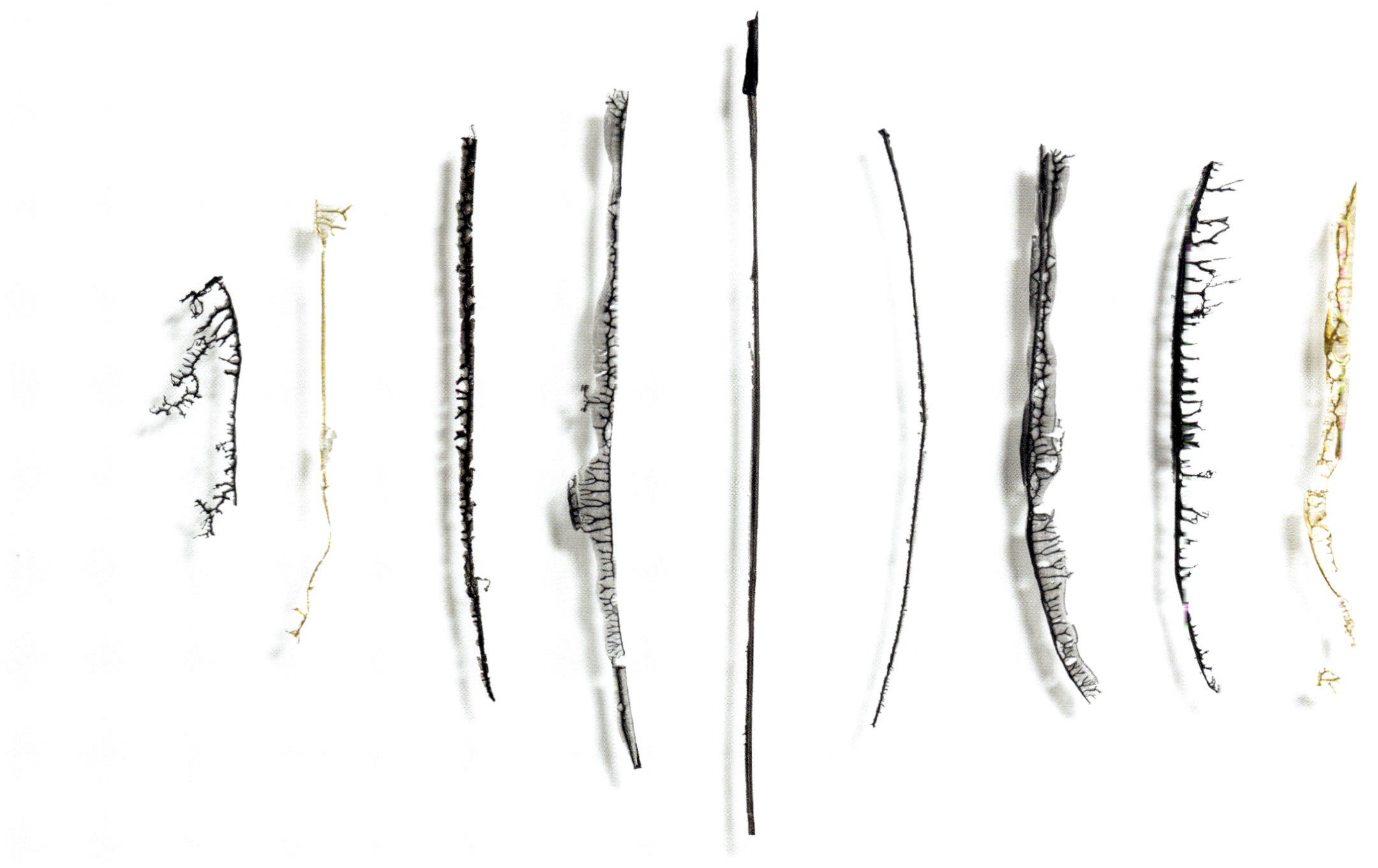

T/R.945 (Incidental Fragments), Recycled Paint Fragments: Graphite, Bronze + Acrylic Gel on Glass, 55 × 44 cm, 2021

T/R.944 (Incidental Fragments), Recycled Paint Fragments: Graphite, Bronze + Acrylic Gel on Glass, 44 × 55 cm, 2020

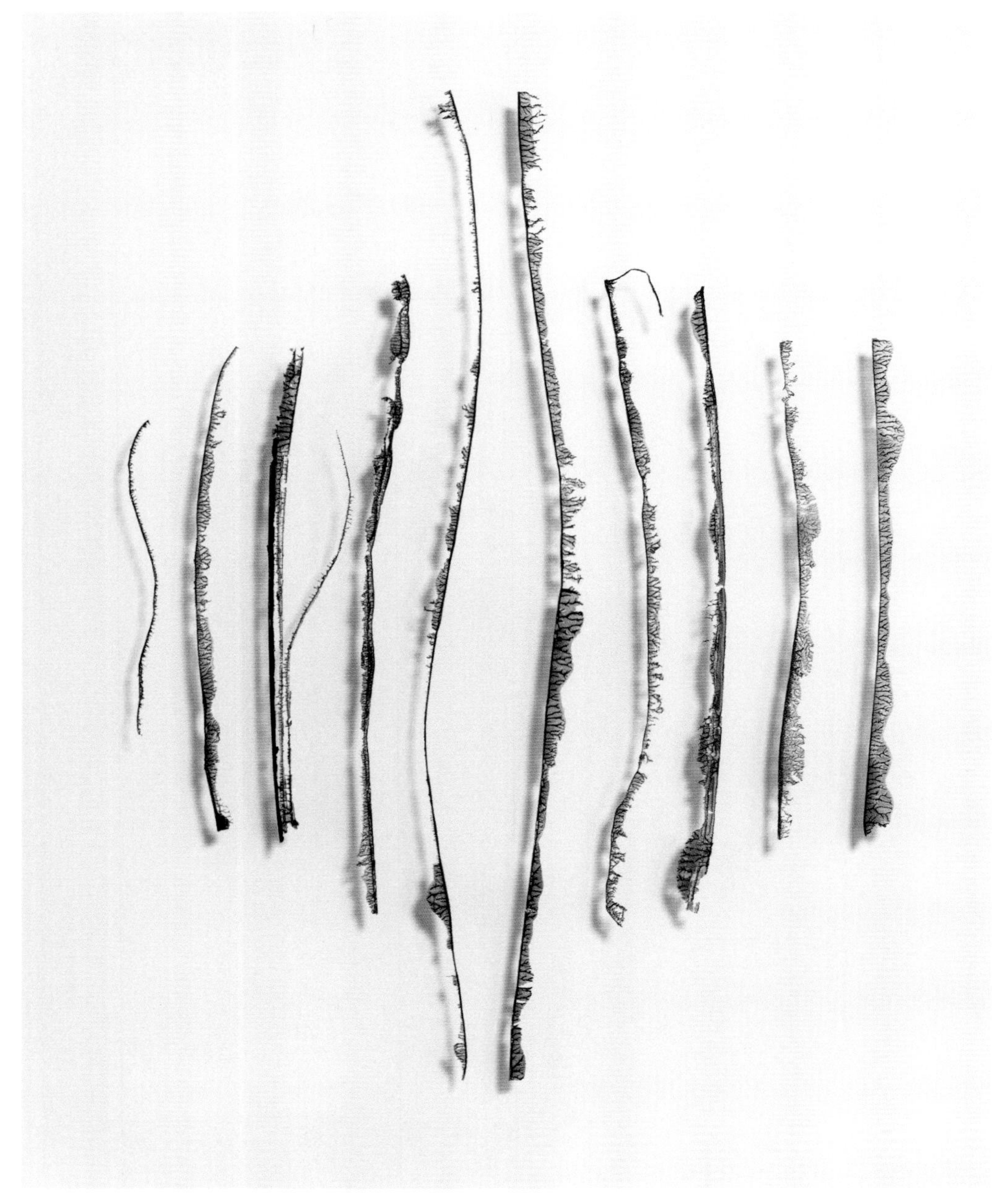

T/R.949 (Incidental Fragments), Recycled Paint Fragments: Graphite, Bronze + Acrylic Gel on Glass, 85×71 cm, 2020

P/R.1085, Studio Detritus: Aluminium, Cardboard, Packing Foam, Plywood, Foamboard, Composite Board in Plexiglas, 70×65 cm, 2025

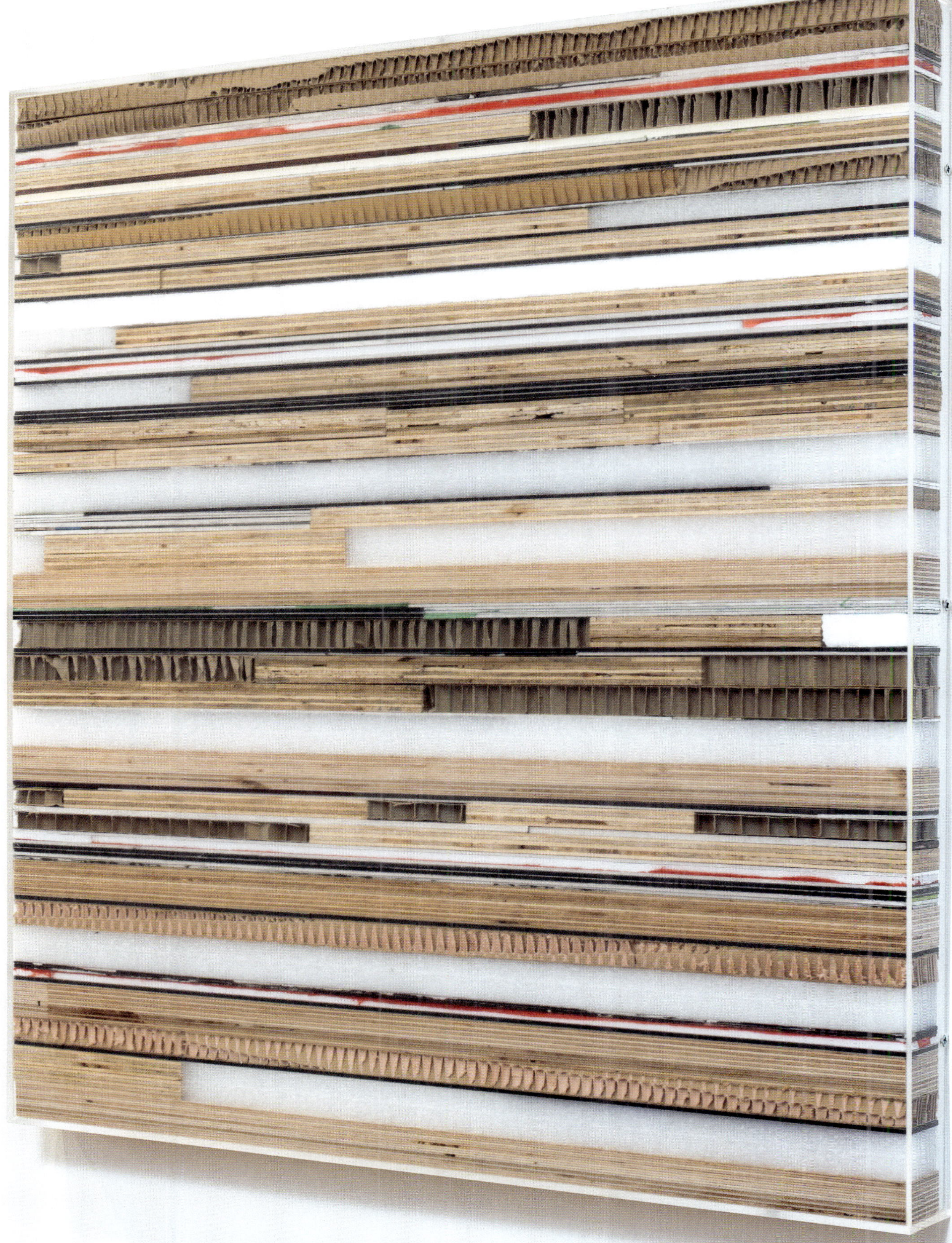

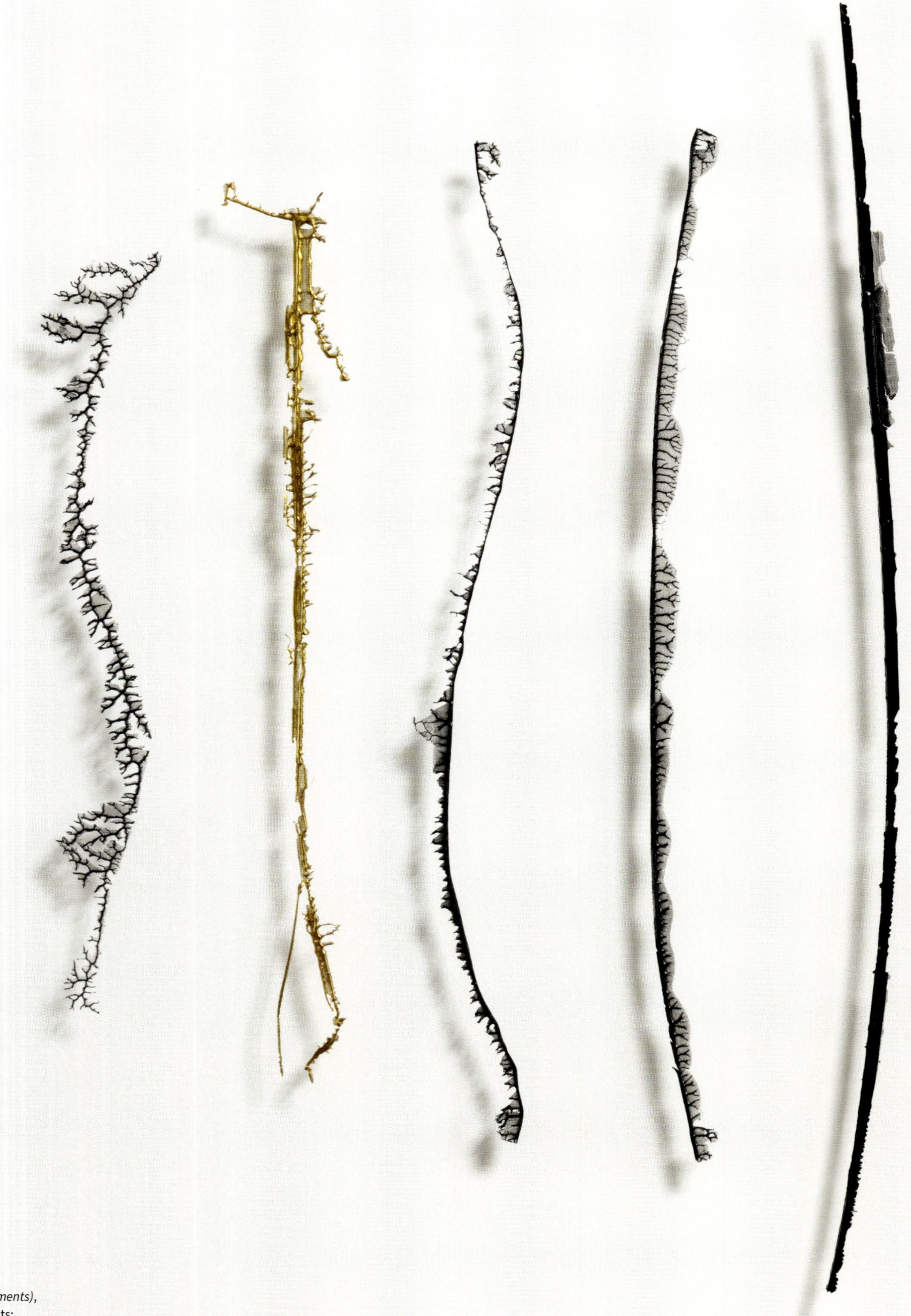

T/R.950 (Incidental Fragments),
Recycled Paint Fragments:
Graphite, Bronze + Acrylic Gel
on Glass, 71×85 cm, 2020

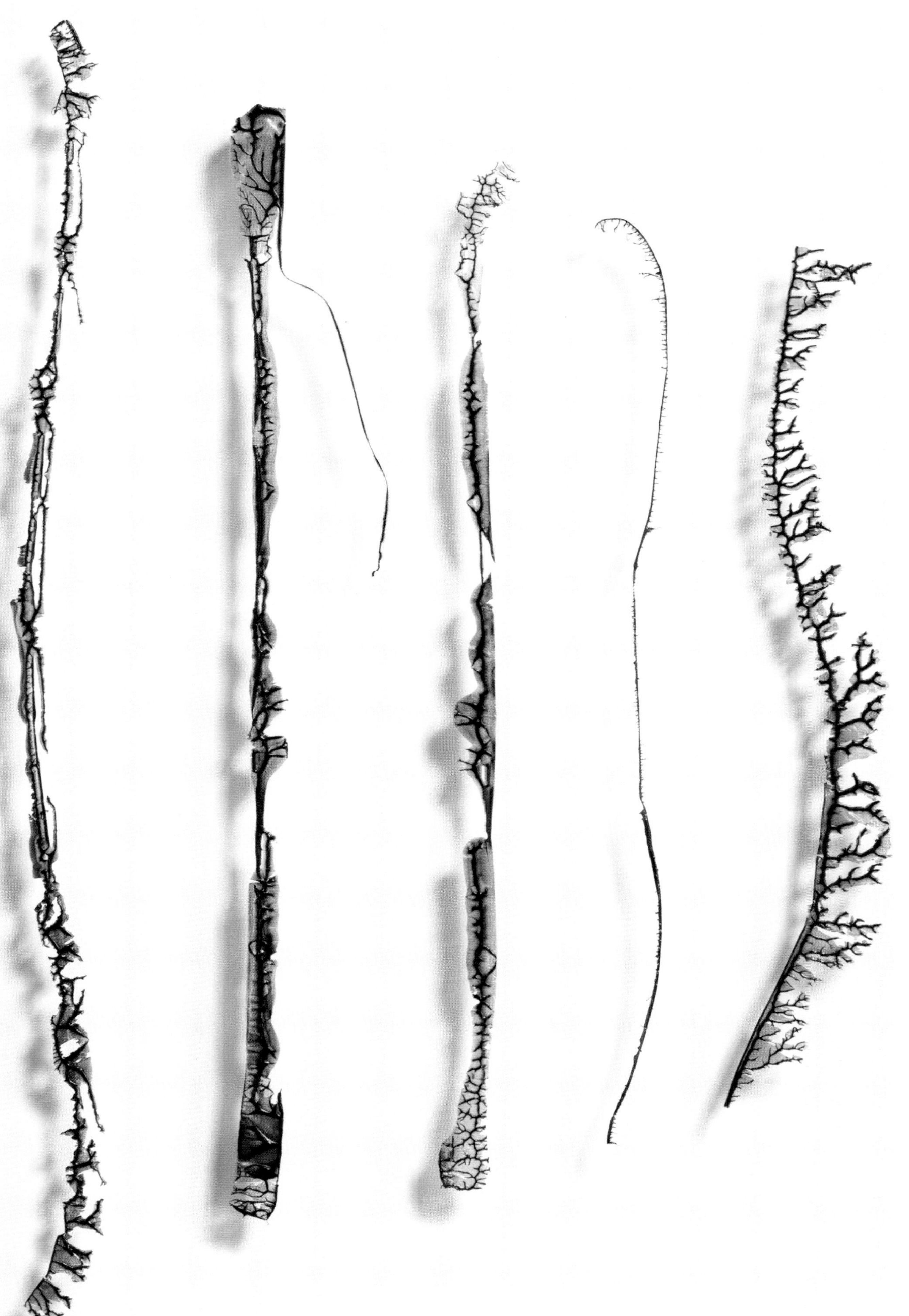

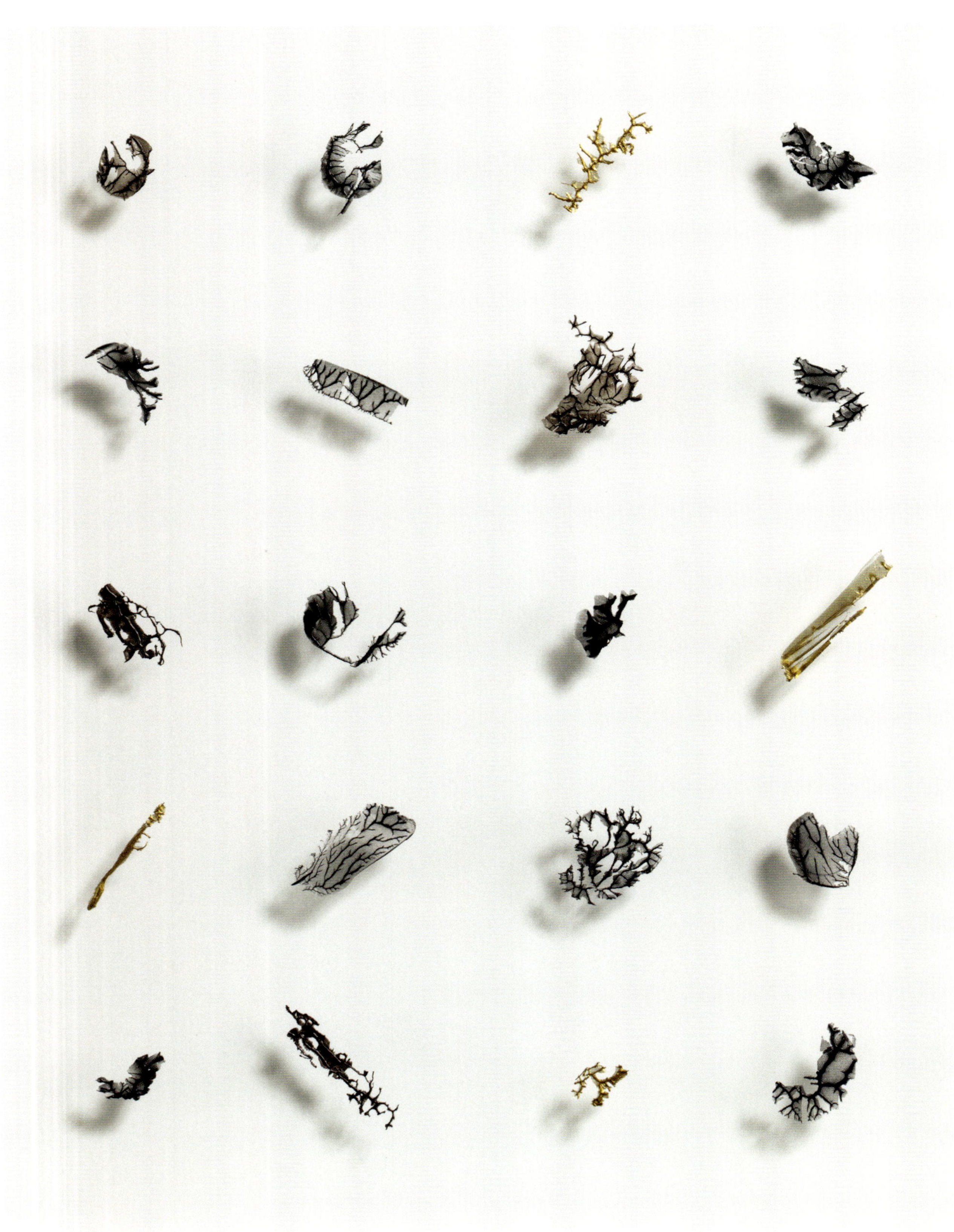

T/R.946 (Incidental Fragments),
Recycled Paint Fragments:
Graphite, Bronze + Acrylic Gel
on Glass, 55 × 44 cm, 2021

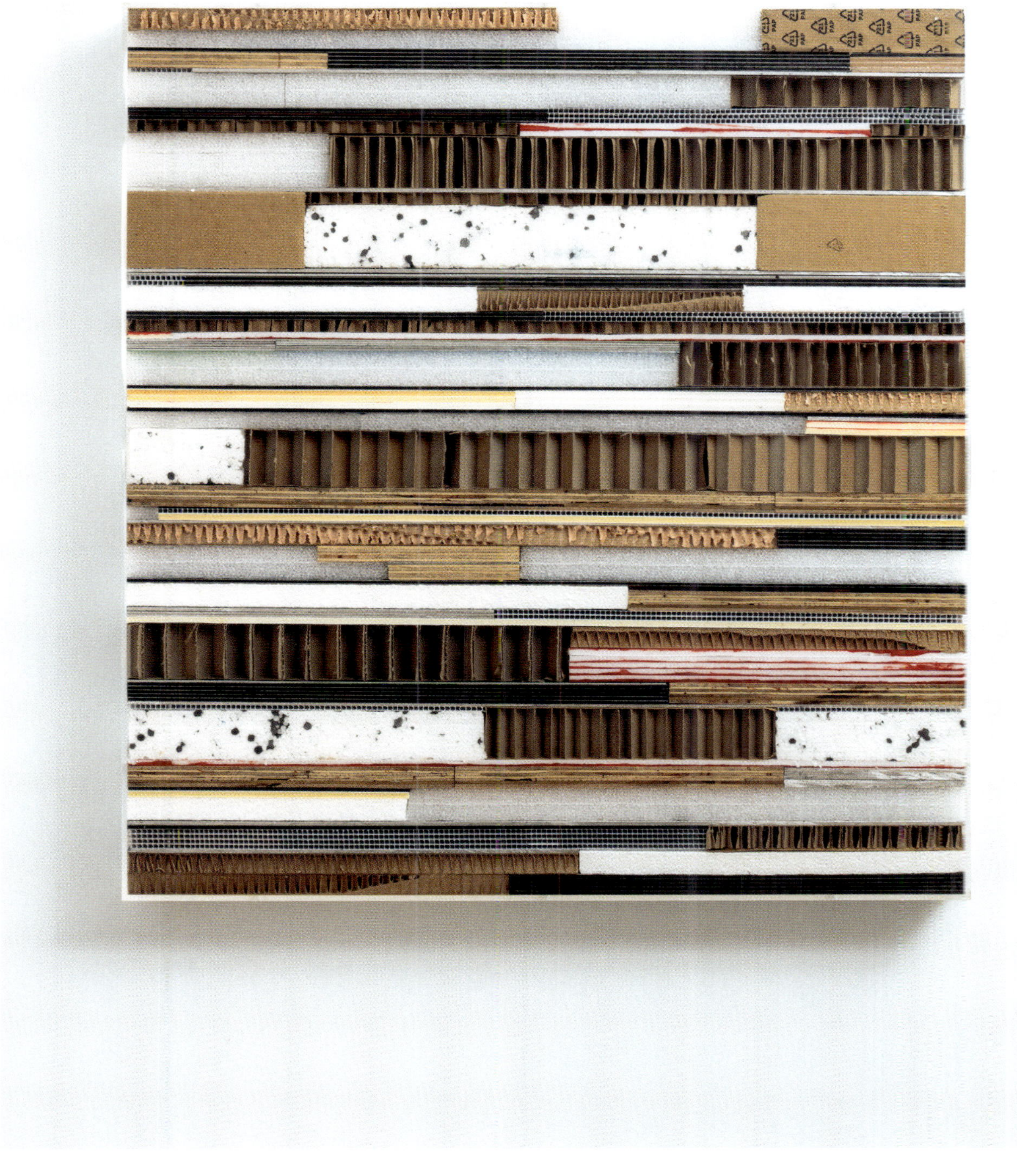

P/R.1113, Studio Detritus:
Aluminium, Cardboard,
Packing Foam, Plywood,
Foamboard, Composite Board
in Plexiglas, 70×65 cm, 2025

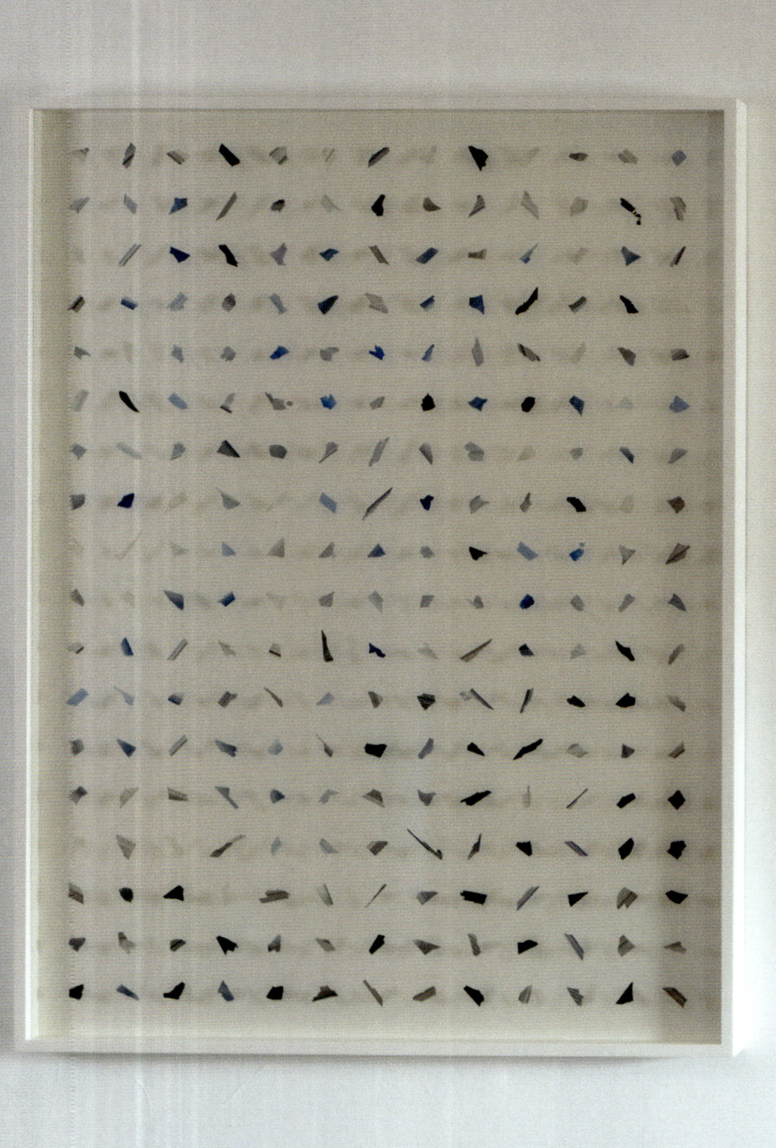
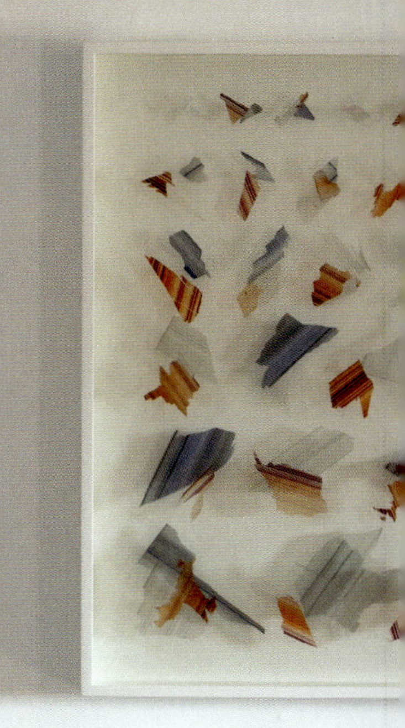

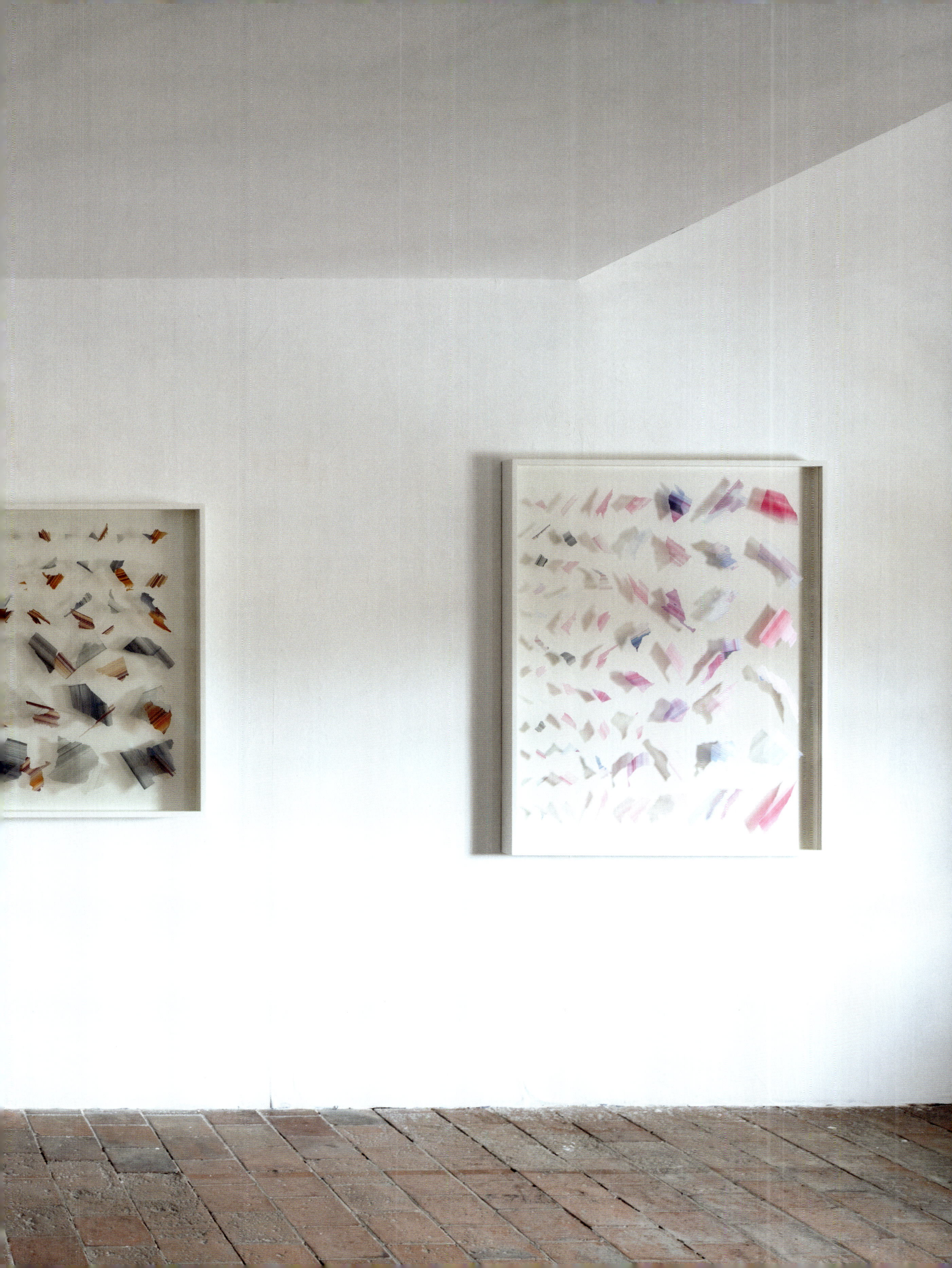

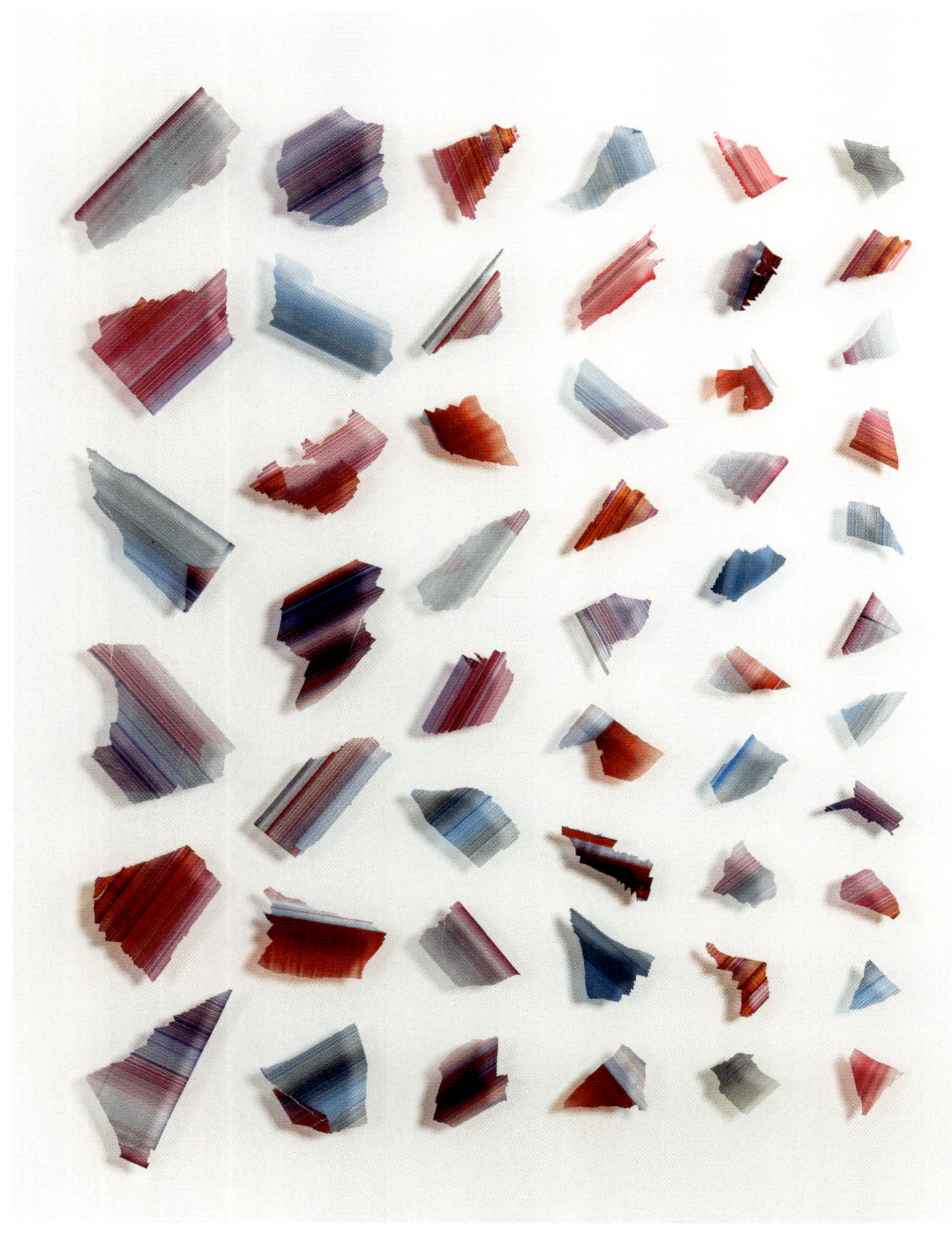

T/R.1040, Recycled Paint Fragments: Acrylic, Graphite + Acrylic Gel on Glass, 109×86 cm, 2024

T/R.1029, Recycled Paint Fragments: Acrylic, Graphite + Acrylic Gel on Glass, 109×86 cm, 2023

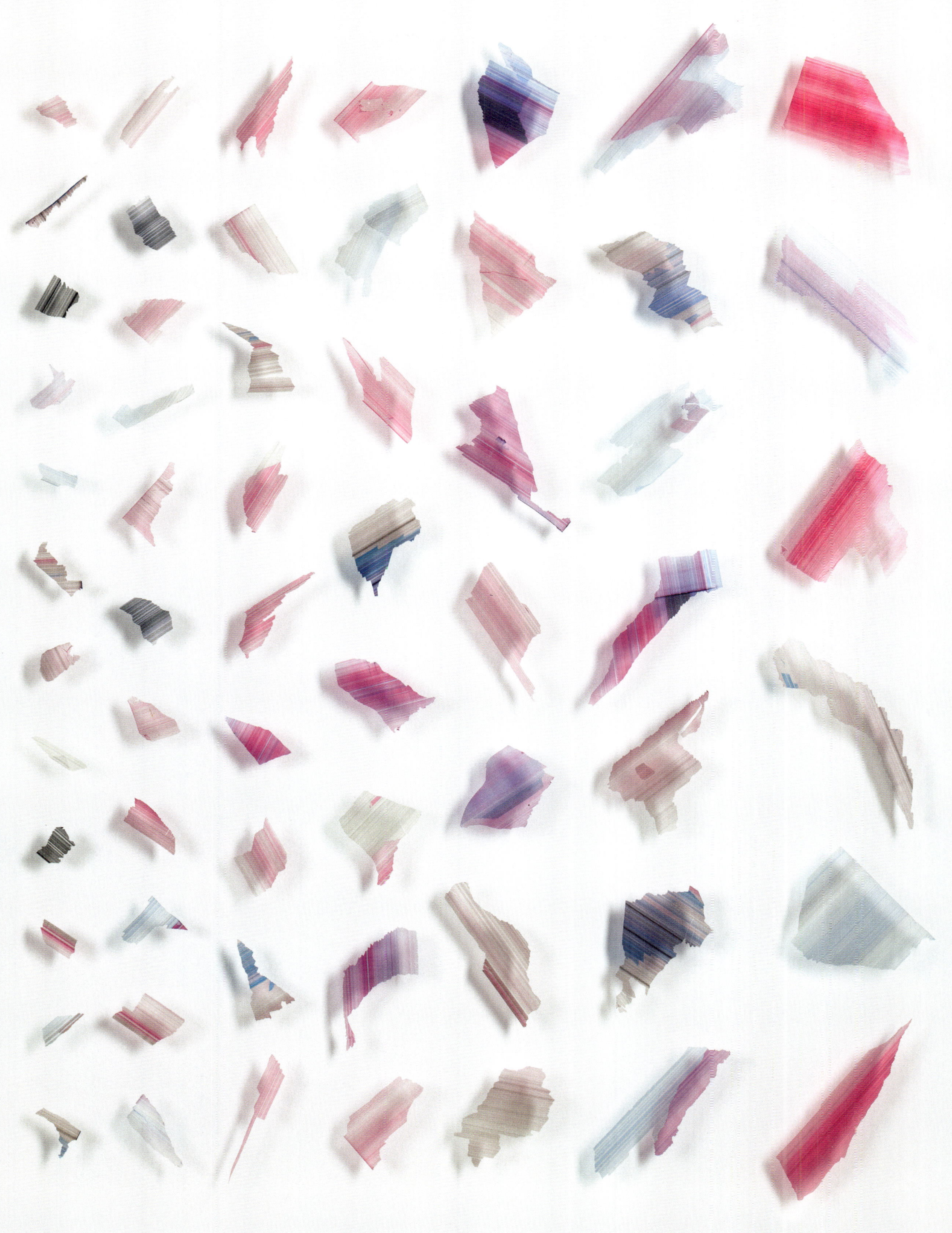

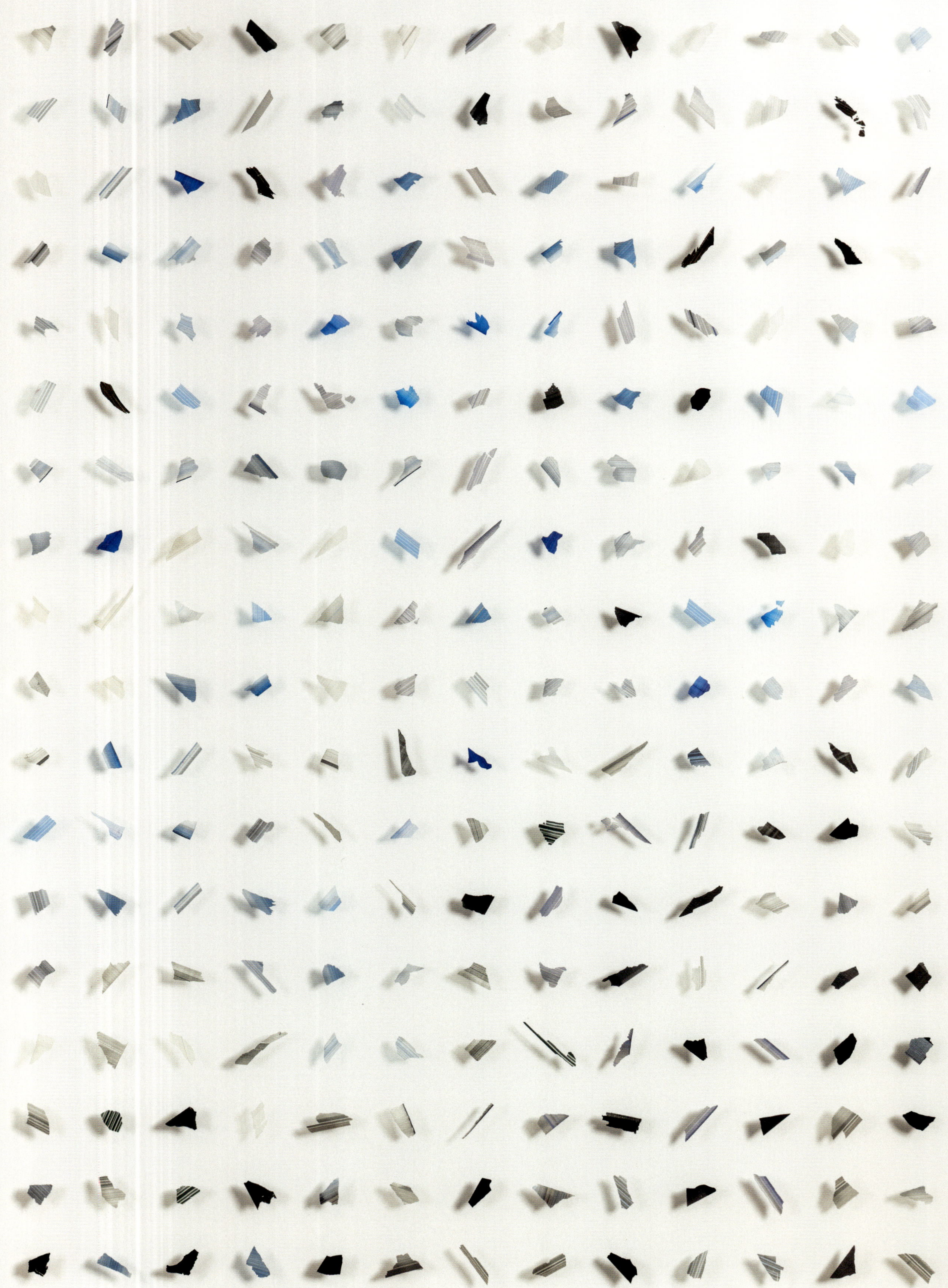

T/R.1037, Recycled Paint
Fragments: Acrylic, Graphite
+ Acrylic Gel on Glass,
140 × 104 cm, 2024

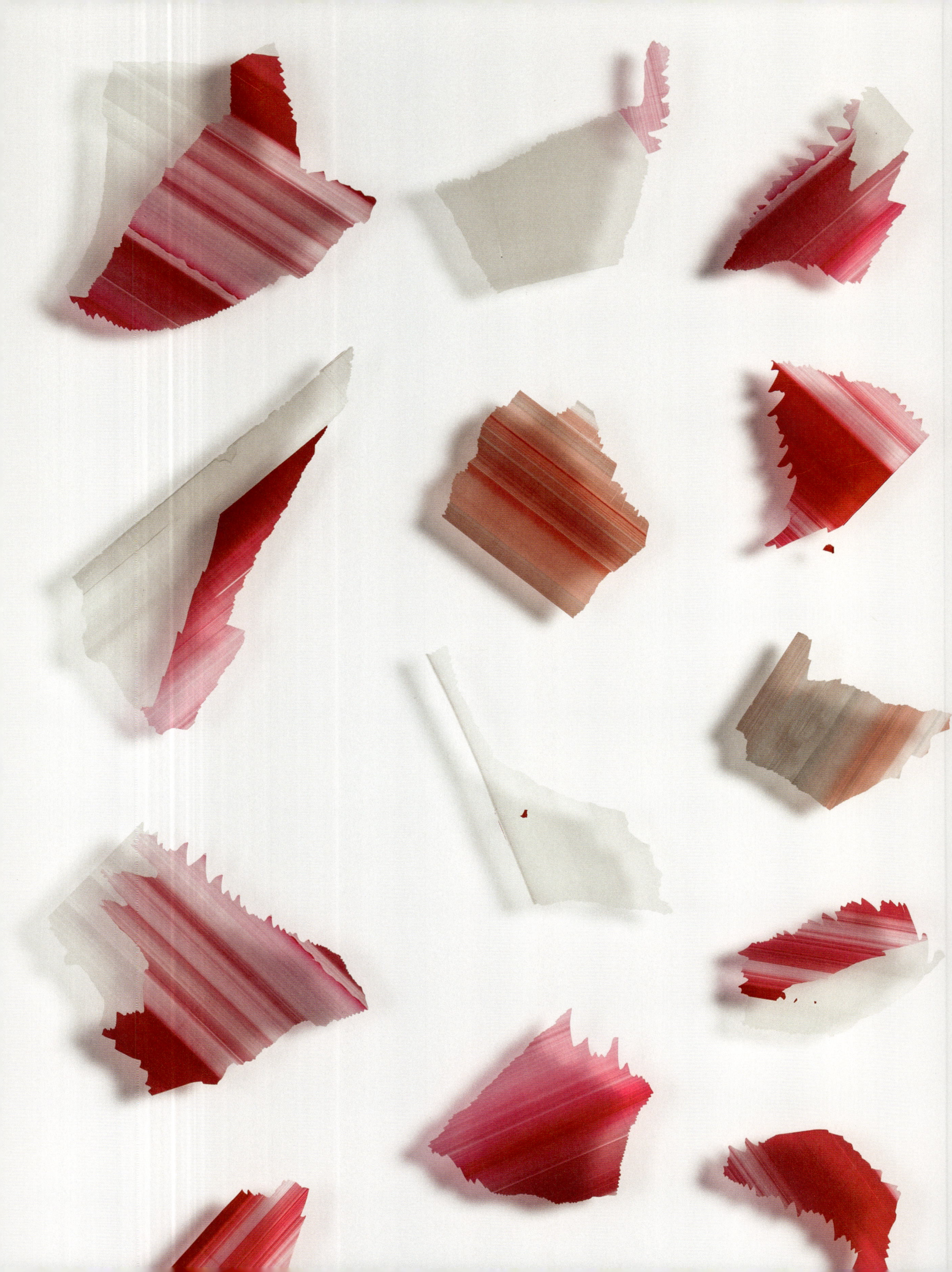

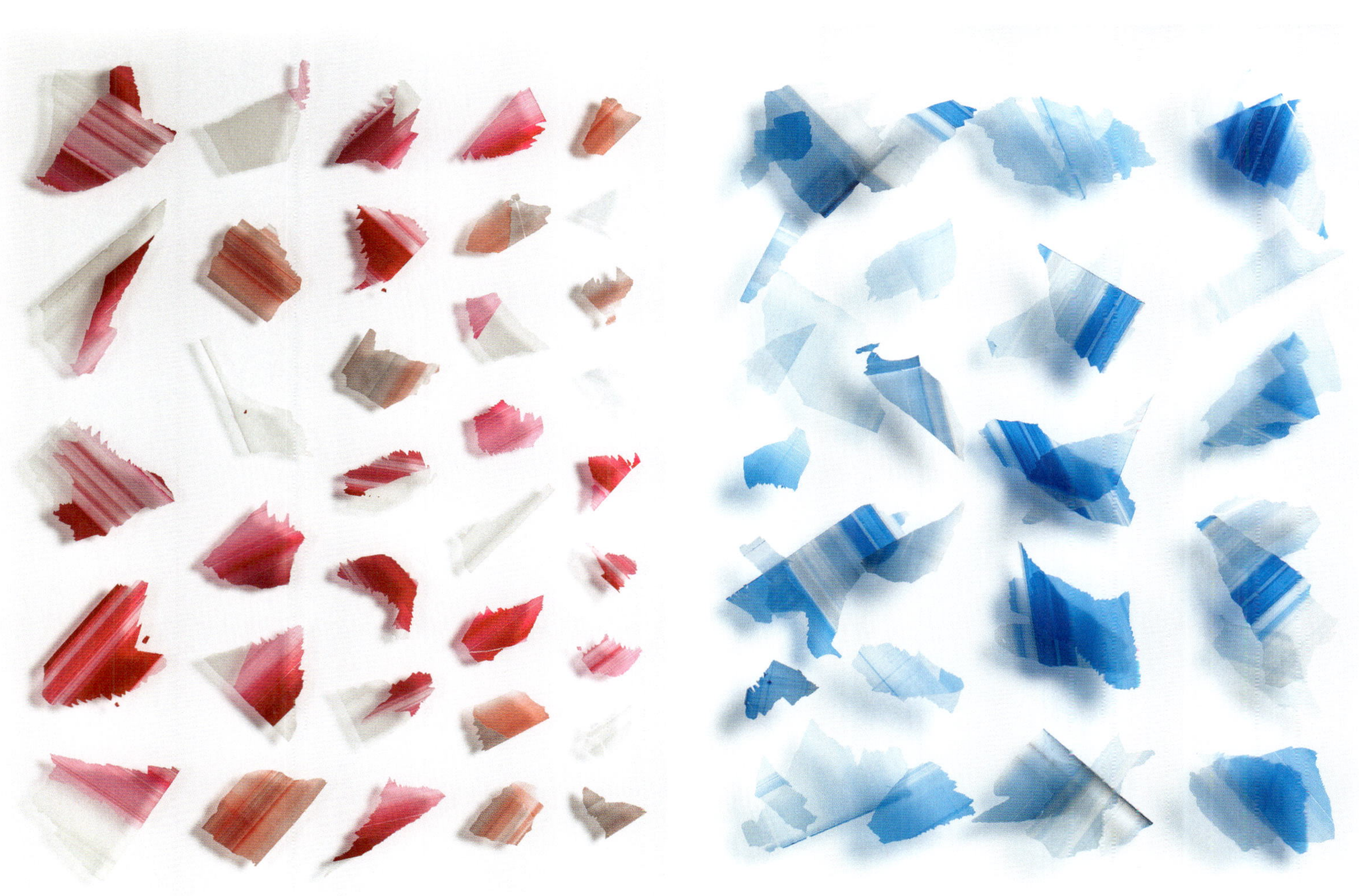

T/R. 1062, Recycled Paint Fragments: Acrylic, Graphite, Tin + Acrylic Gel on Glass, 109×86 cm, 2025

T/R.1068, Recycled Paint Fragments: Acrylic, Graphite, Tin + Acrylic Gel on Glass, 55×44 cm, 2025

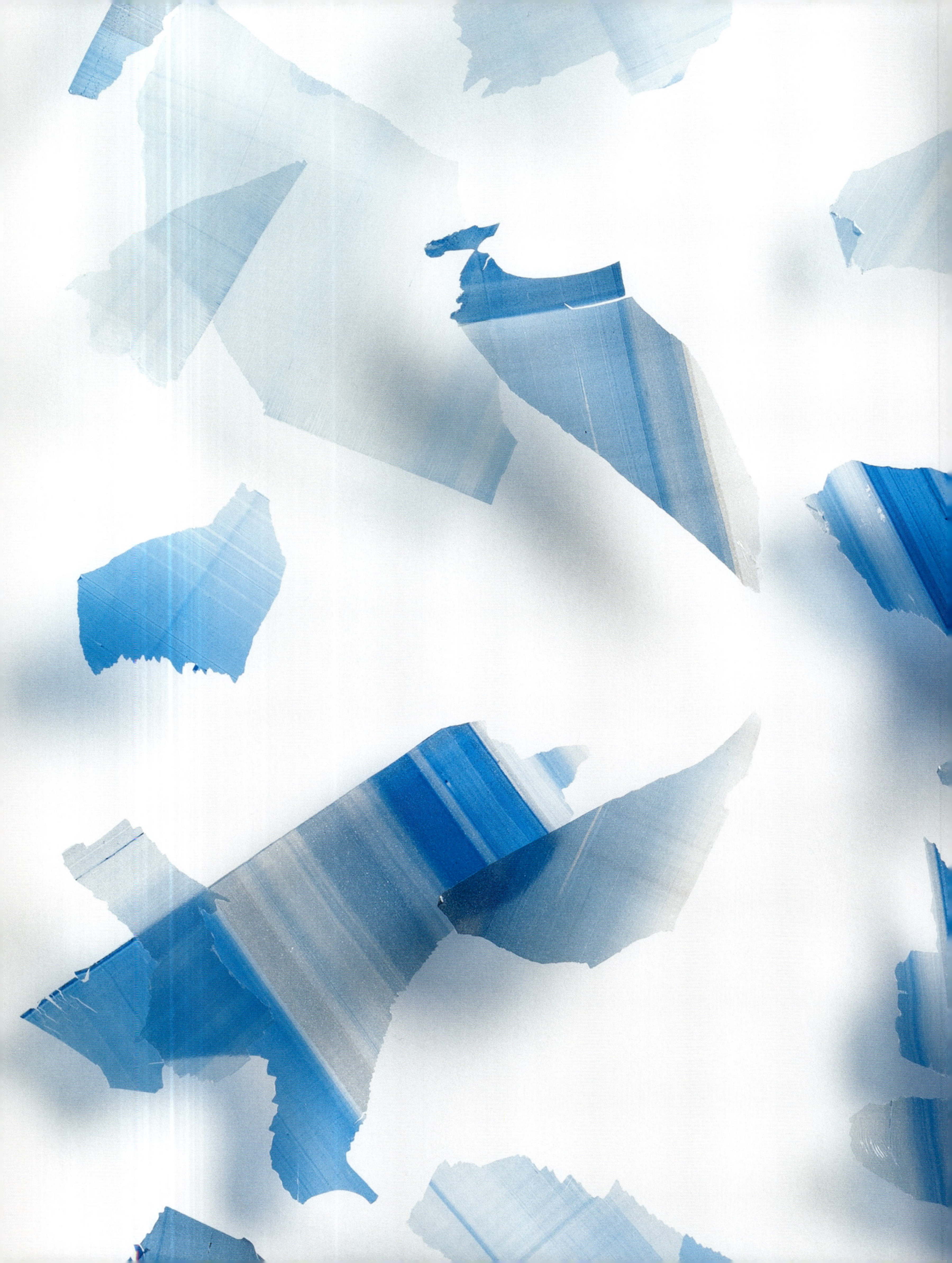

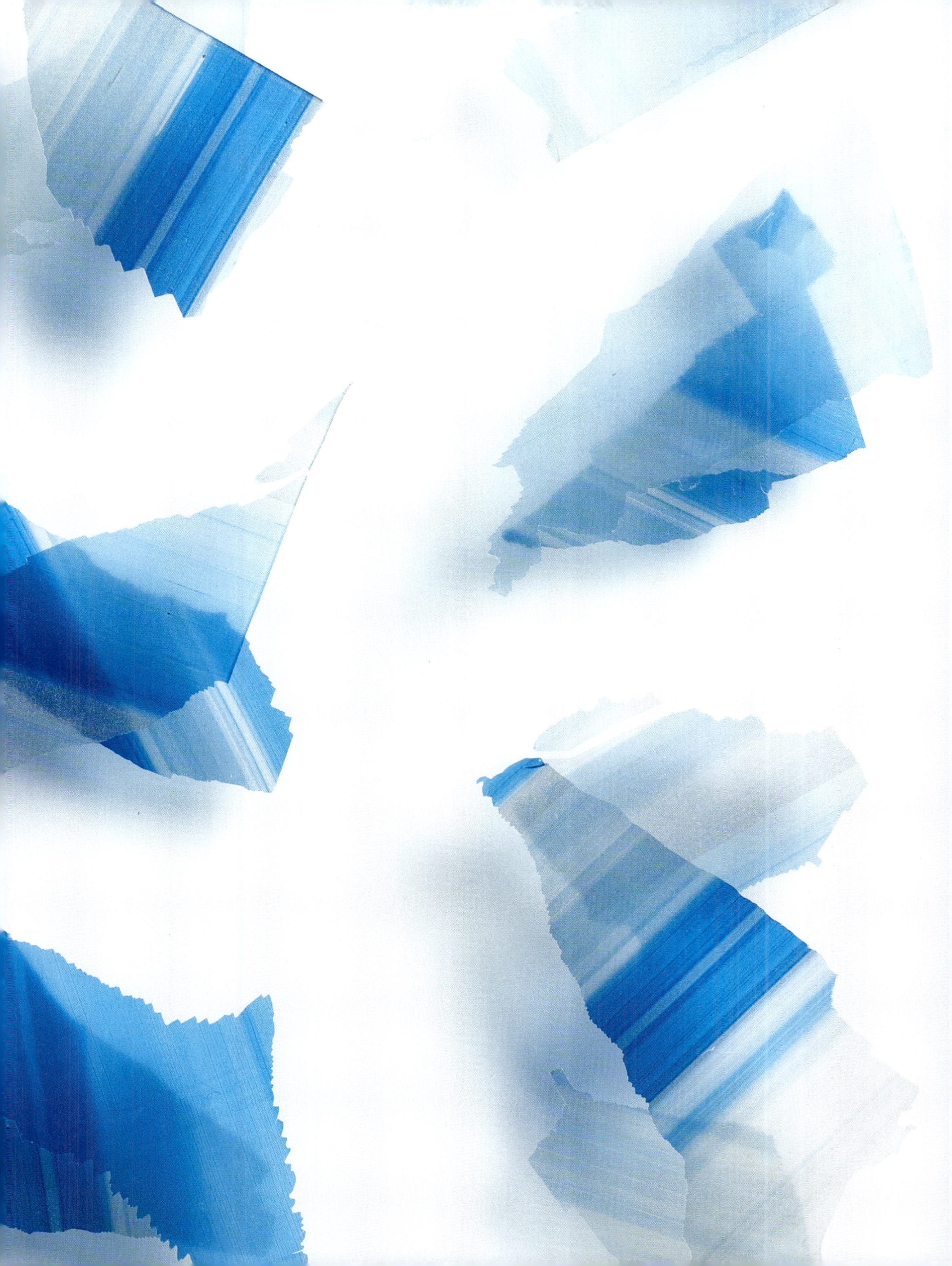

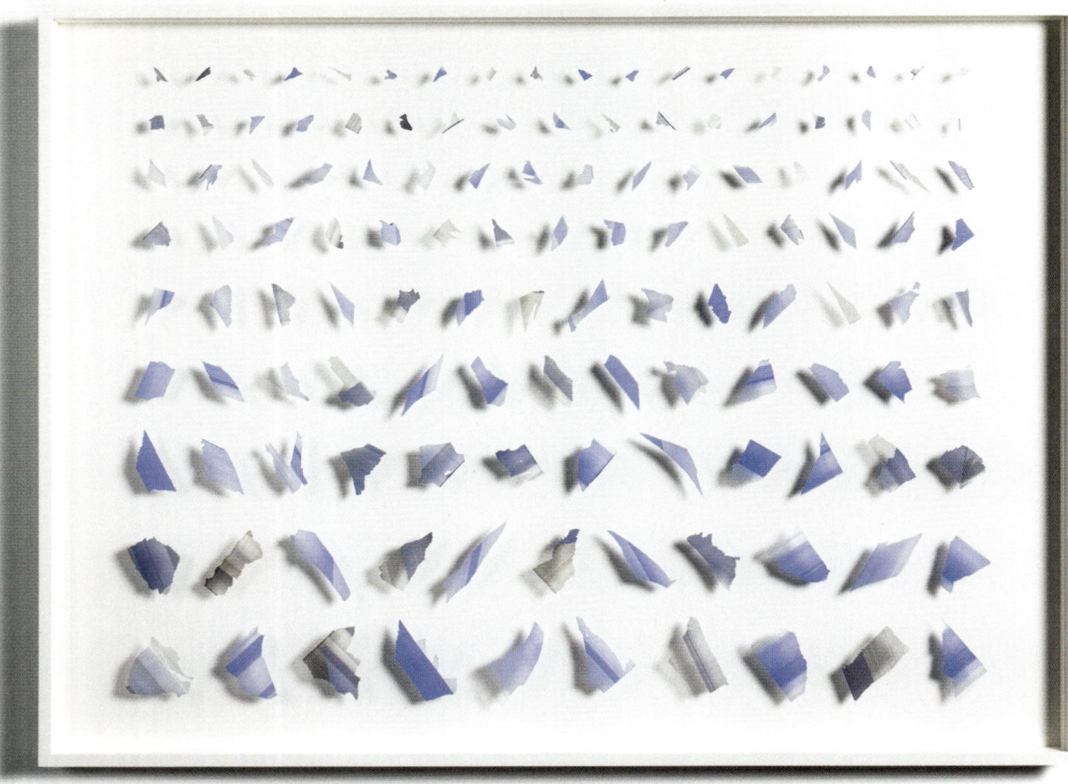

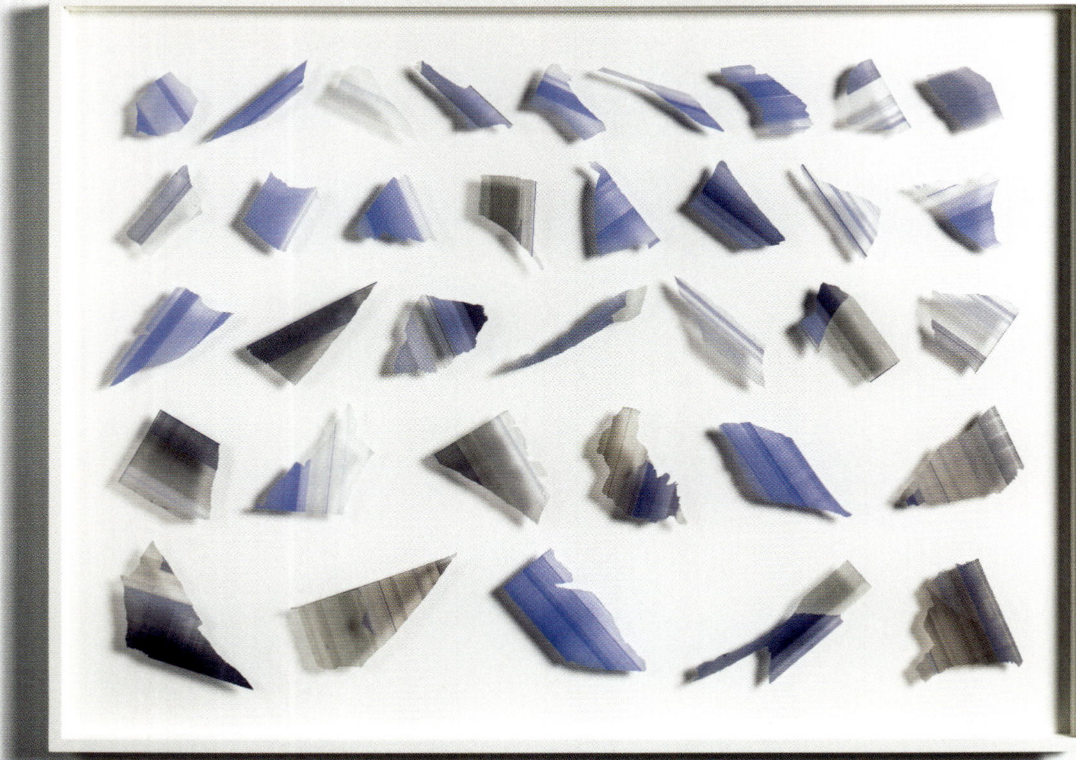

T/R. 1061, Recycled Paint Fragments: Acrylic, Graphite, Tin + Acrylic Gel on Glass, 219 × 140 cm, 2025

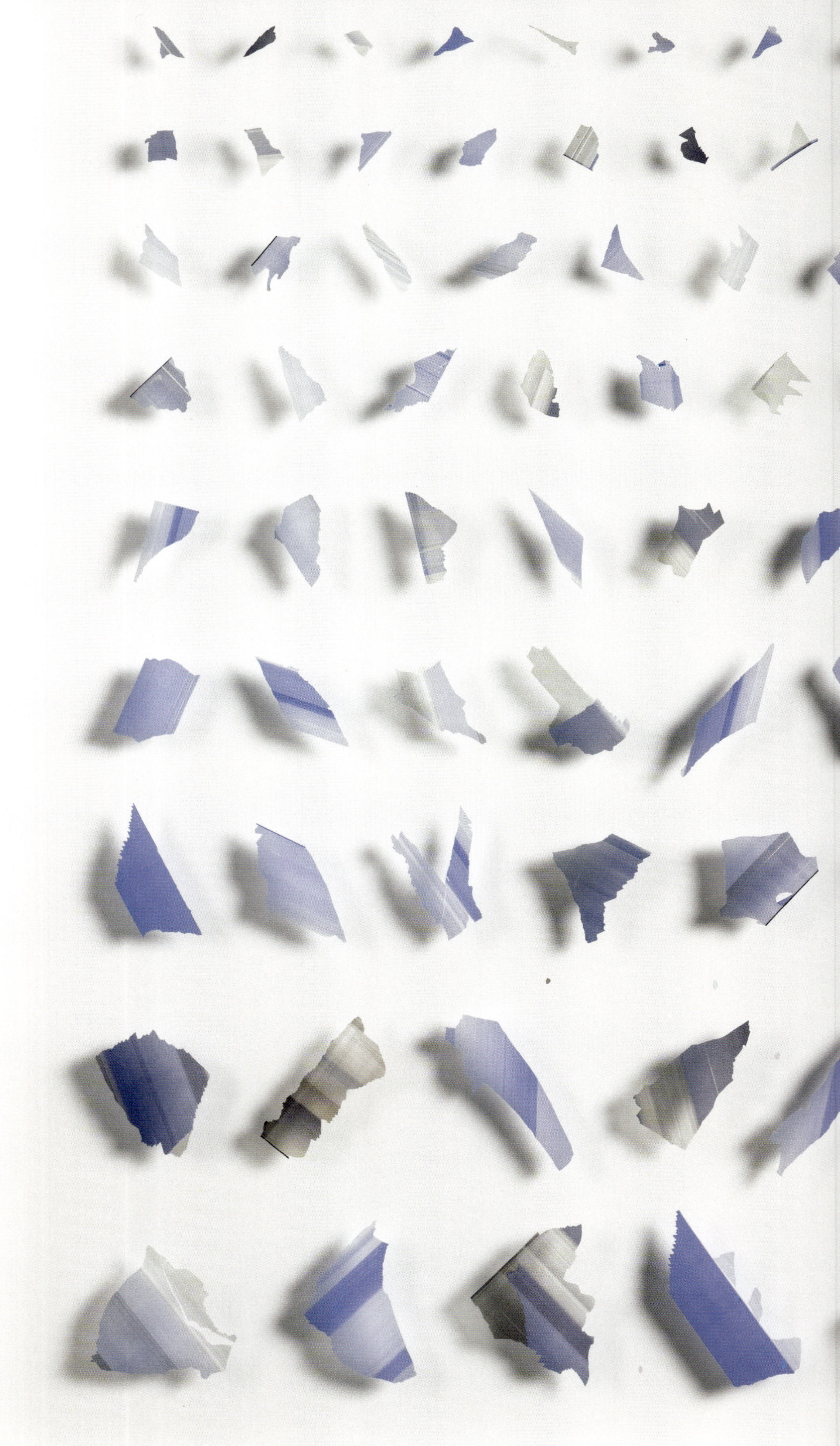

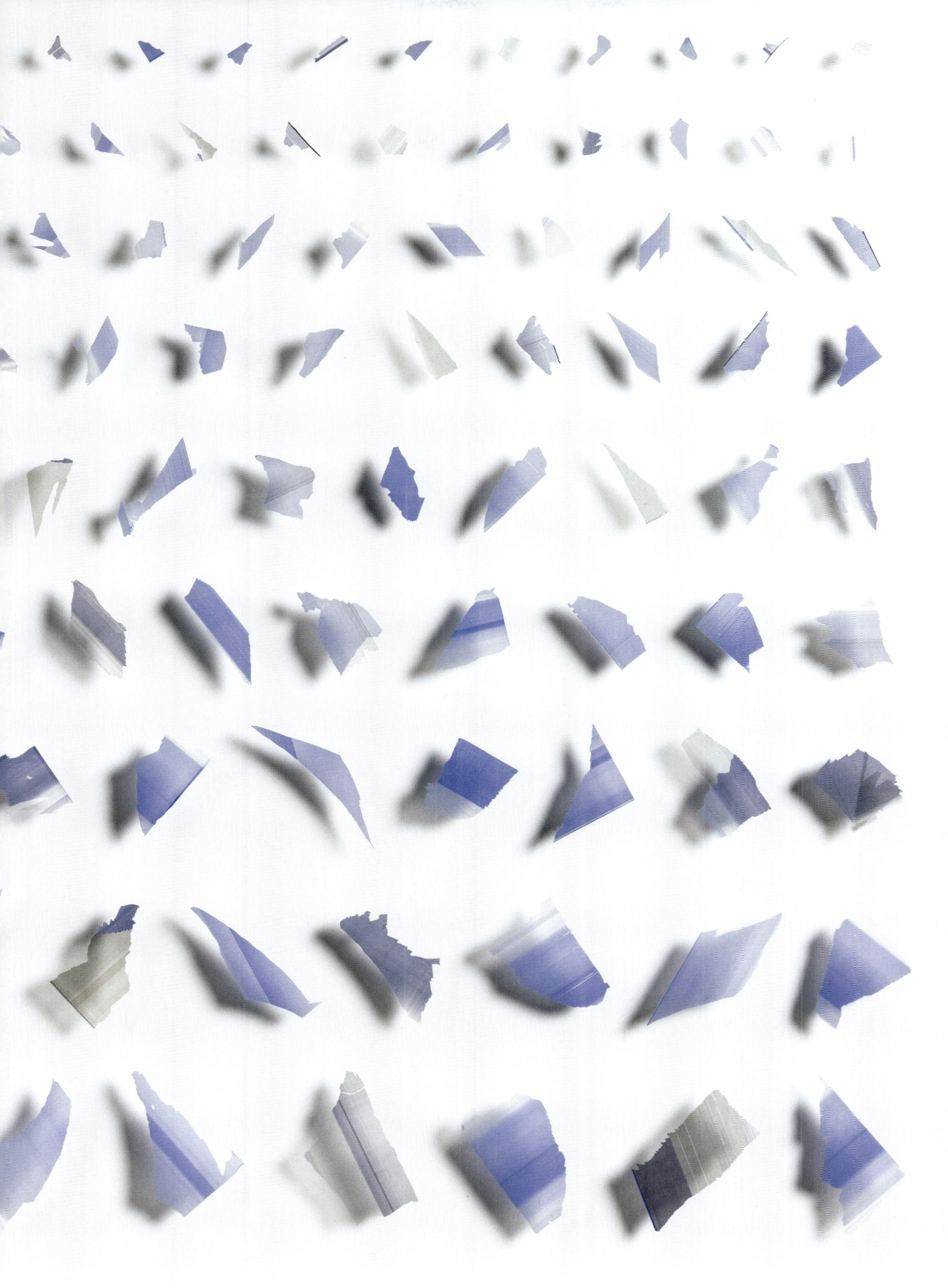

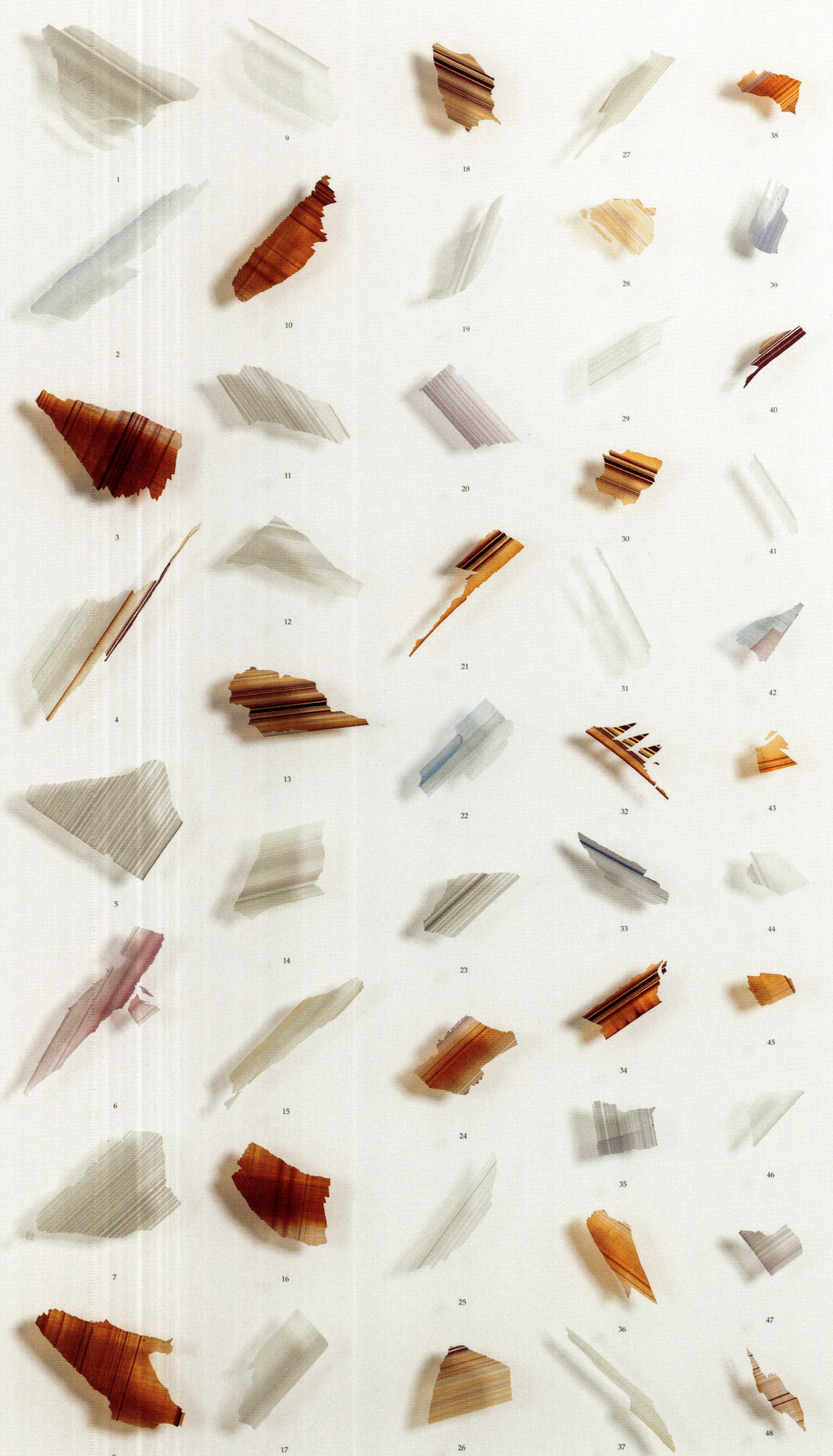

1, 2, 5, 7, 9, 11, 12, 14, 15, 17, 19, 23, 25, 27, 29, 31, 37, 41
44, 46
P/R. 969, Acrylic + Acrylic Gel on Glass, 2020
(Destroyed)

3, 8, 10, 13, 16, 18, 20, 26, 28, 38, 45, 47, 48
P/R. 892, Acrylic + Acrylic Gel on Aluminium, 2019
(Destroyed)

4, 6, 21, 24, 30, 32, 34, 36, 40, 43
P/R. 923, Acrylic + Acrylic Gel on Glass, 2020
(Destroyed)

22, 35, 42
P/R. 964, Acrylic, Graphite + Acrylic Gel on Glass, 2020
(Destroyed)

33, 39
P/R. 962, Acrylic, Graphite + Acrylic Gel on Glass, 2021
(Destroyed)

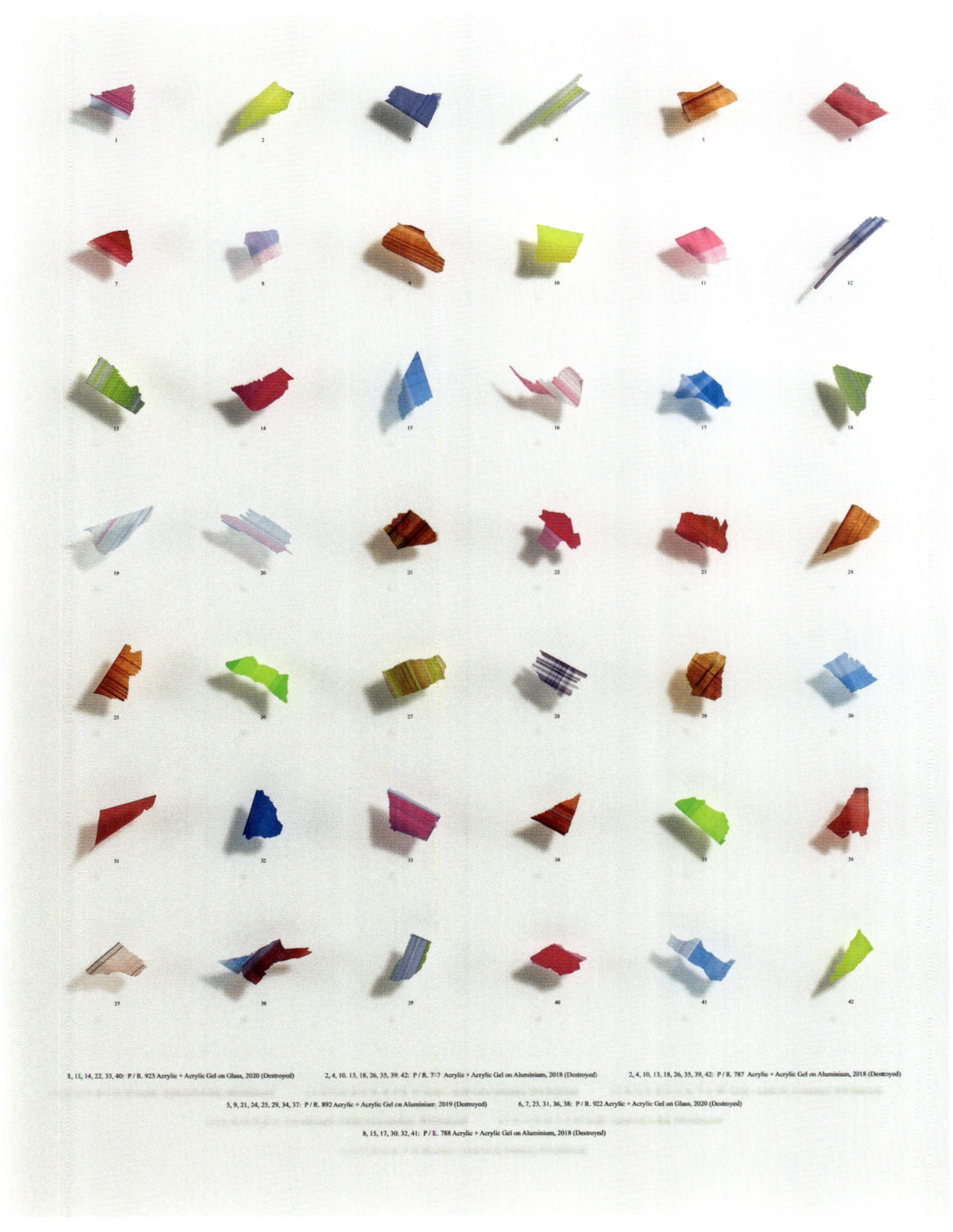

T/R.1046, Recycled Paint Fragments: Acrylic, Graphite, Acrylic Gel + Text on Glass, 109×86 cm, 2024

T/R.1011, Recycled Paint Fragments: Acrylic,Graphite, Acrylic Gel + Text on Glass, 109×86 cm, 2022

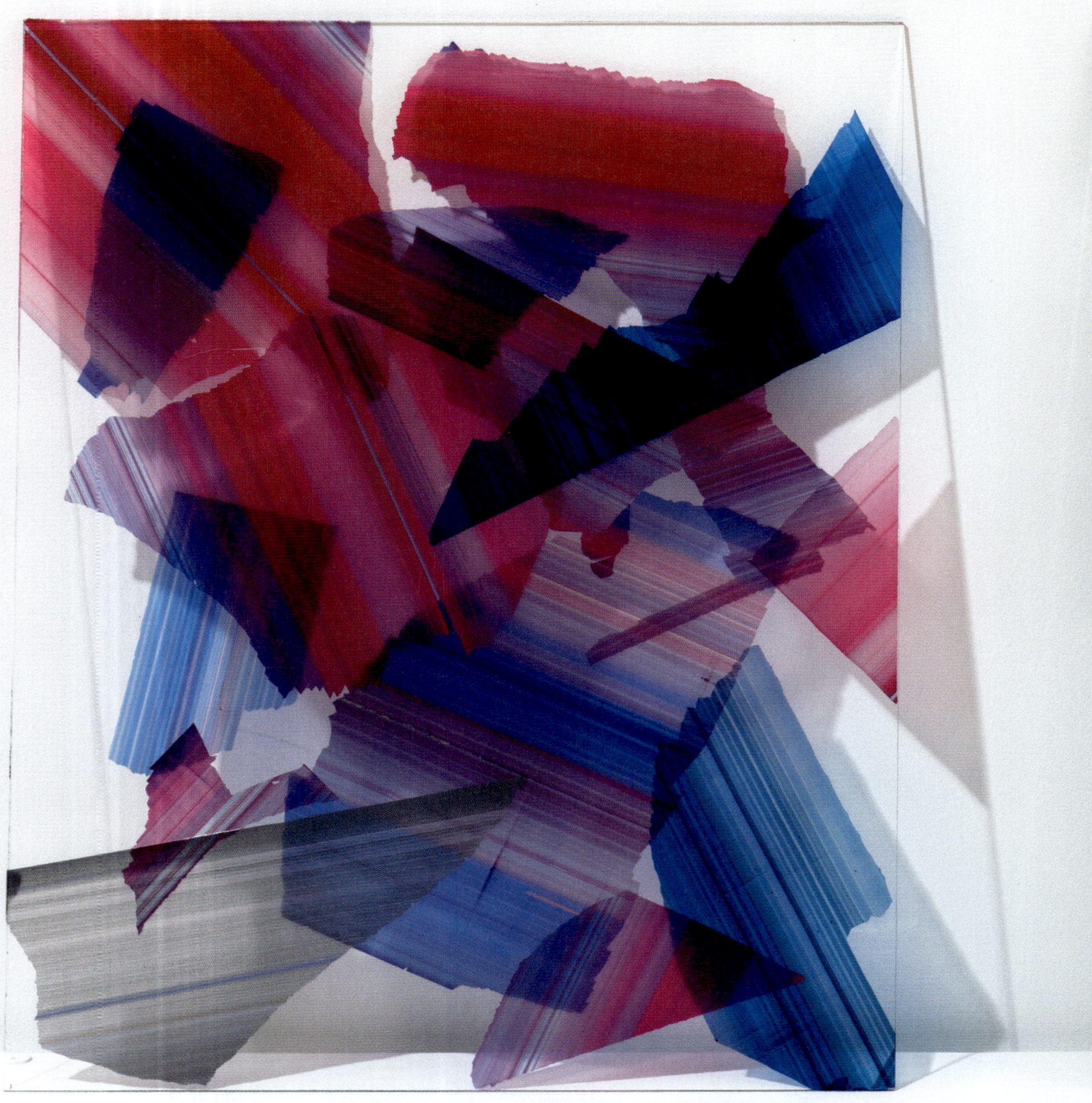

T/R.1117-1119, Recycled Paint Fragments: Acrylic, Graphite, Tin + Acrylic Gel on Glass, 32 × 26 cm (each), 2025

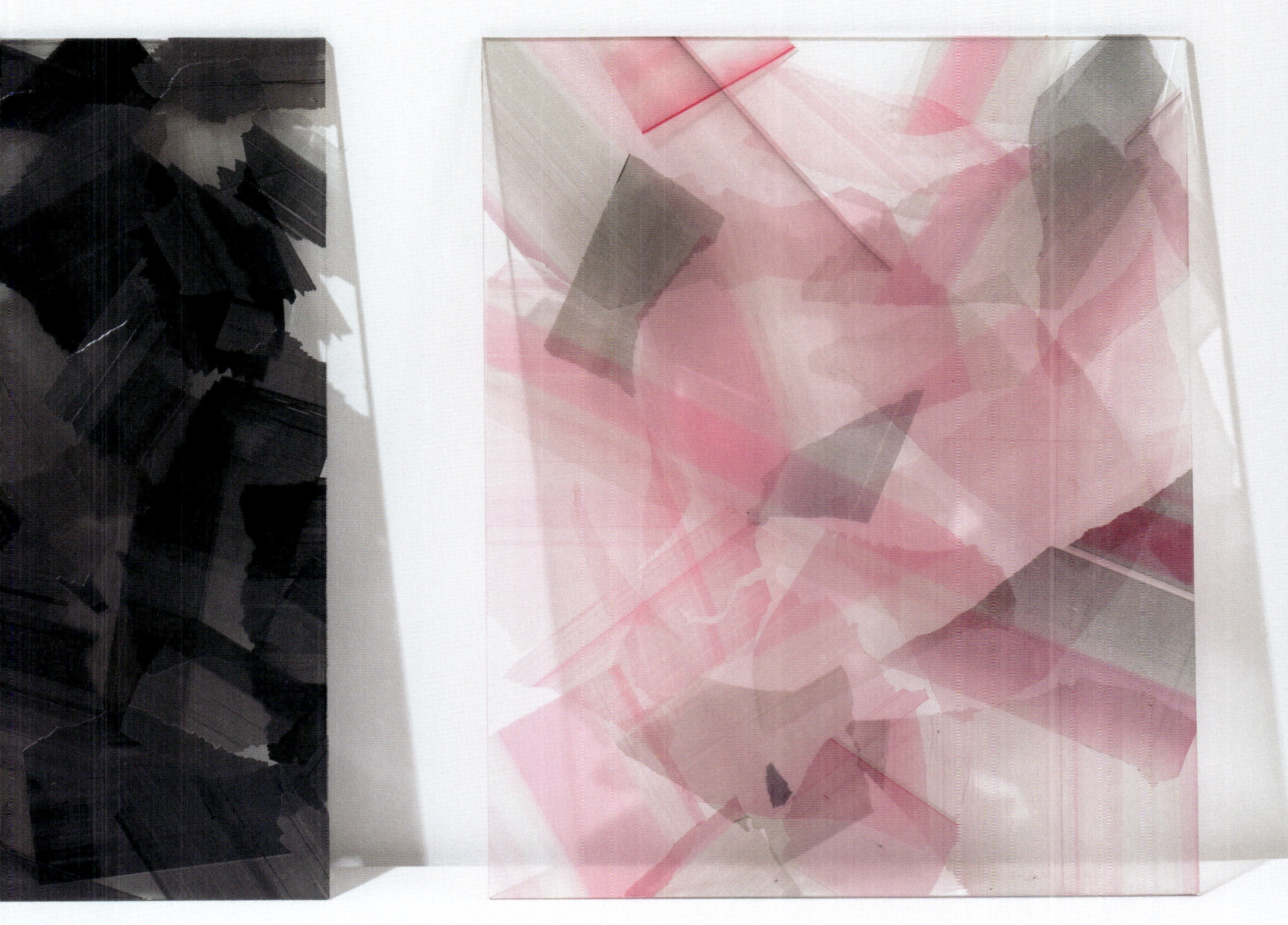

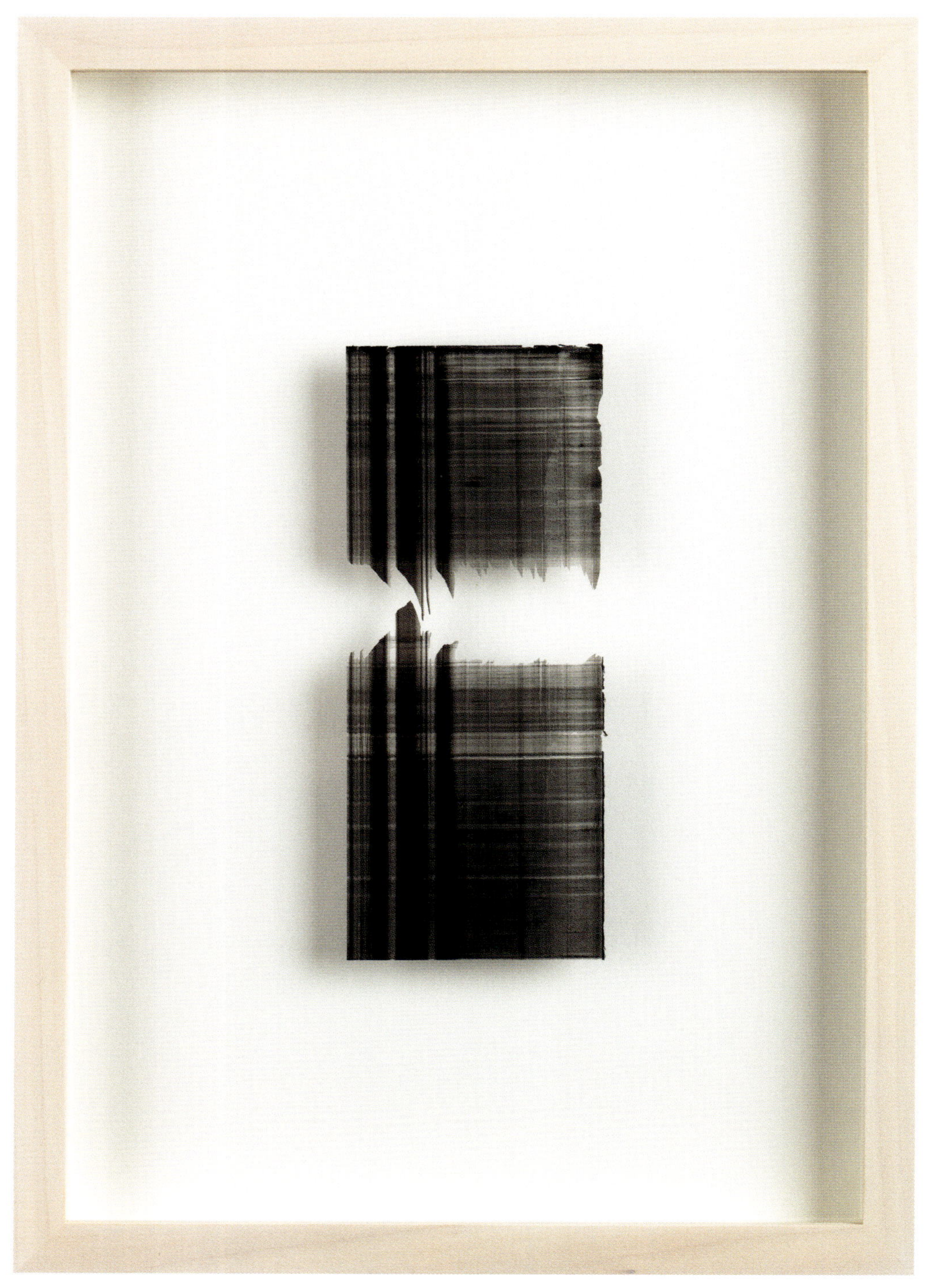

T/R.927, Recycled Paint Fragments: Graphite + Acrylic Gel on Glass, 31×22 cm, 2020

T/R.1032, Recycled Paint Fragments: Graphite, Bronze + Acrylic Gel on Glass, 55×44 cm, 2023

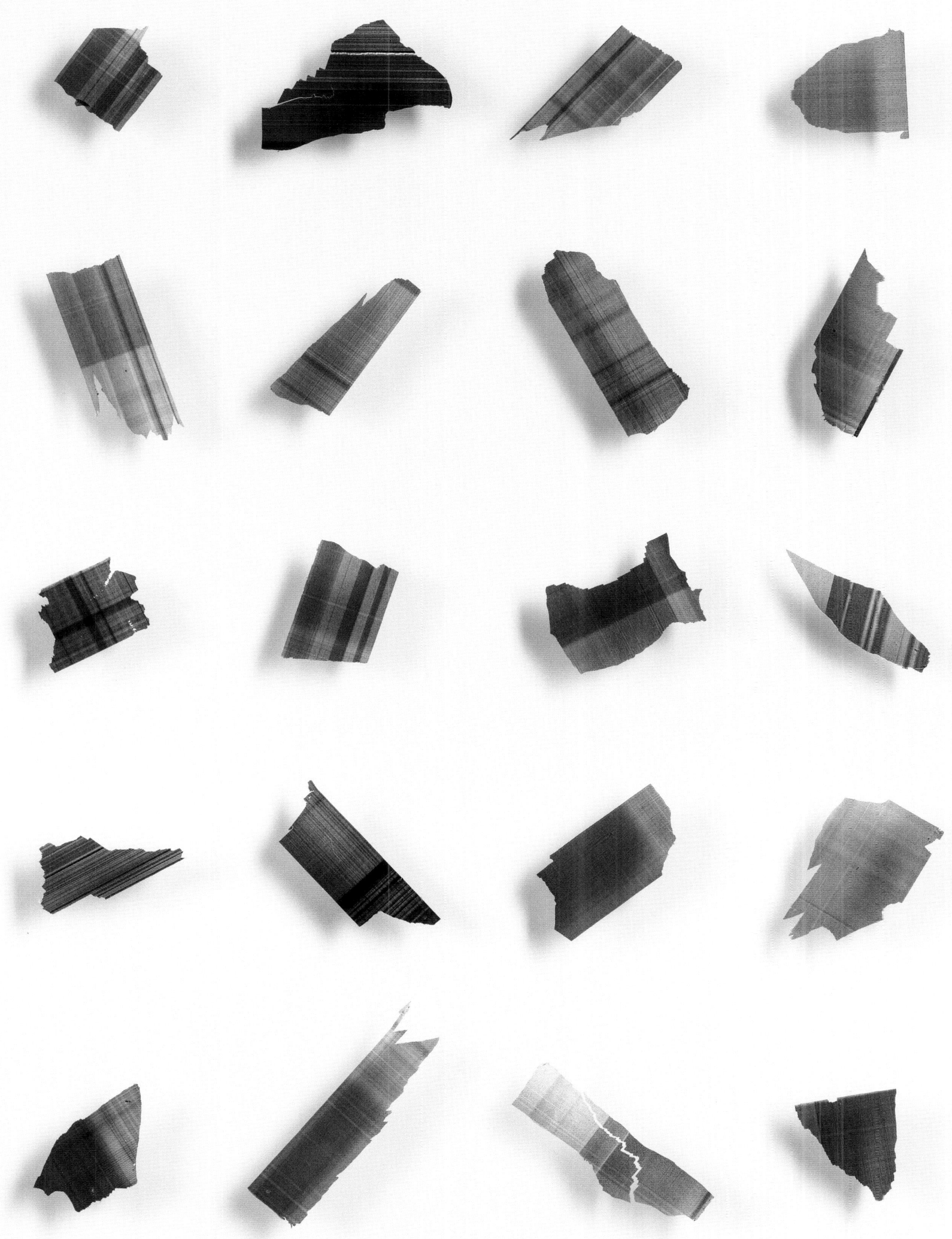

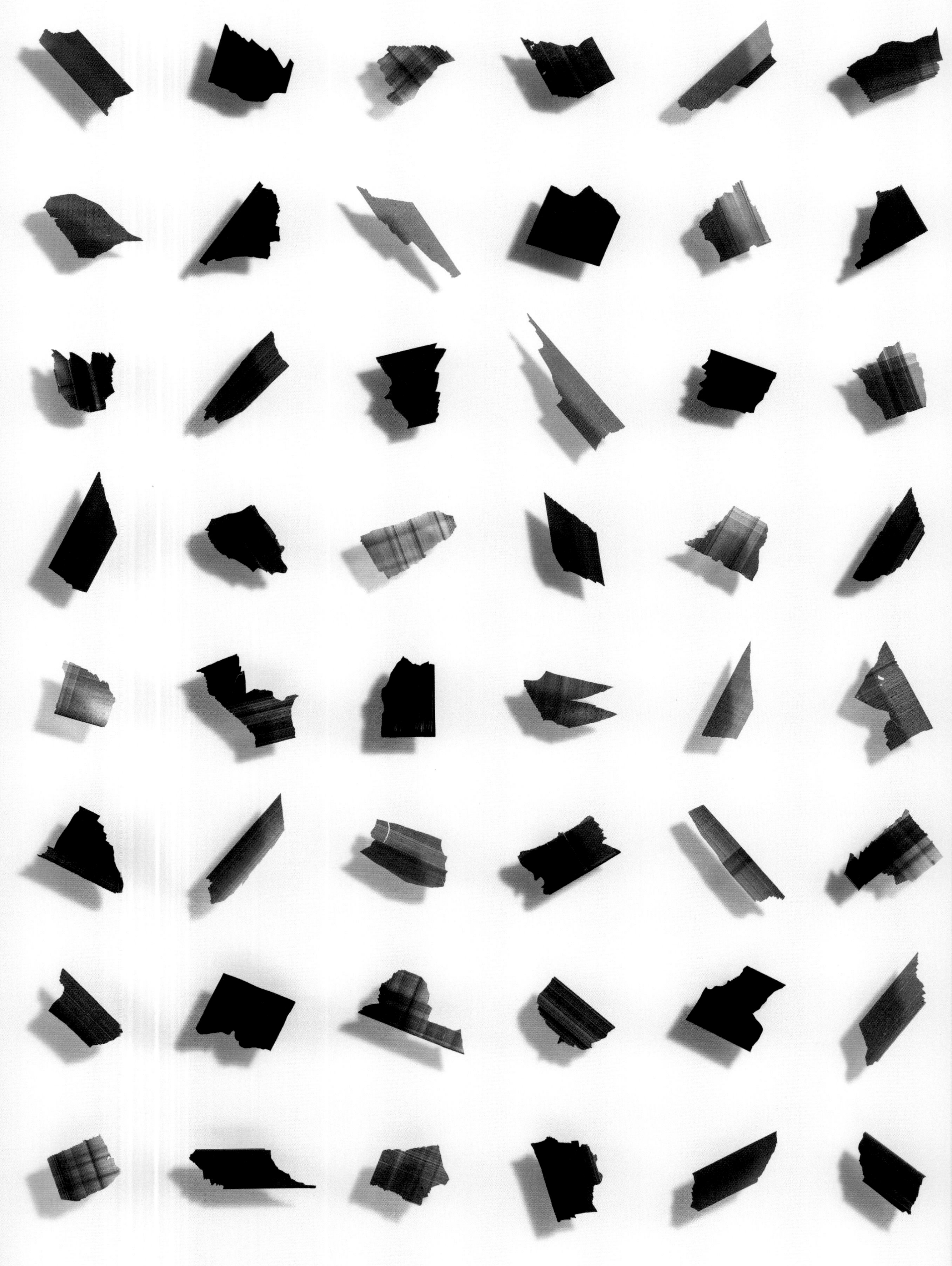

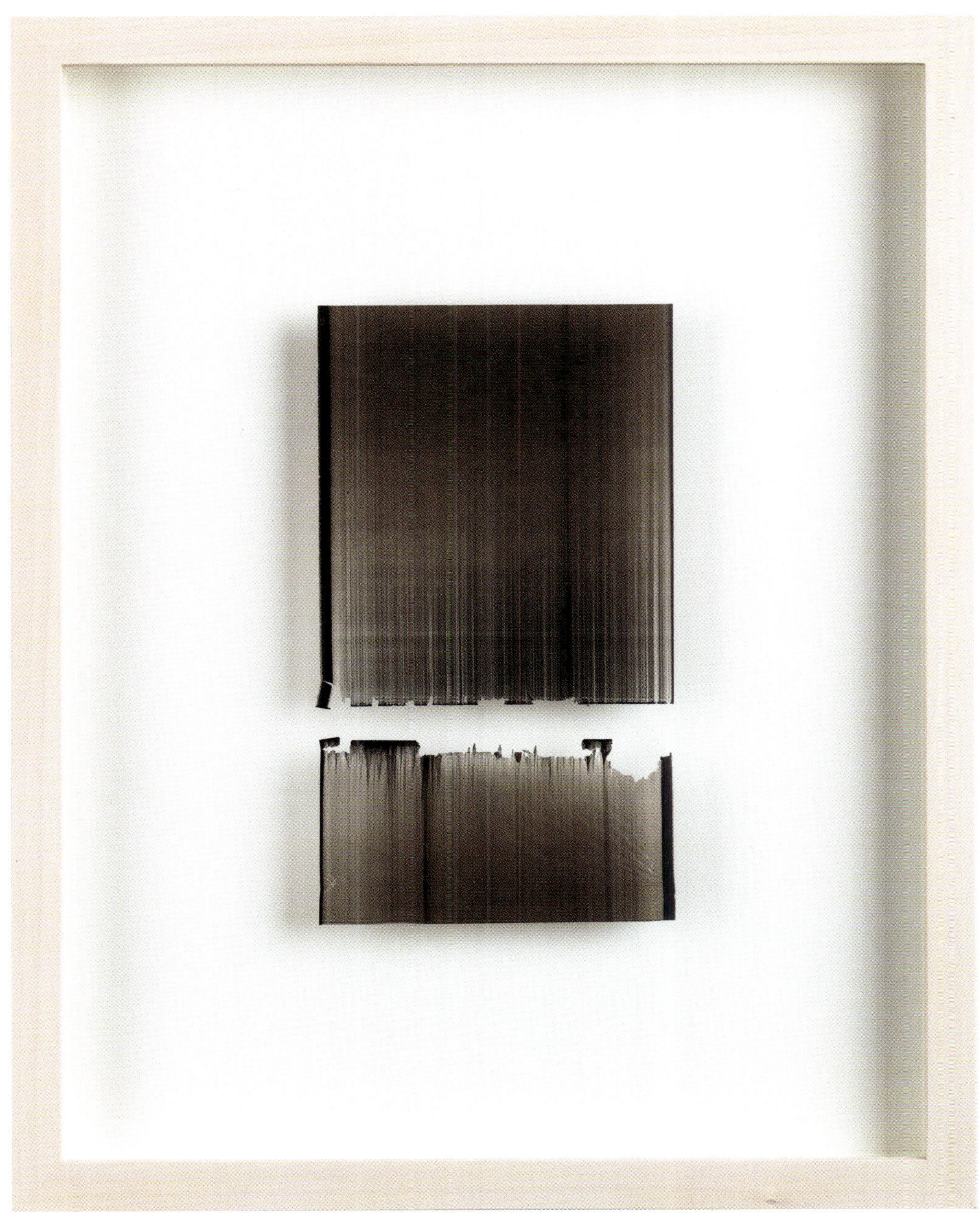

T/R.1009, Recycled Paint Fragments: Graphite, Bronze + Acrylic Gel on Glass, 109×86 cm, 2022

T/R.925, Recycled Paint Fragments: Graphite + Acrylic Gel on Glass, 31×25 cm, 2020

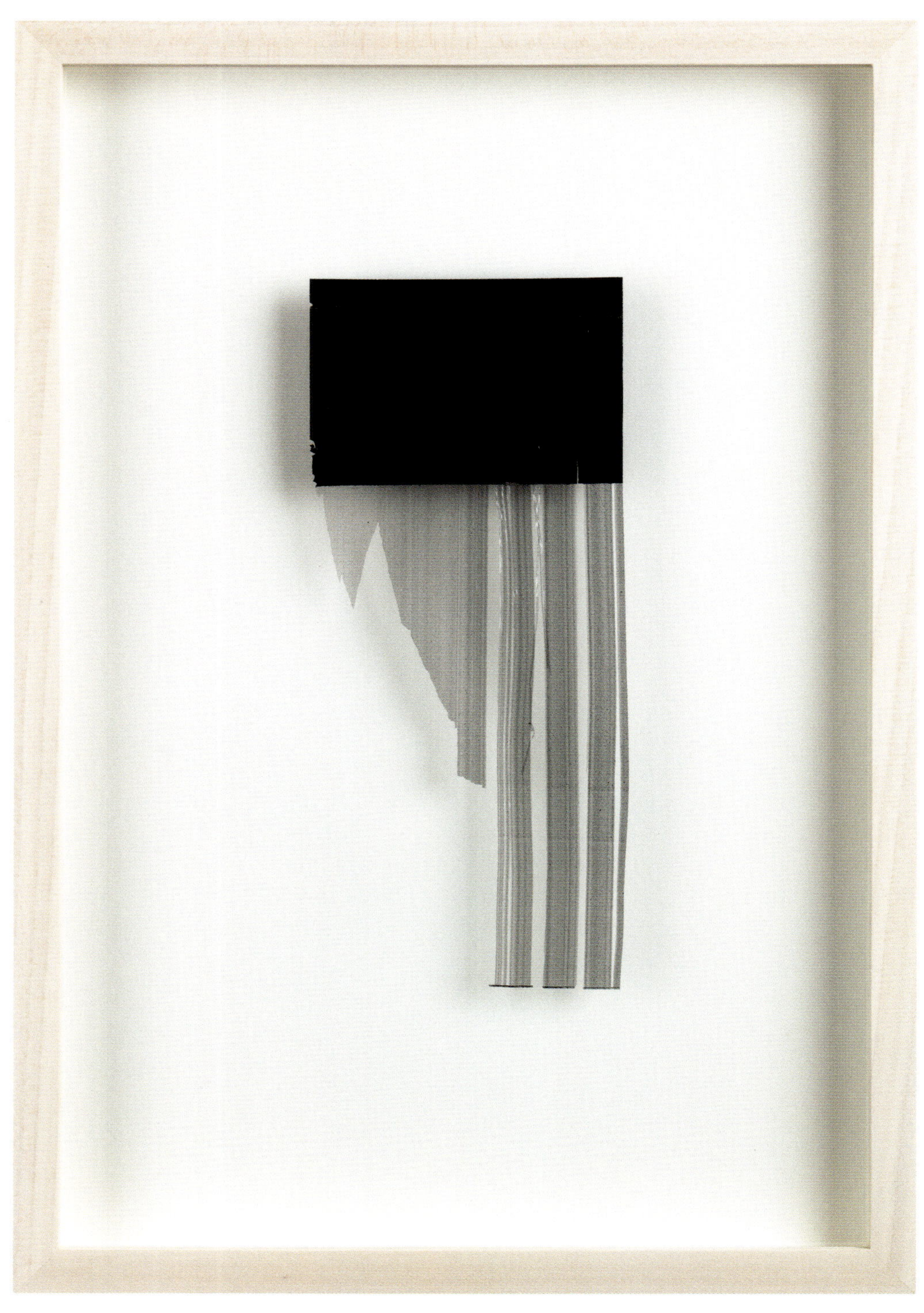

T/R.928, Recycled Paint Fragment: Graphite, Acrylic Gel, Oil + Resin on Glass, 36×25 cm, 2020

T/R.947, Recycled Paint Fragments: Graphite, Bronze, Acrylic Gel, Oil + Resin on Glass, 85×71 cm, 2020

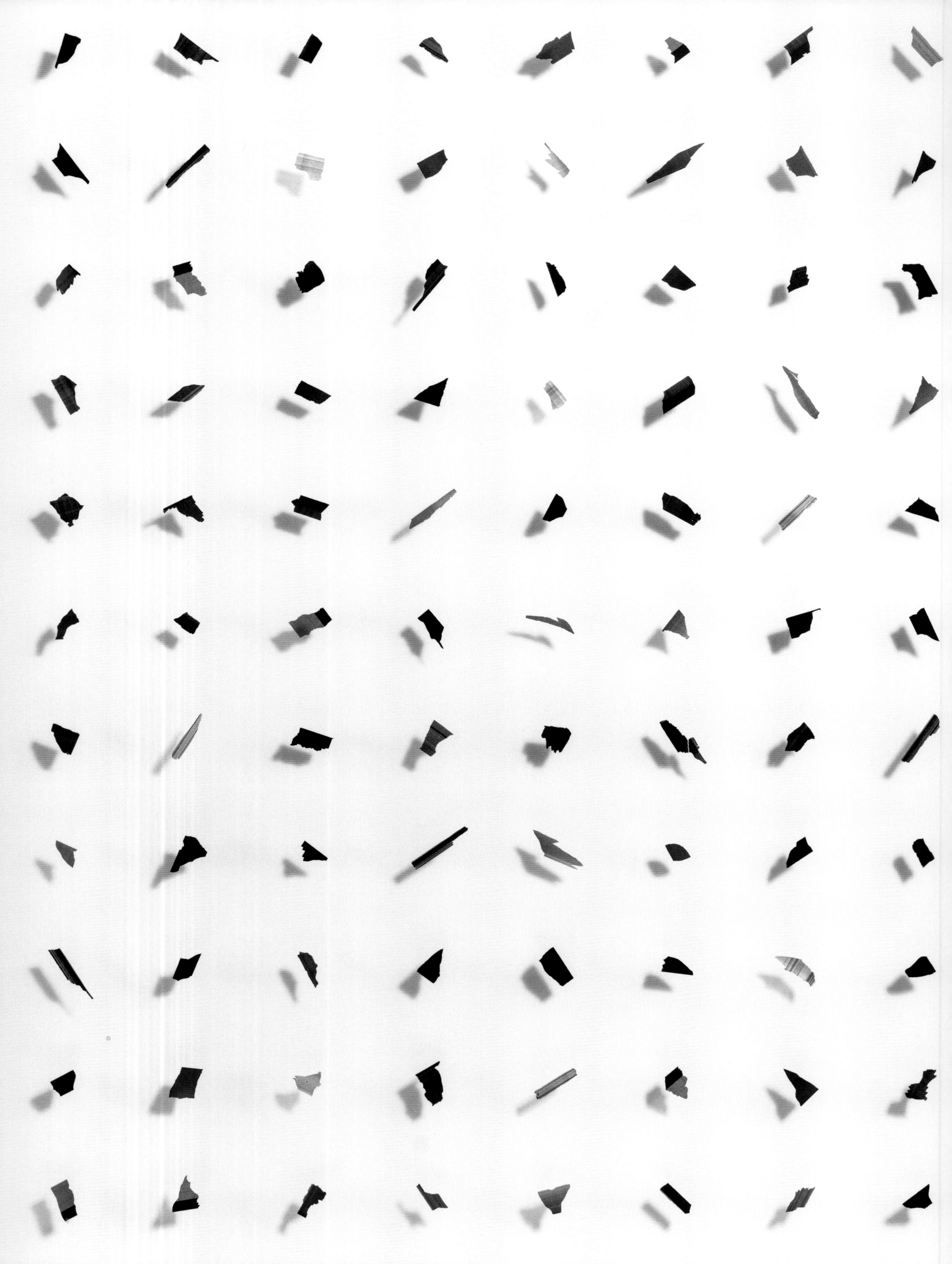

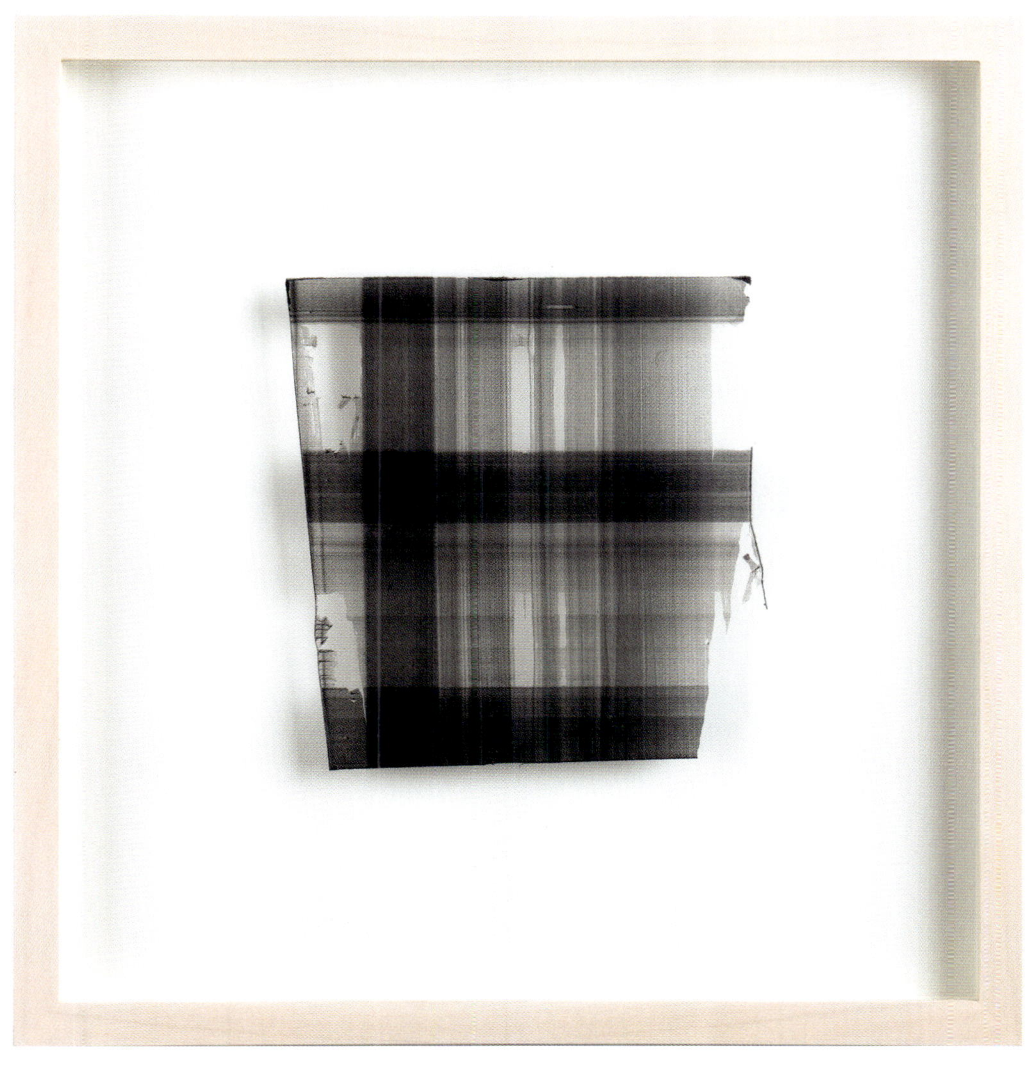

T/R.1007, Recycled Paint Fragments: Graphite, Bronze + Acrylic Gel on Glass, 109 × 86 cm, 2022

T/R.929, Recycled Paint Fragment: Graphite + Acrylic Gel on Glass, 30 × 29 cm, 2020

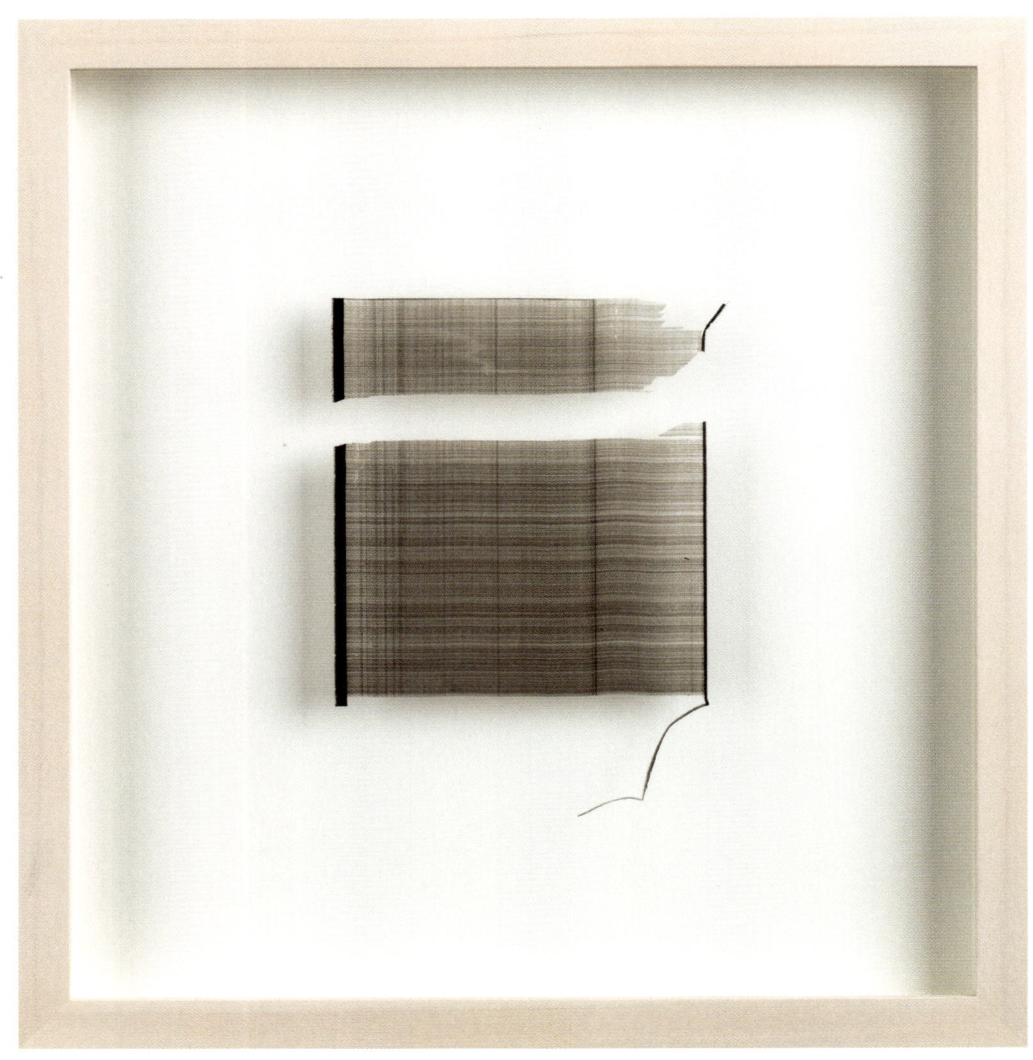

T/R.926, Recycled Paint Fragments: Graphite + Acrylic Gel on Glass, 26×25 cm, 2020

T/R.1033, Recycled Paint Fragments: Graphite, Bronze + Acrylic Gel on Glass, 55×44 cm, 2023

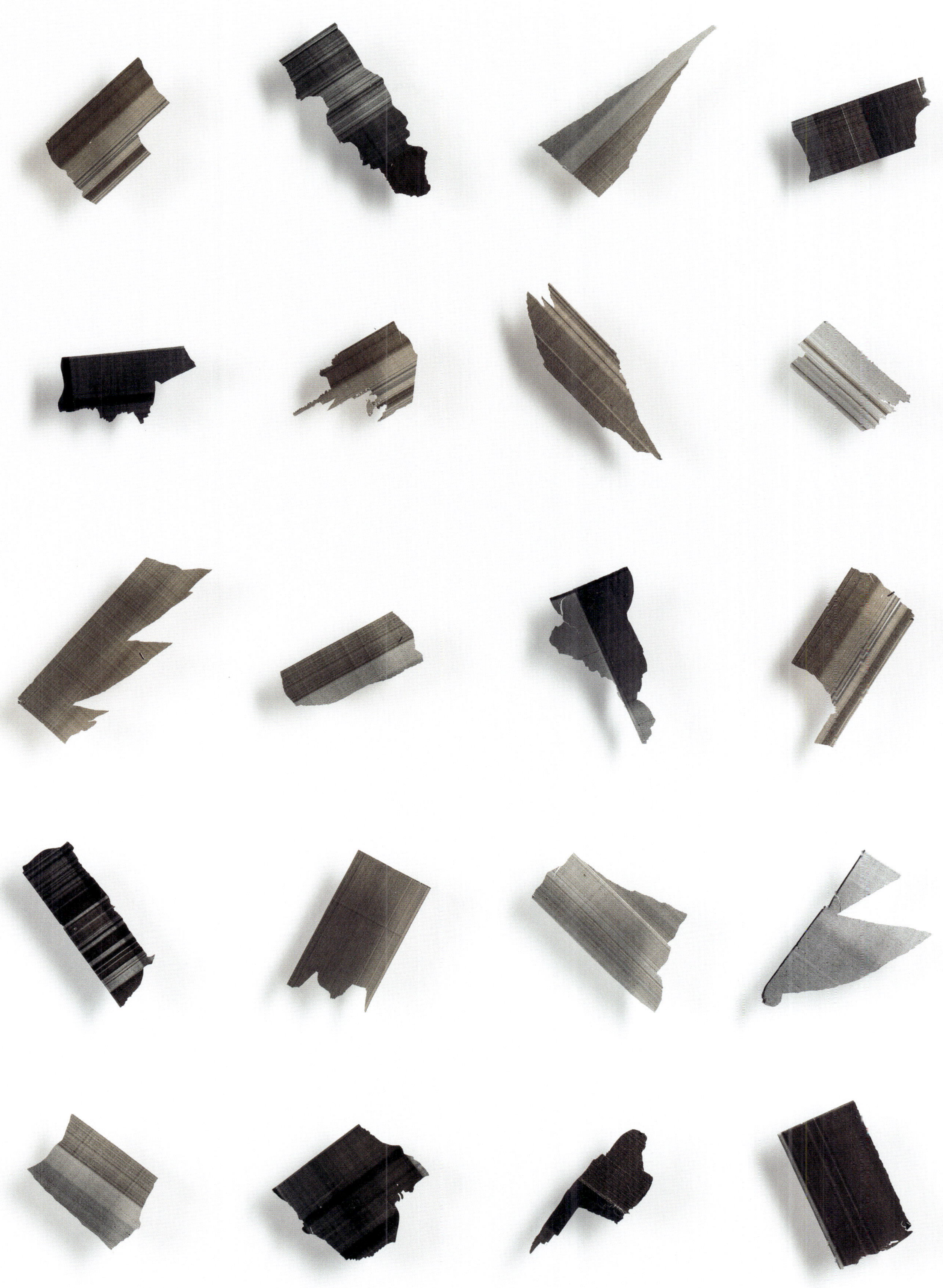

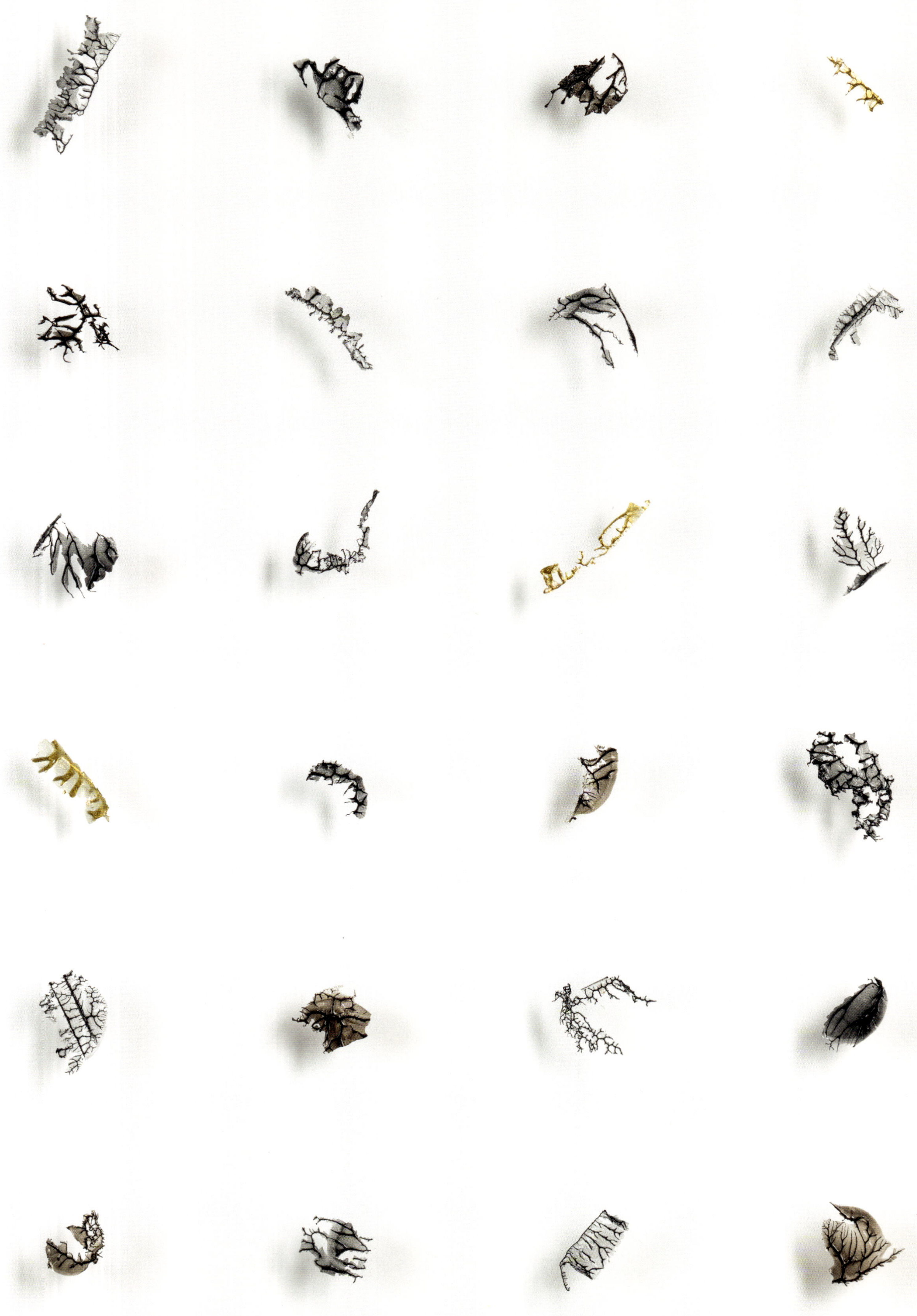

T/R.1030 (Incidental Fragments),
Recycled Paint Fragments:
Graphite, Bronze, Tin + Acrylic
Gel on Glass, 55 × 44 cm, 2023

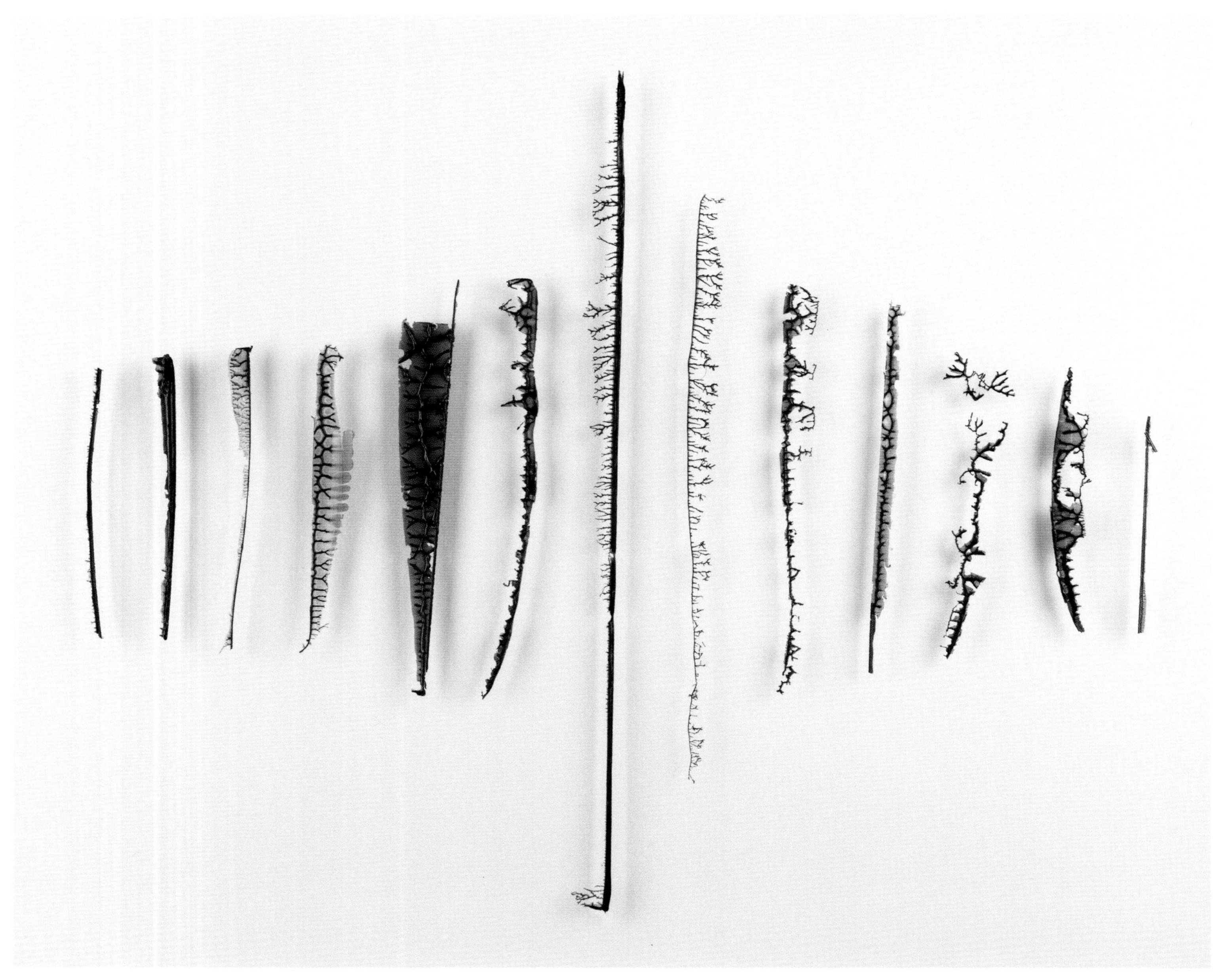

T/R.937 (Incidental Fragments), Recycled Paint Fragments: Graphite, Bronze + Acrylic Gel on Glass, 49×60 cm, 2020

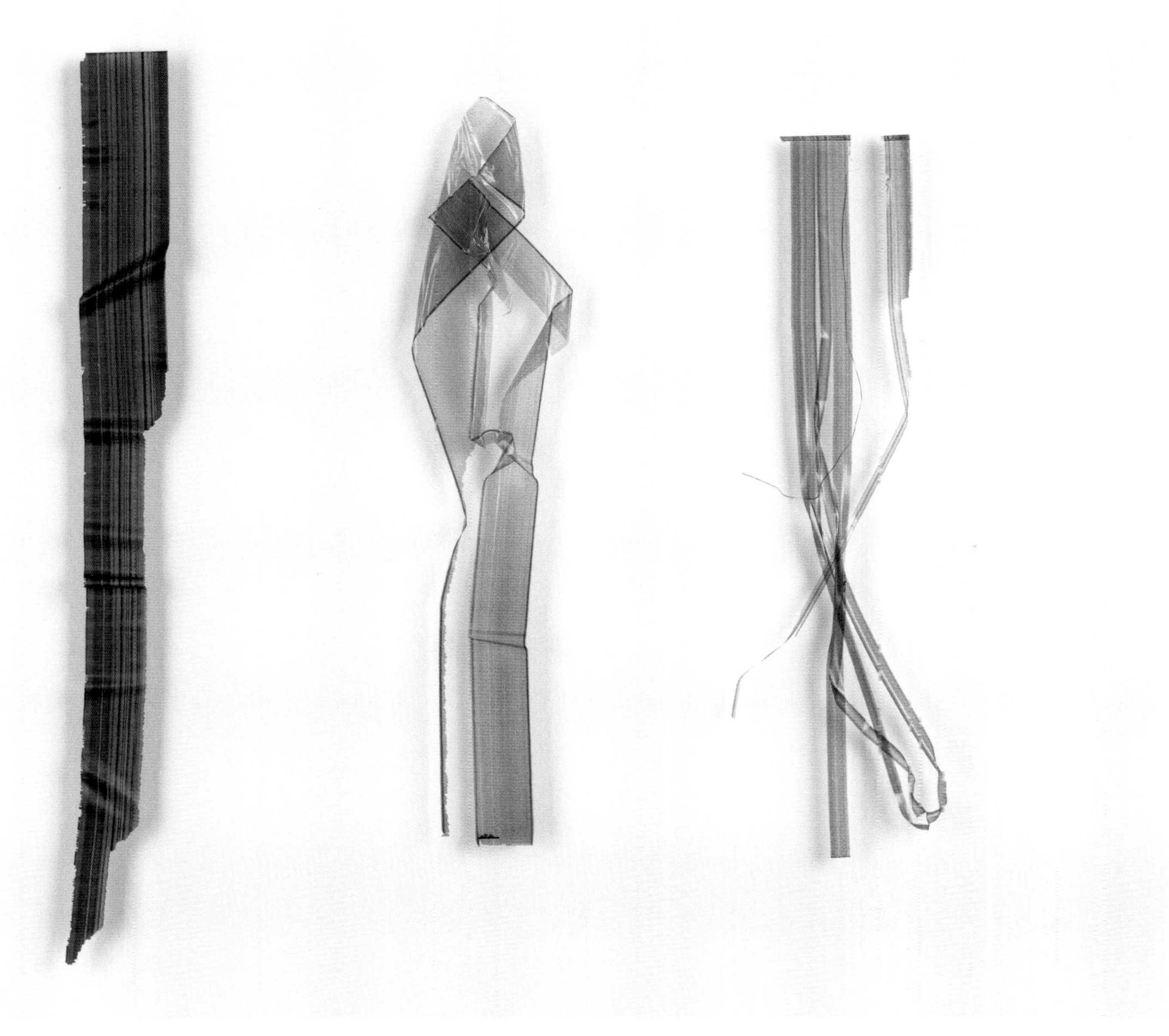

T/R.930, Recycled Paint
Fragments: Graphite
+ Acrylic Gel on Glass,
36 × 48 cm, 2020

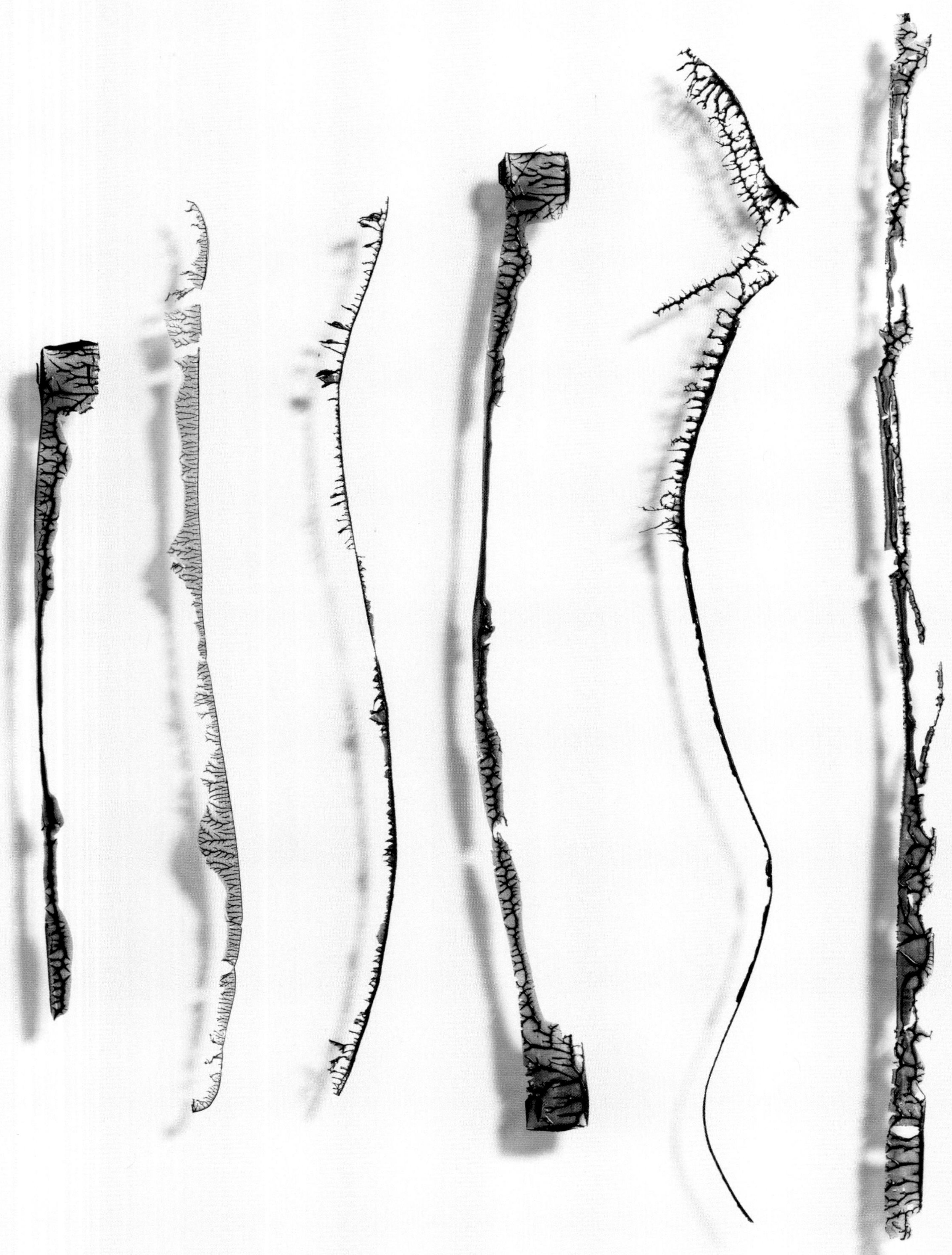

T/R.951 (Incidental Fragments),
Recycled Paint Fragments:
Graphite, Bronze + Acrylic Gel
on Glass, 71 × 85 cm, 2020

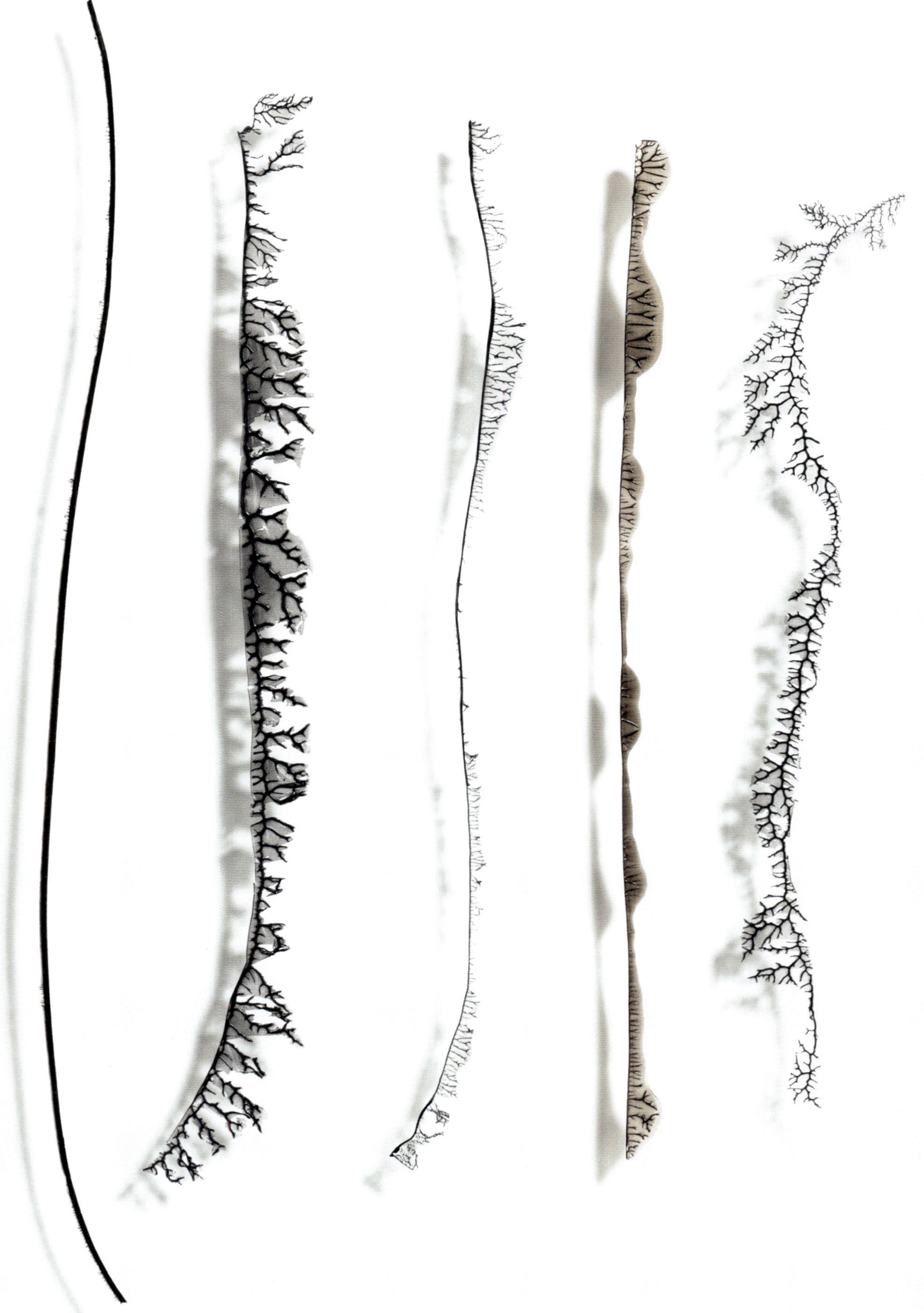

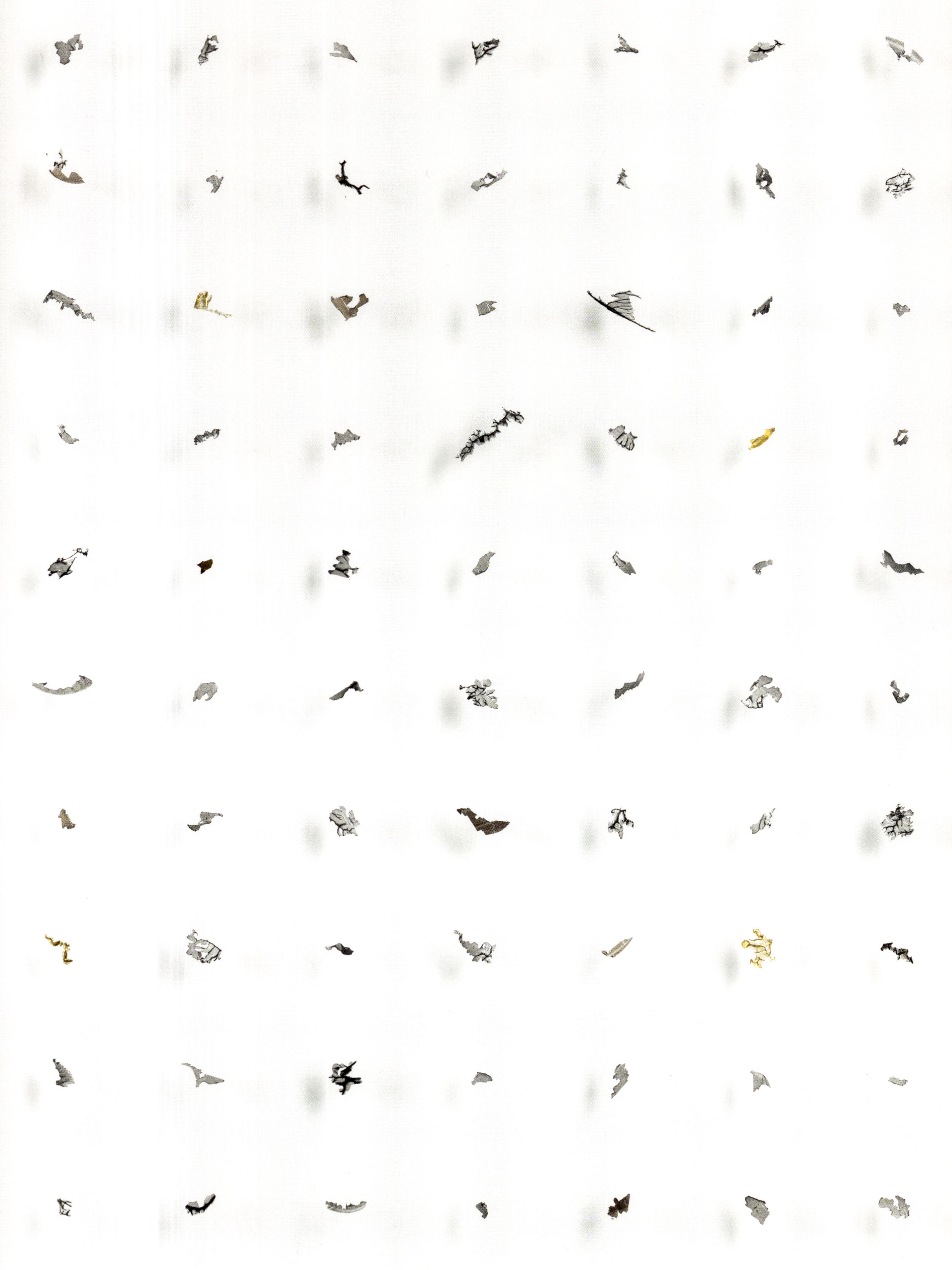

T/R.1031 (Incidental Fragments),
Recycled Paint Fragments:
Graphite, Bronze
+ Acrylic Gel on Glass,
55 × 44 cm, 2023

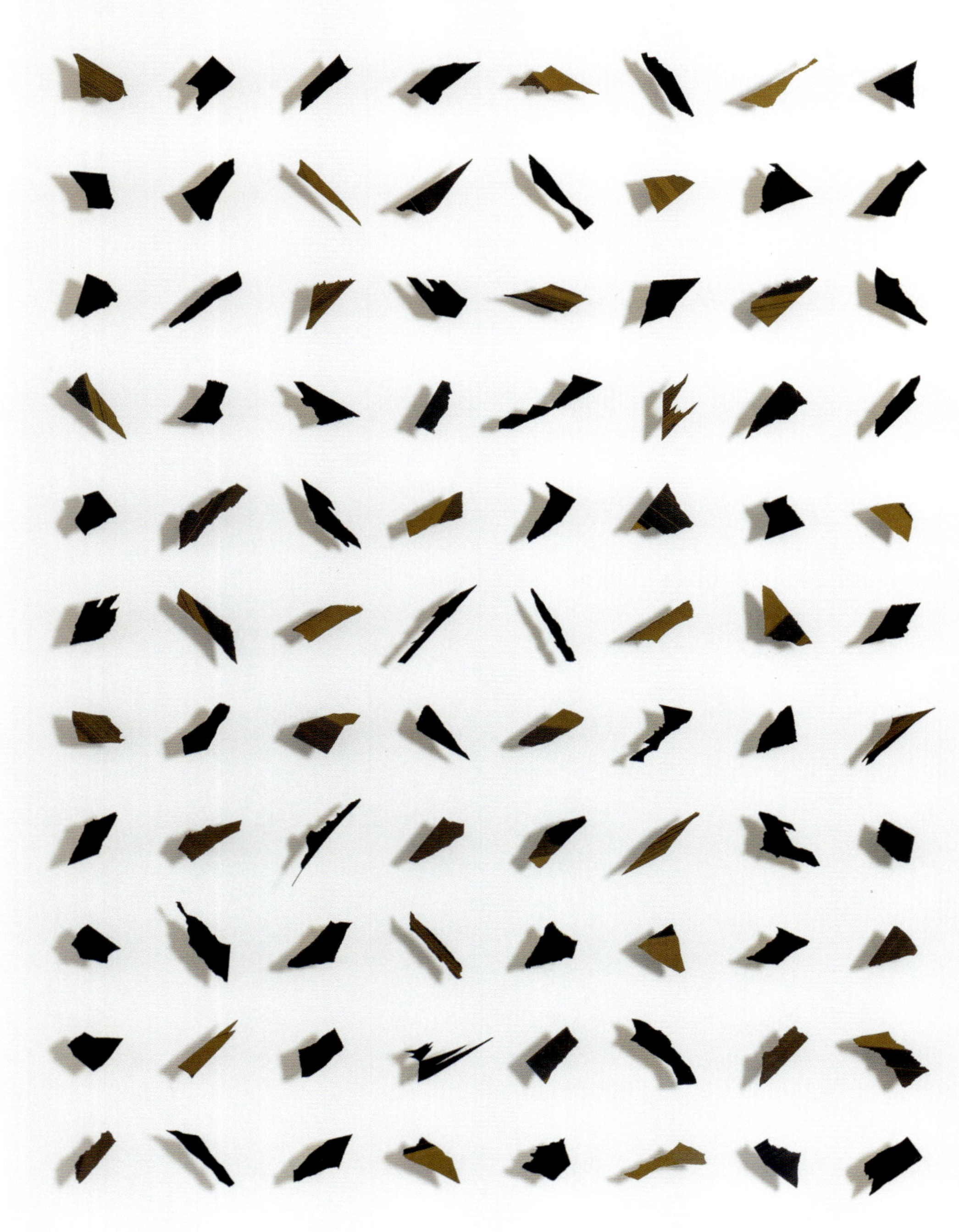

T/R.1035, Recycled Paint
Fragments: Graphite, Bronze,
Acrylic Gel, Oil + Resin on Glass,
109 × 86 cm, 2023

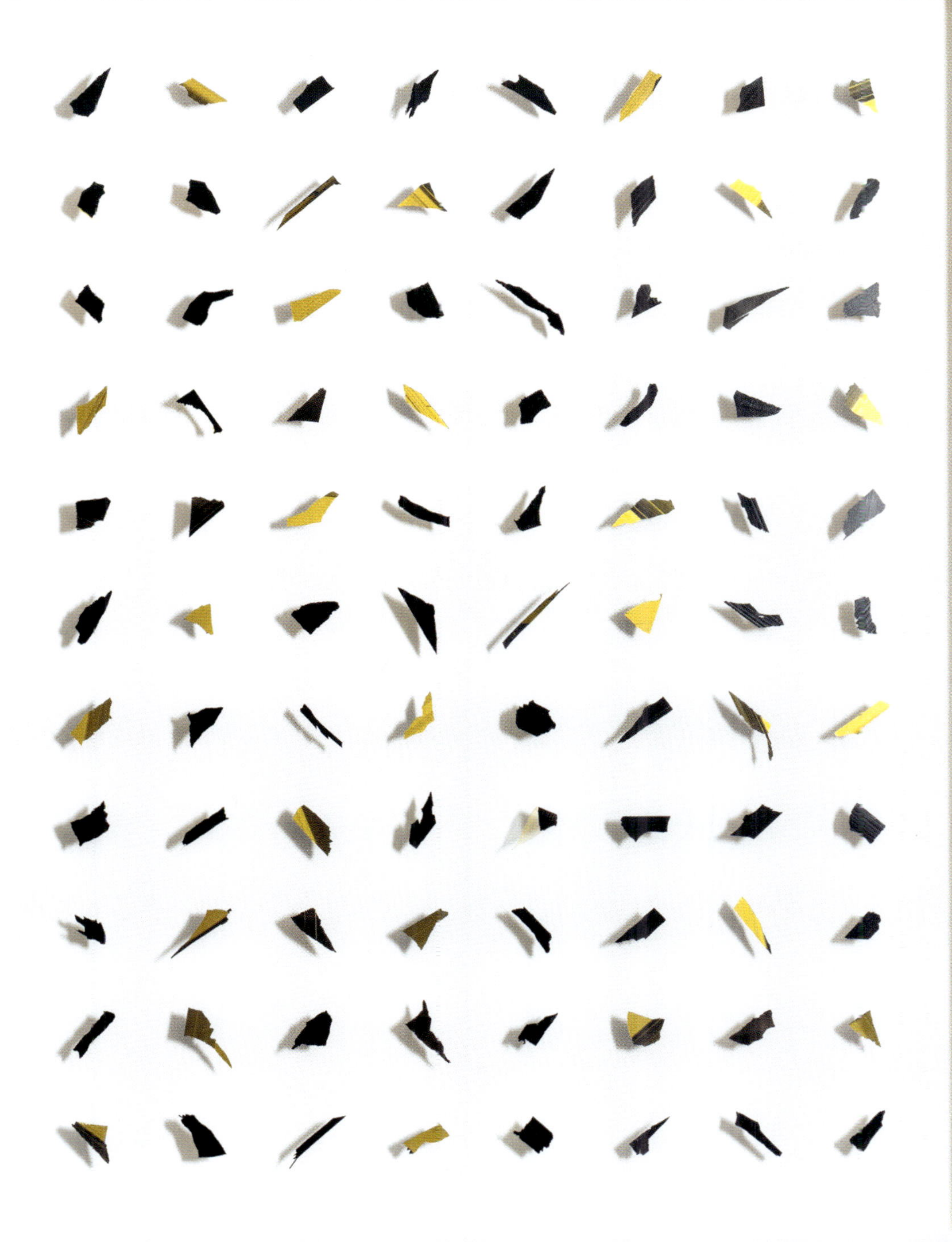

T/R.1036, Recycled Paint Fragments: Graphite, Bronze, Acrylic Gel, Oil + Resin on Glass, 109 × 86 cm, 2023

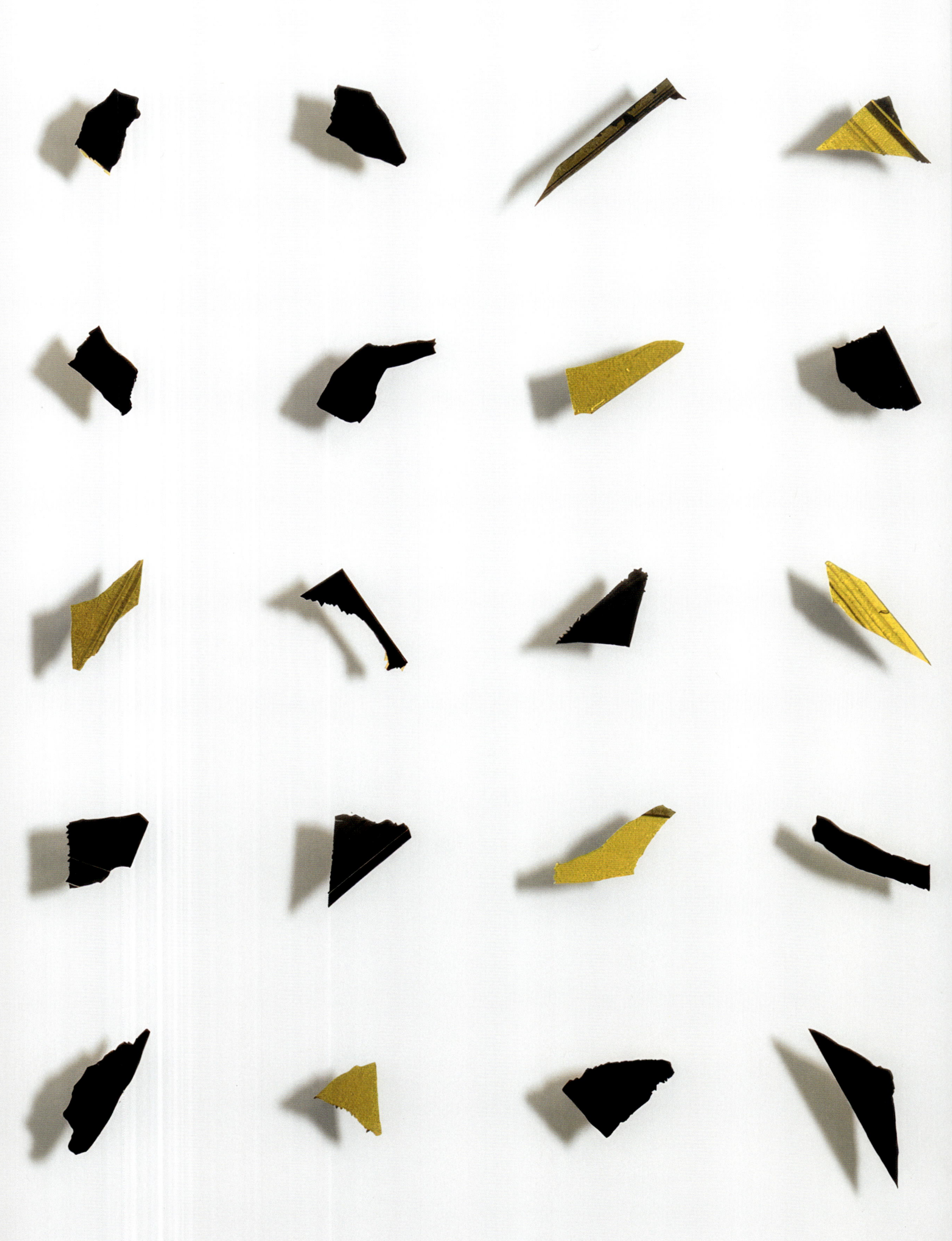

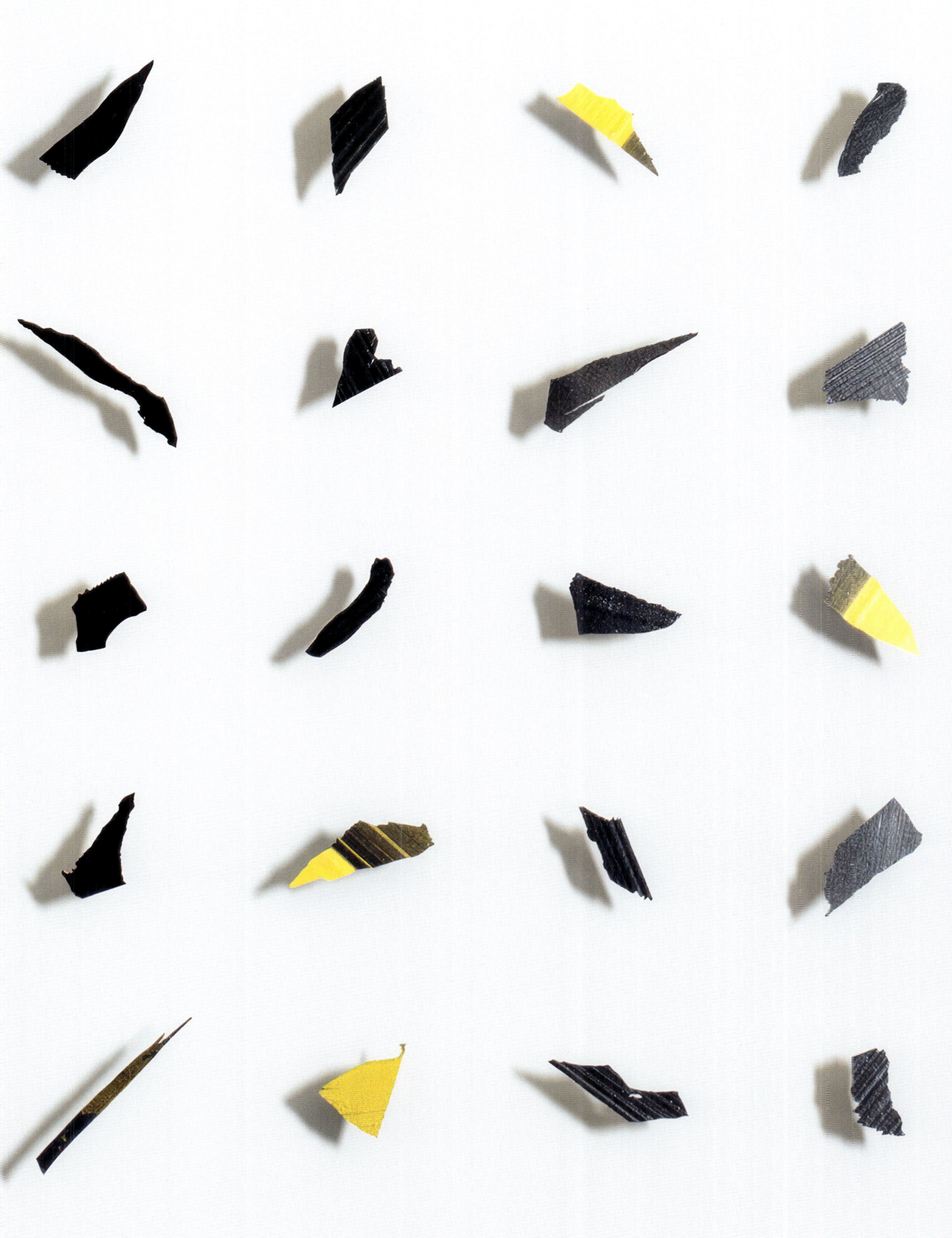

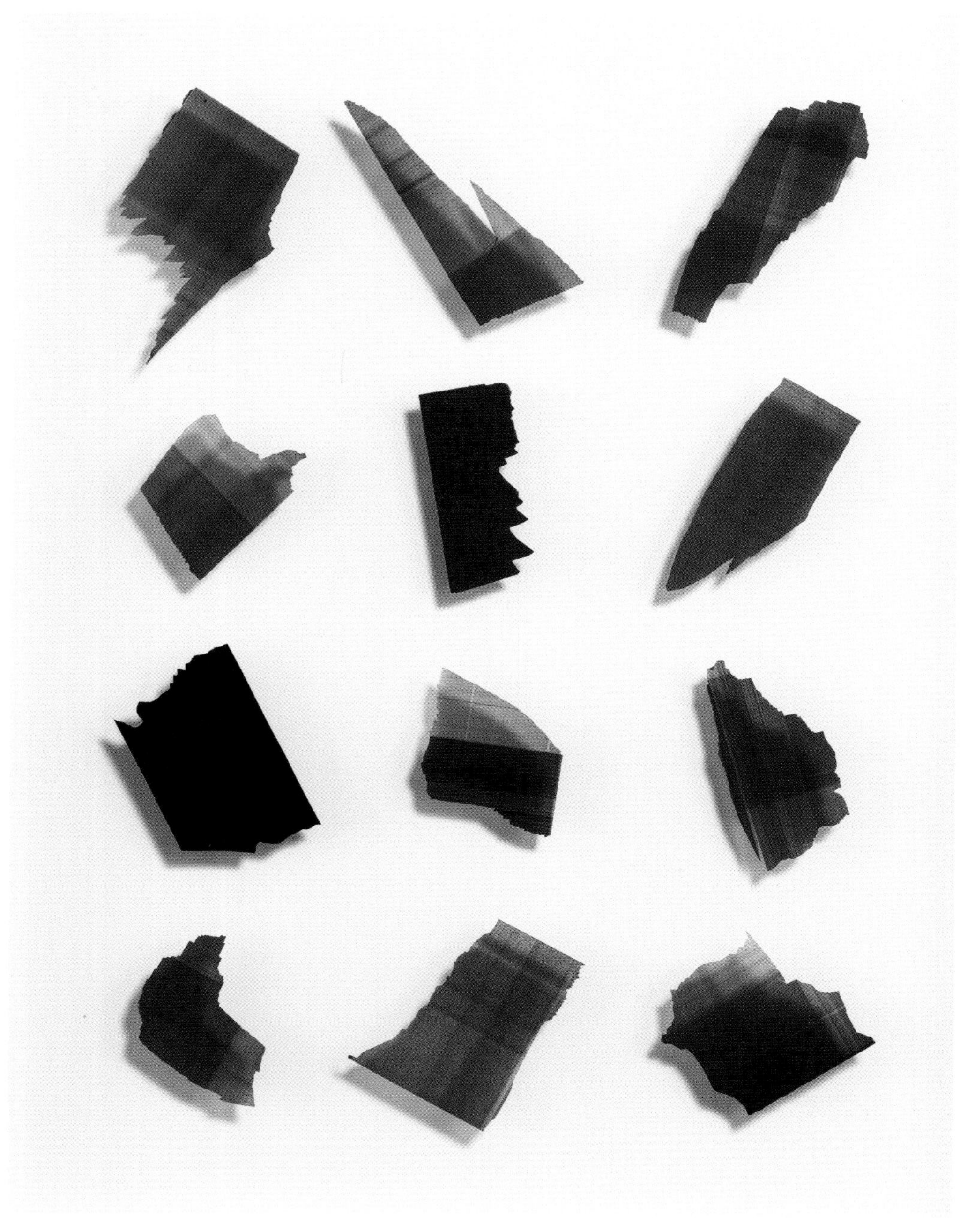

T/R.938, Recycled Paint Fragments: Graphite, Bronze + Acrylic Gel on Glass, 55×44 cm, 2020

T/R.1041, Recycled Paint Fragments: Acrylic, Graphite, Bronze + Acrylic Gel on Glass, 140×104 cm, 2024

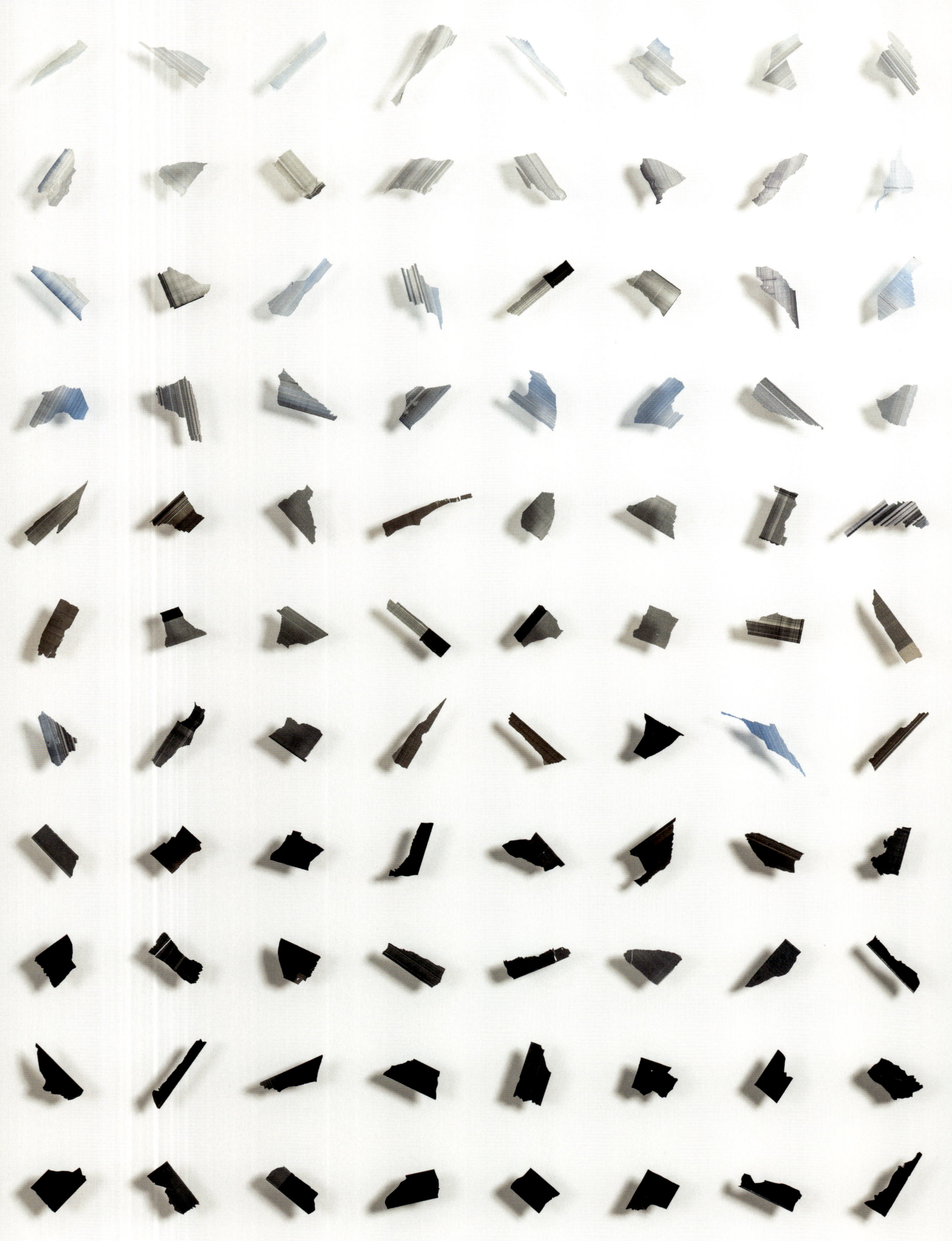

T/R.1042, Recycled Paint Fragments: Acrylic, Graphite, Bronze + Acrylic Gel on Glass, 109 × 86 cm, 2024

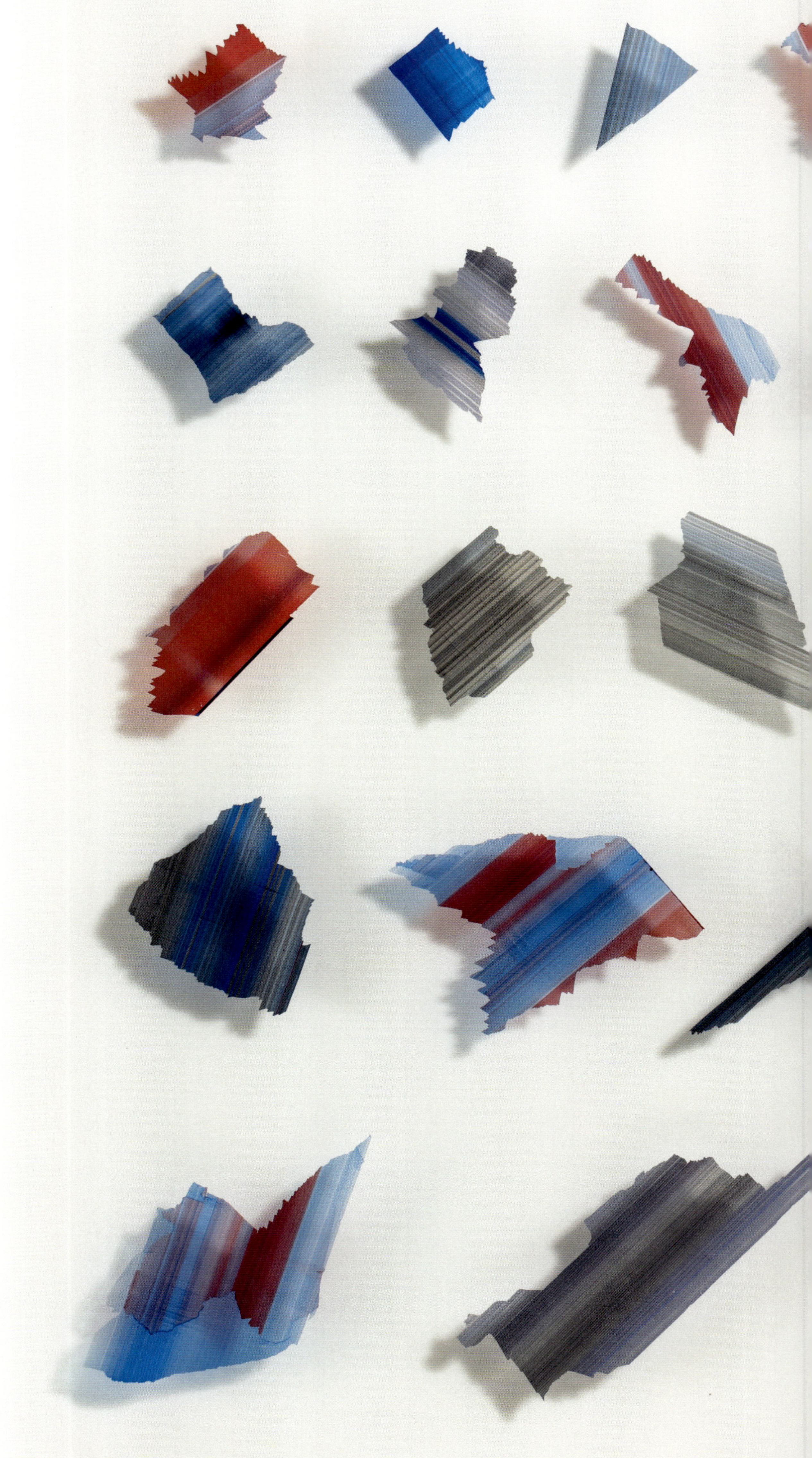

T/R.1012, Recycled Paint Fragments: Acrylic, Graphite + Acrylic Gel on Glass, 86×109 cm, 2022

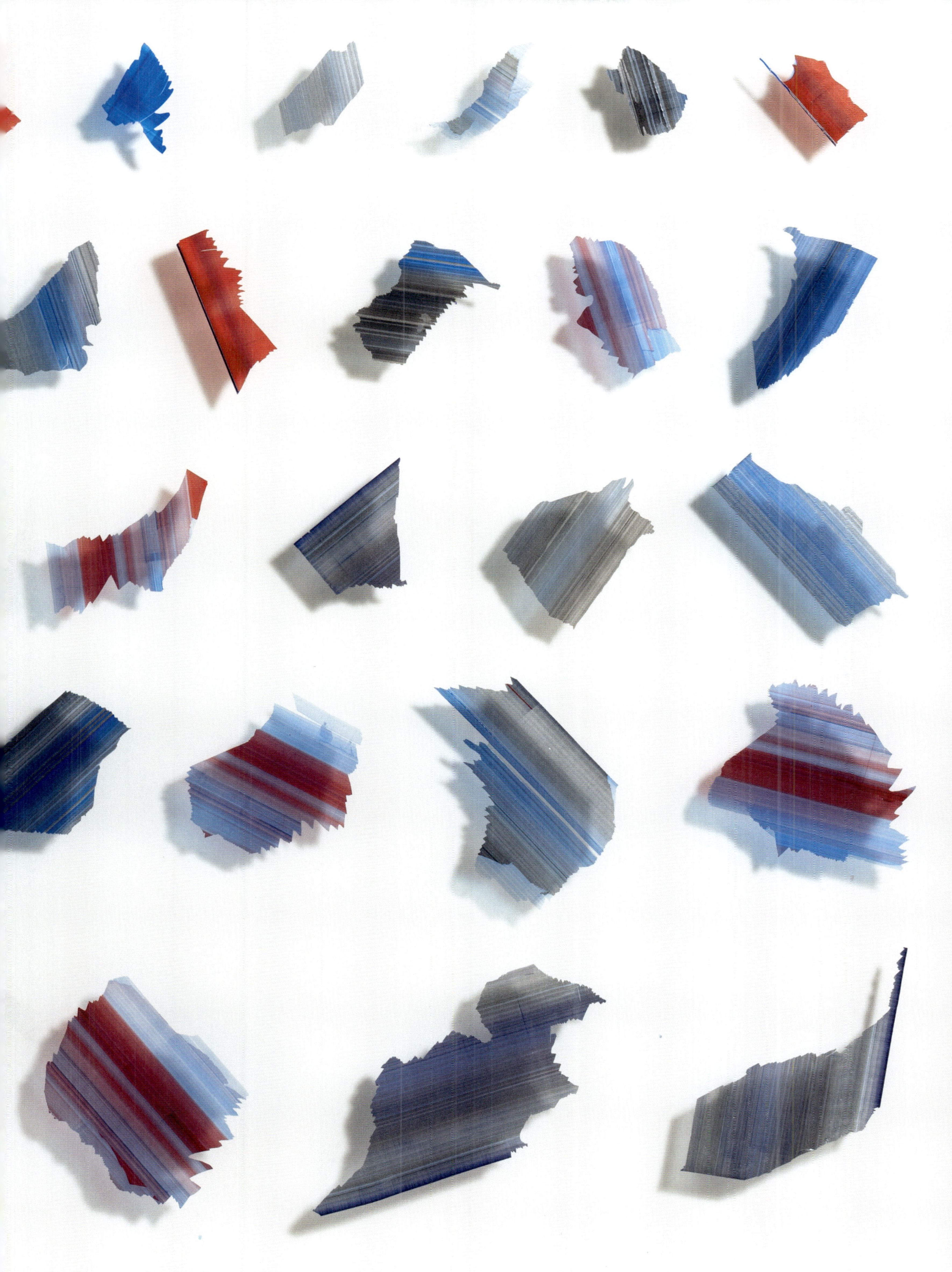

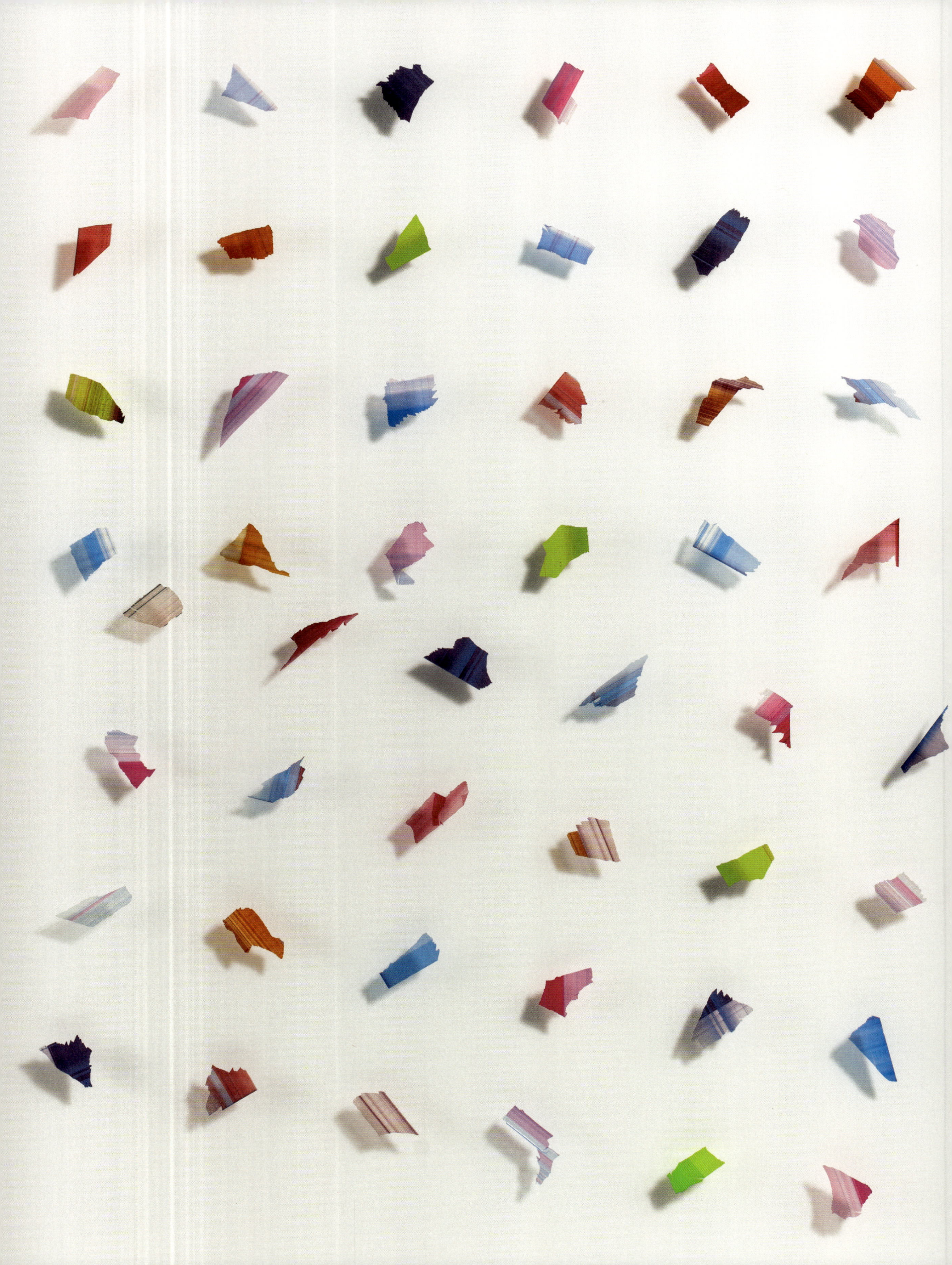

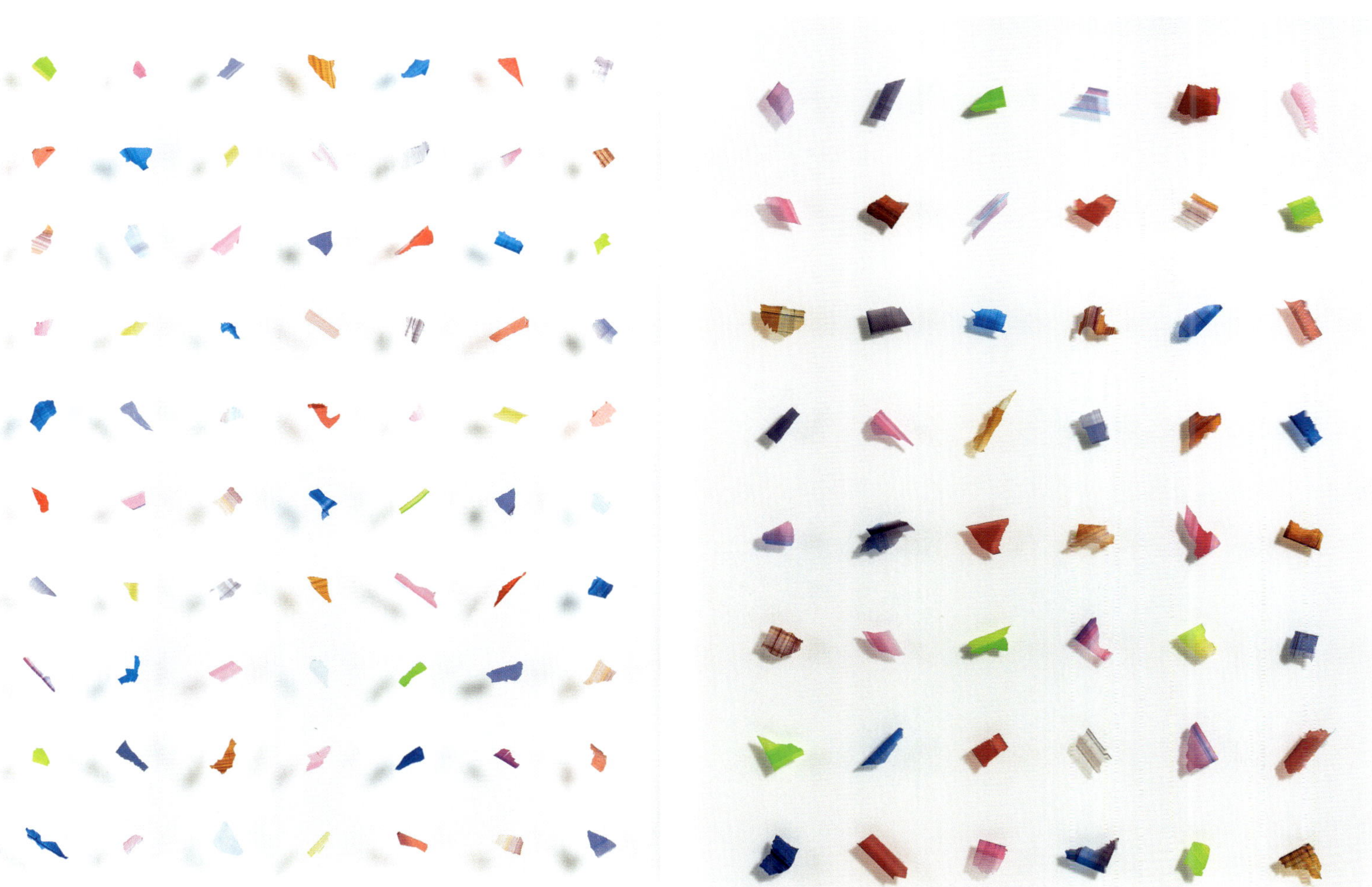

T/R.1005, Recycled Paint
Fragments: Acrylic, Graphite
+ Acrylic Gel on Glass,
109 × 86 cm, 2022

T/R.977, Recycled Paint
Fragments: Acrylic
+ Acrylic Gel on Glass,
55 × 44 cm, 2022

T/R.1021, Recycled Paint
Fragments: Acrylic
+ Acrylic Gel on Glass,
140 × 104 cm, 2022

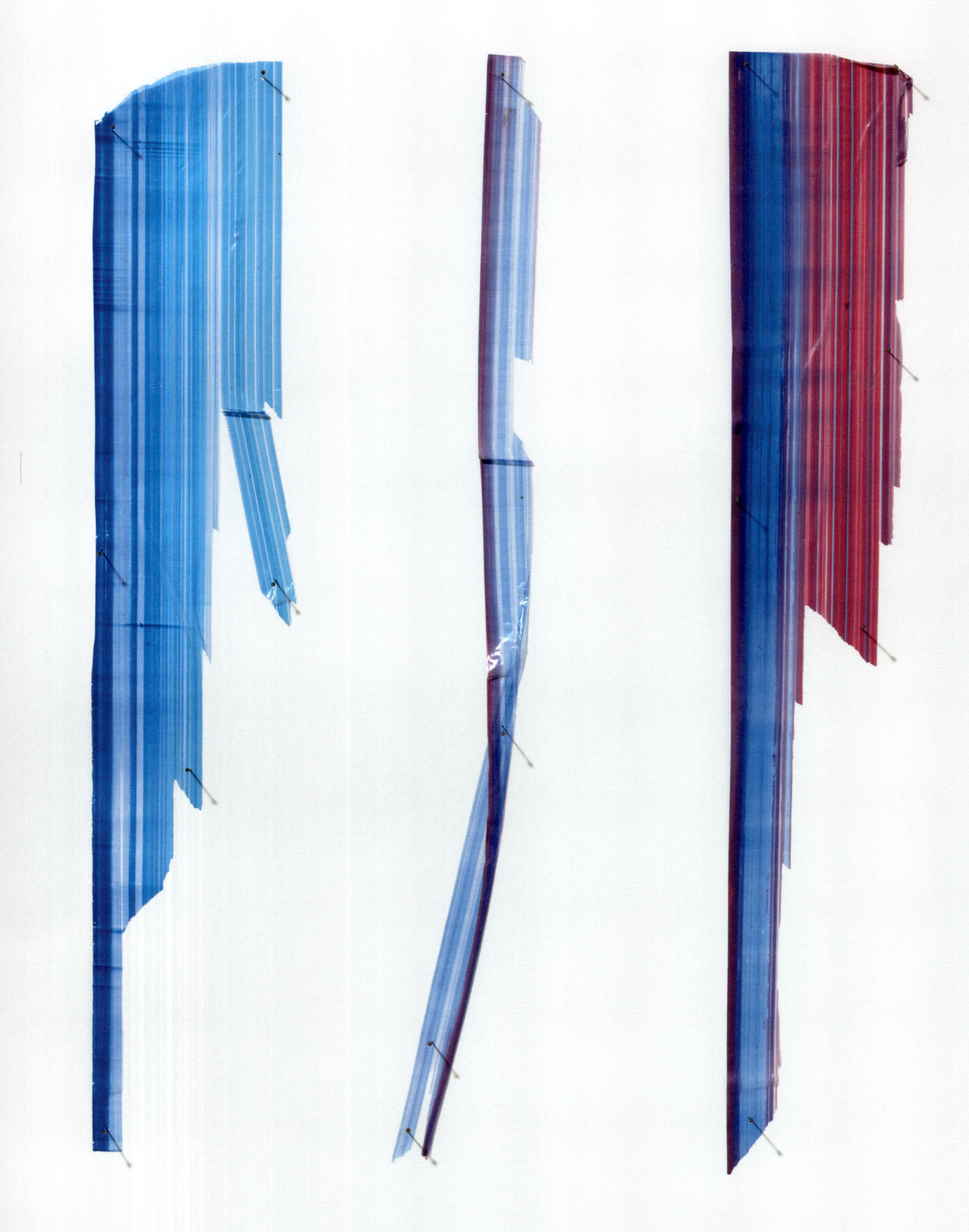

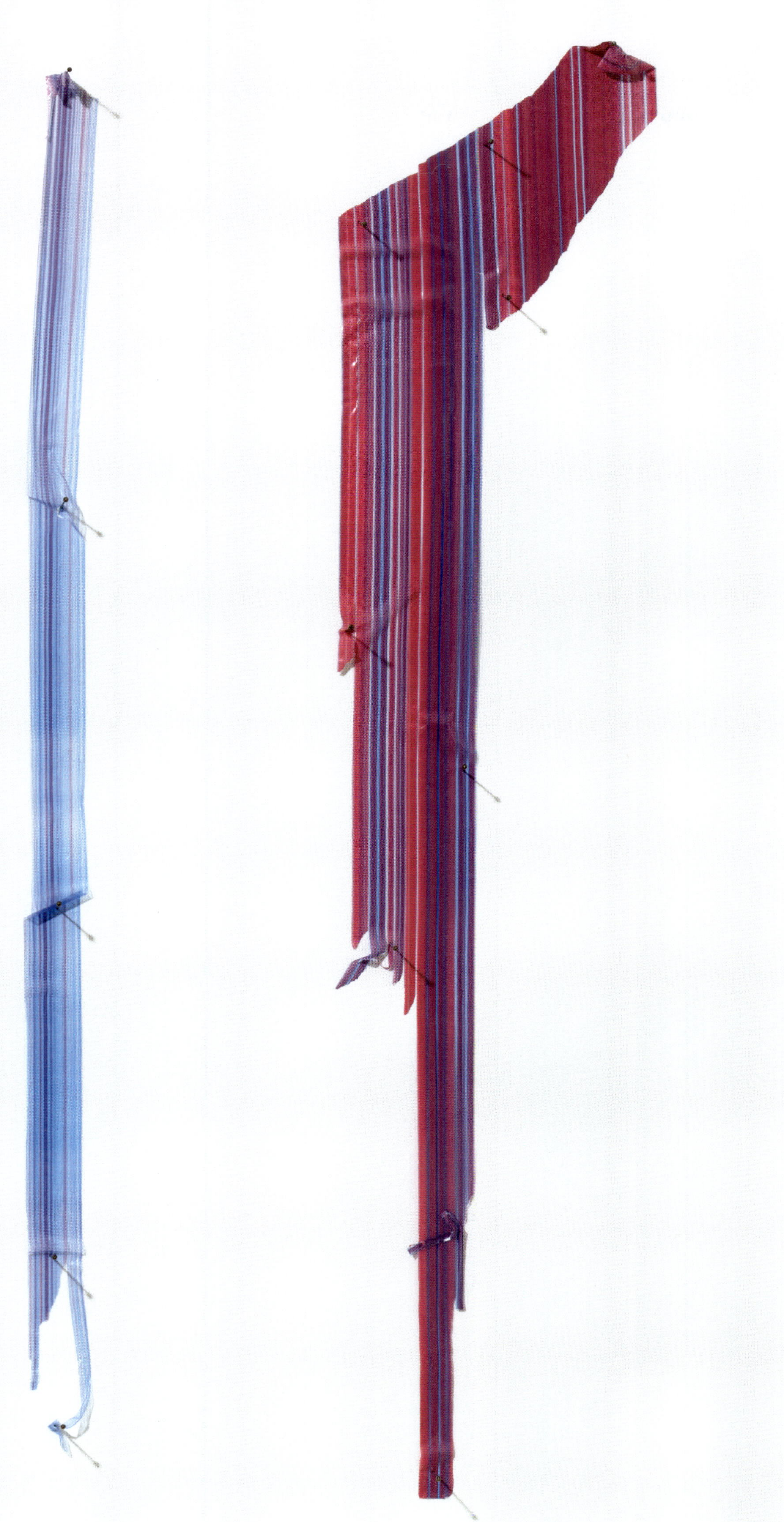

T/R_1115, Recycled Paint Fragments: Acrylic, Graphite, Pins + Acrylic Gel on Glass, 55×64 cm, 2025

T/R.1059, Recycled Paint
Fragments: Acrylic, Graphite
+ Acrylic Gel on Glass,
55 × 44 cm, 2025

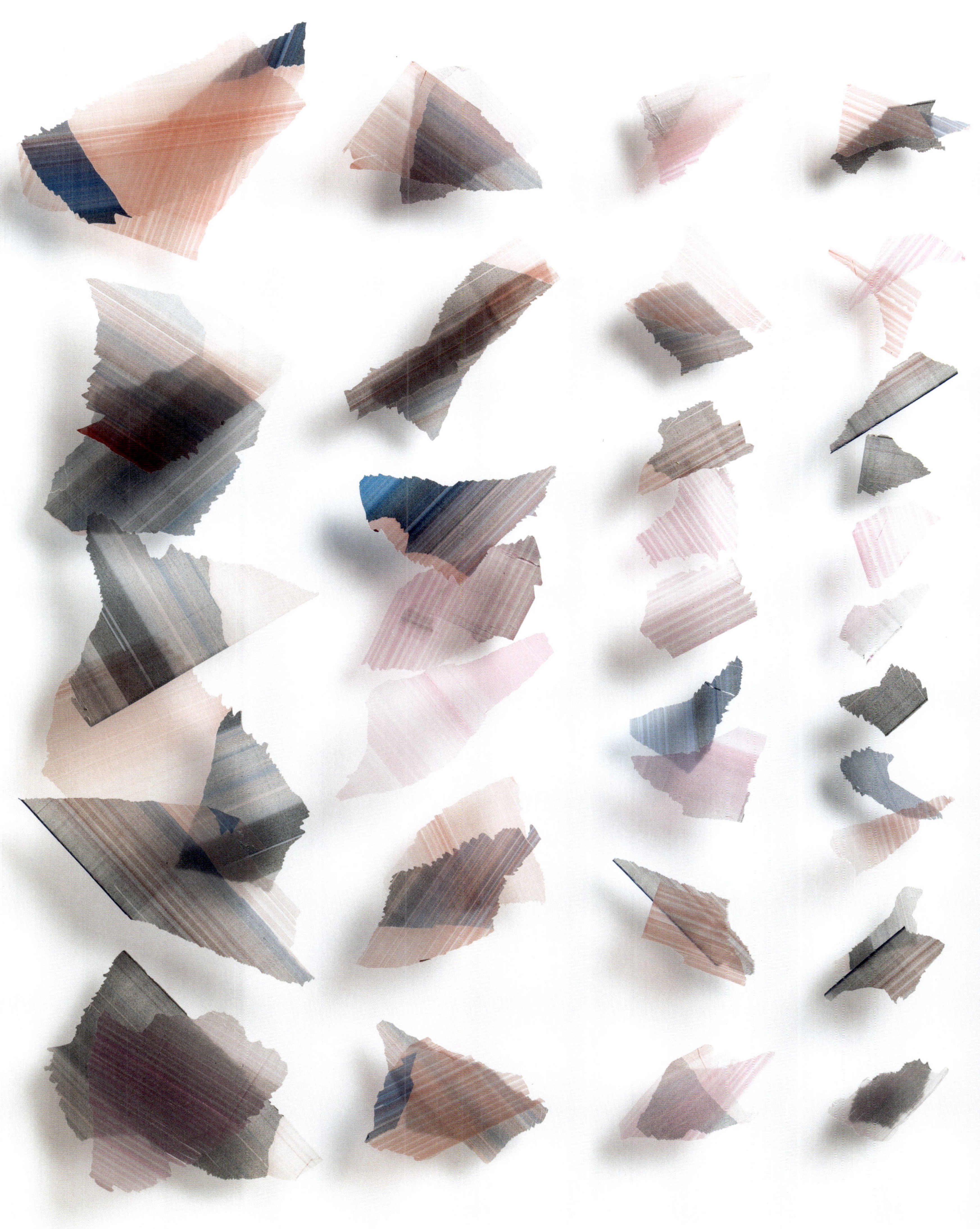

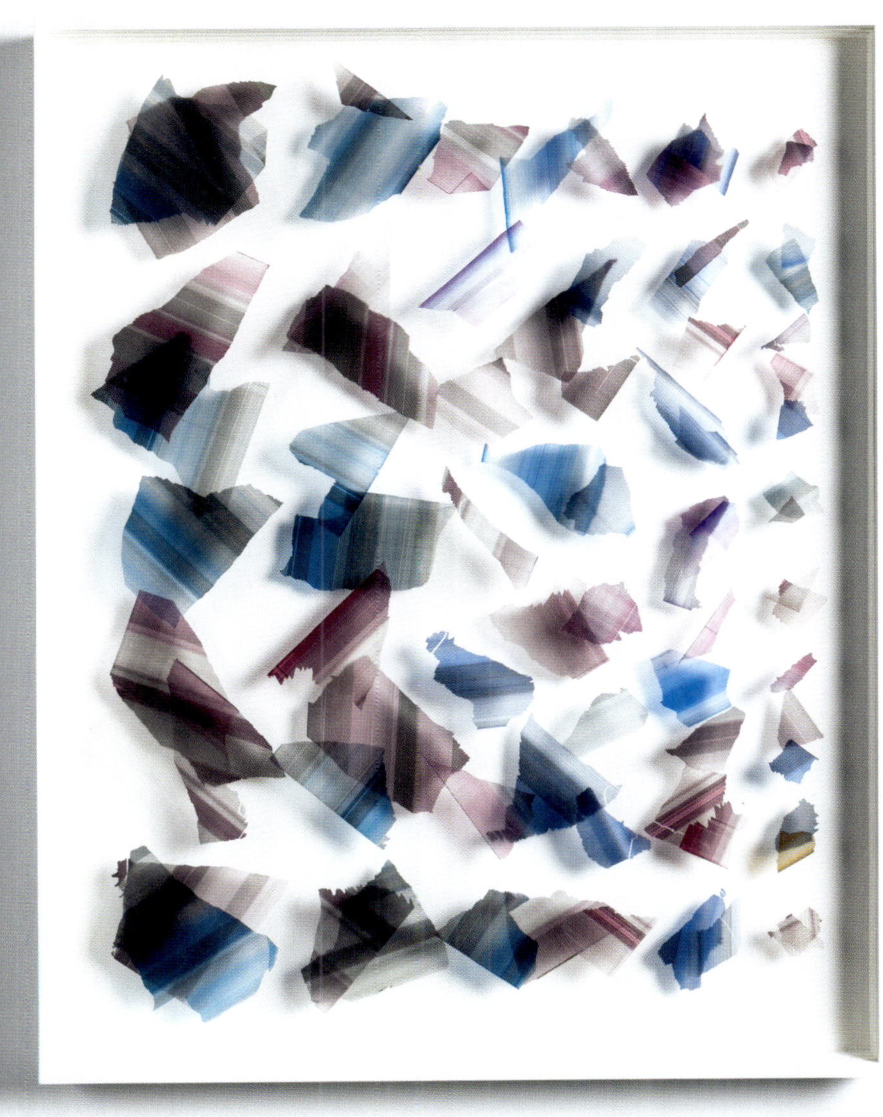

T/R.1064, Recycled Paint Fragments: Acrylic, Graphite + Acrylic Gel on Glass, 55×44 cm, 2025

T/R.1060, Recycled Paint Fragments: Acrylic, Graphite, Tin + Acrylic Gel on Glass, 109×86 cm, 2025

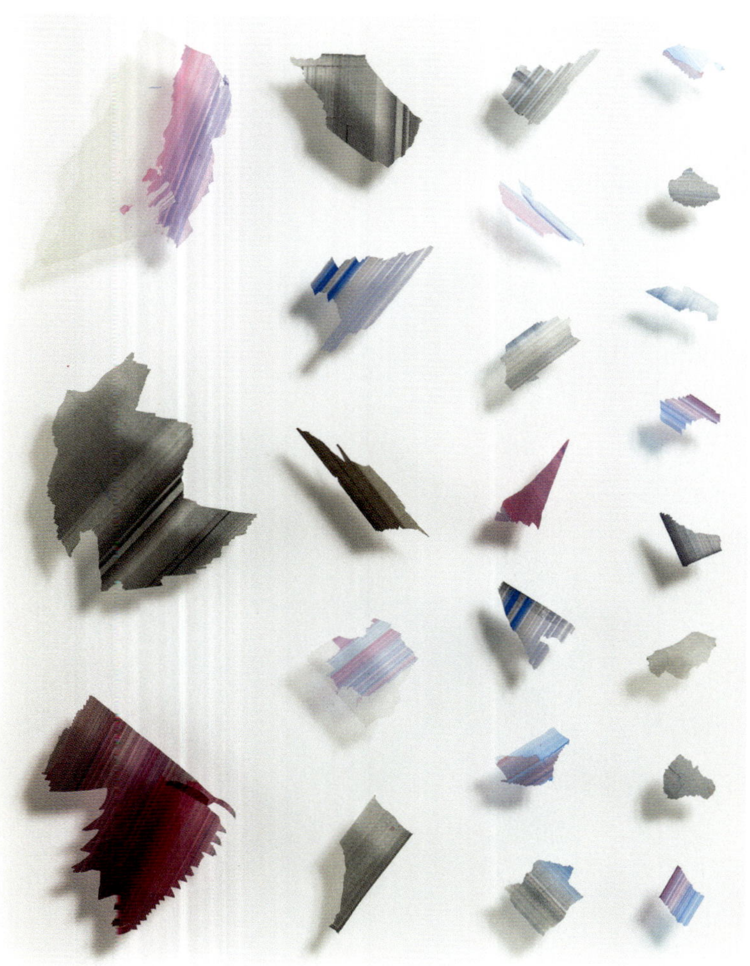

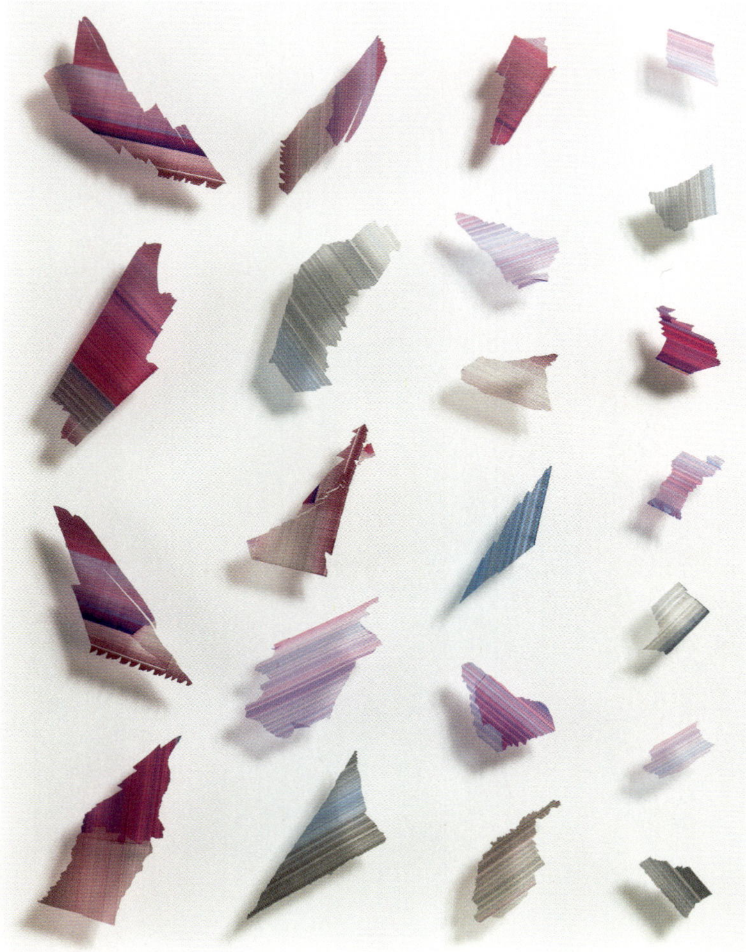

T/R.1017, Recycled Paint Fragments: Acrylic, Graphite + Acrylic Gel on Glass, 55 × 44 cm, 2022

T/R.1018, Recycled Paint Fragments: Acrylic, Graphite + Acrylic Gel on Glass, 55 × 44 cm, 2022

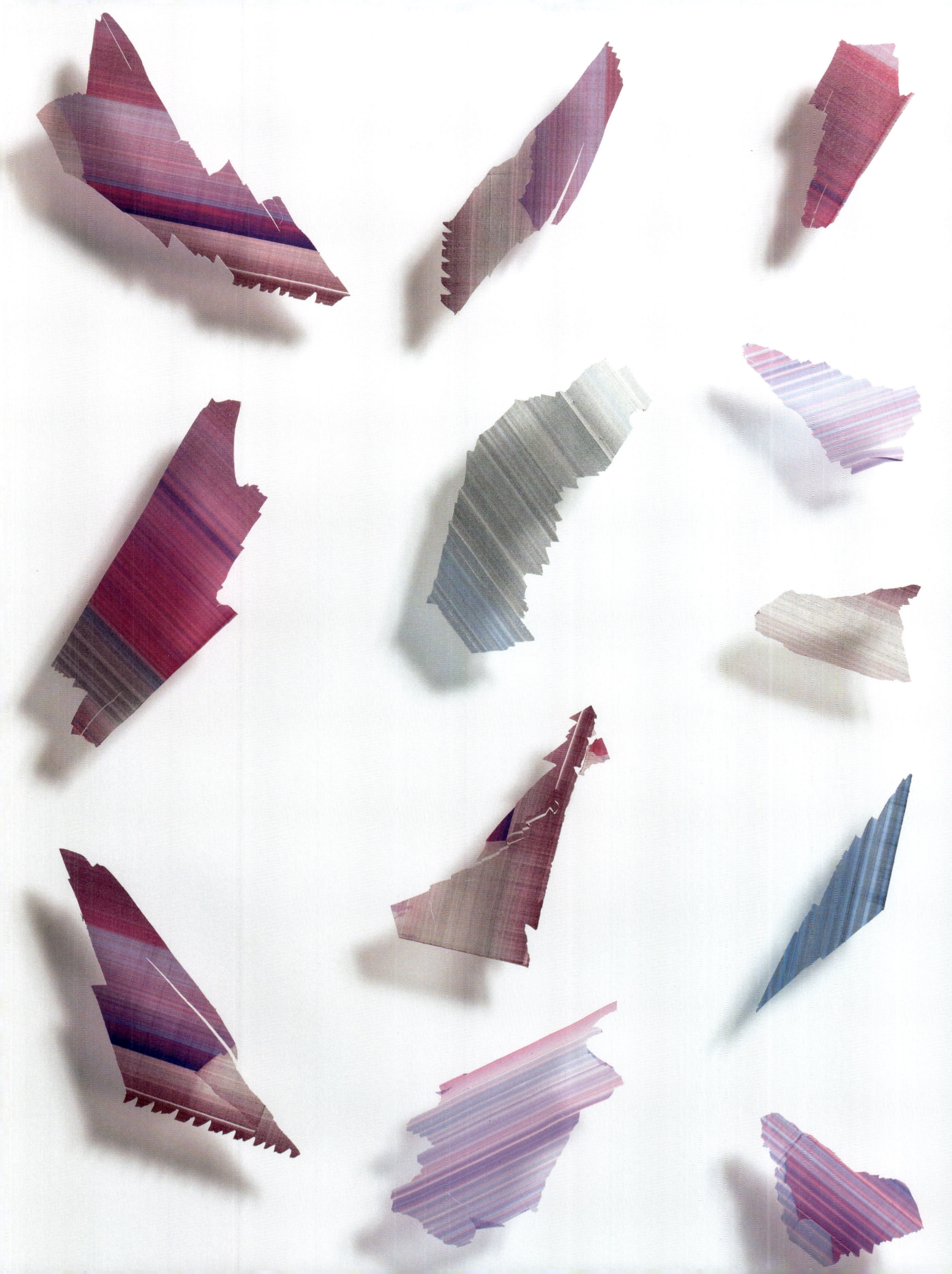

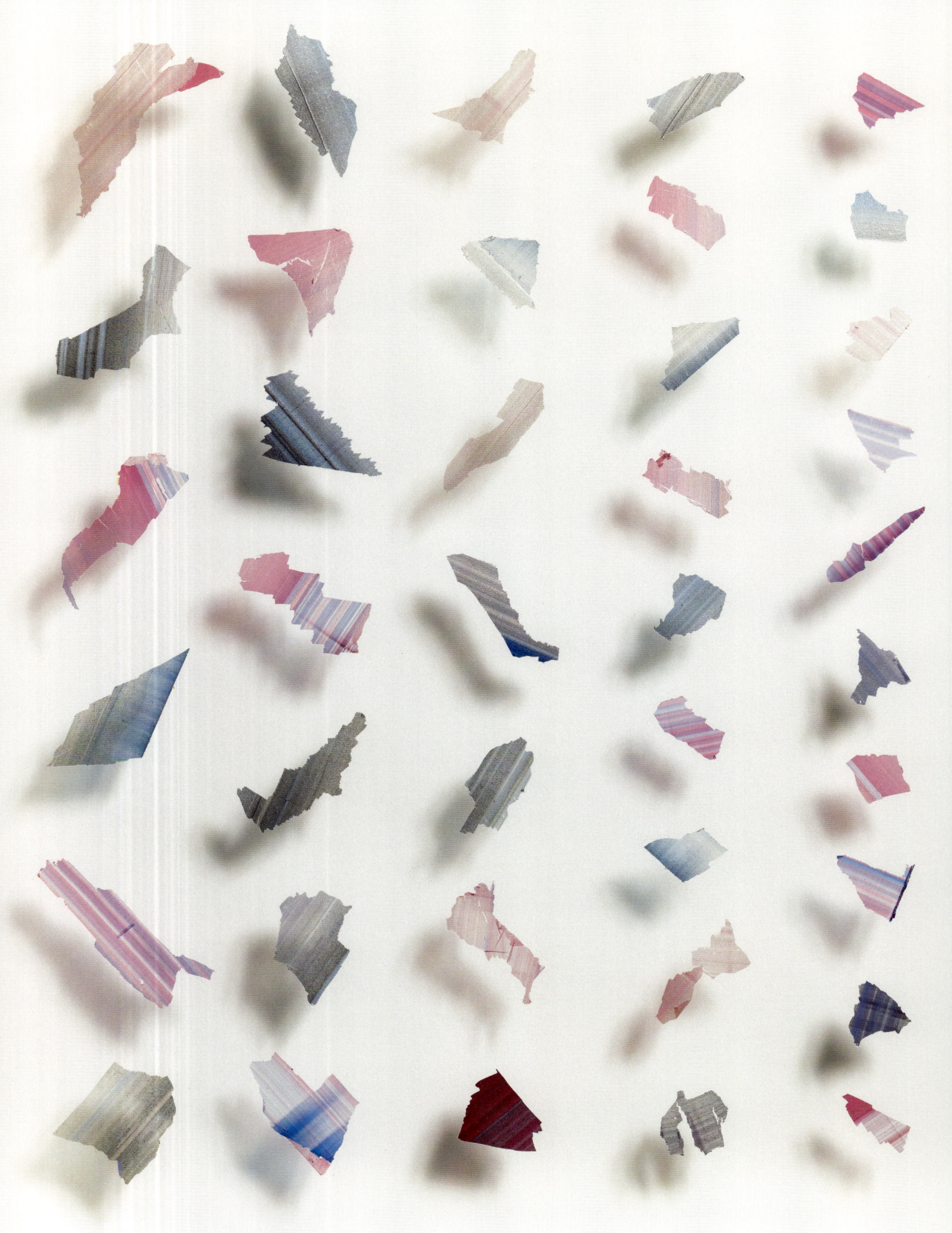

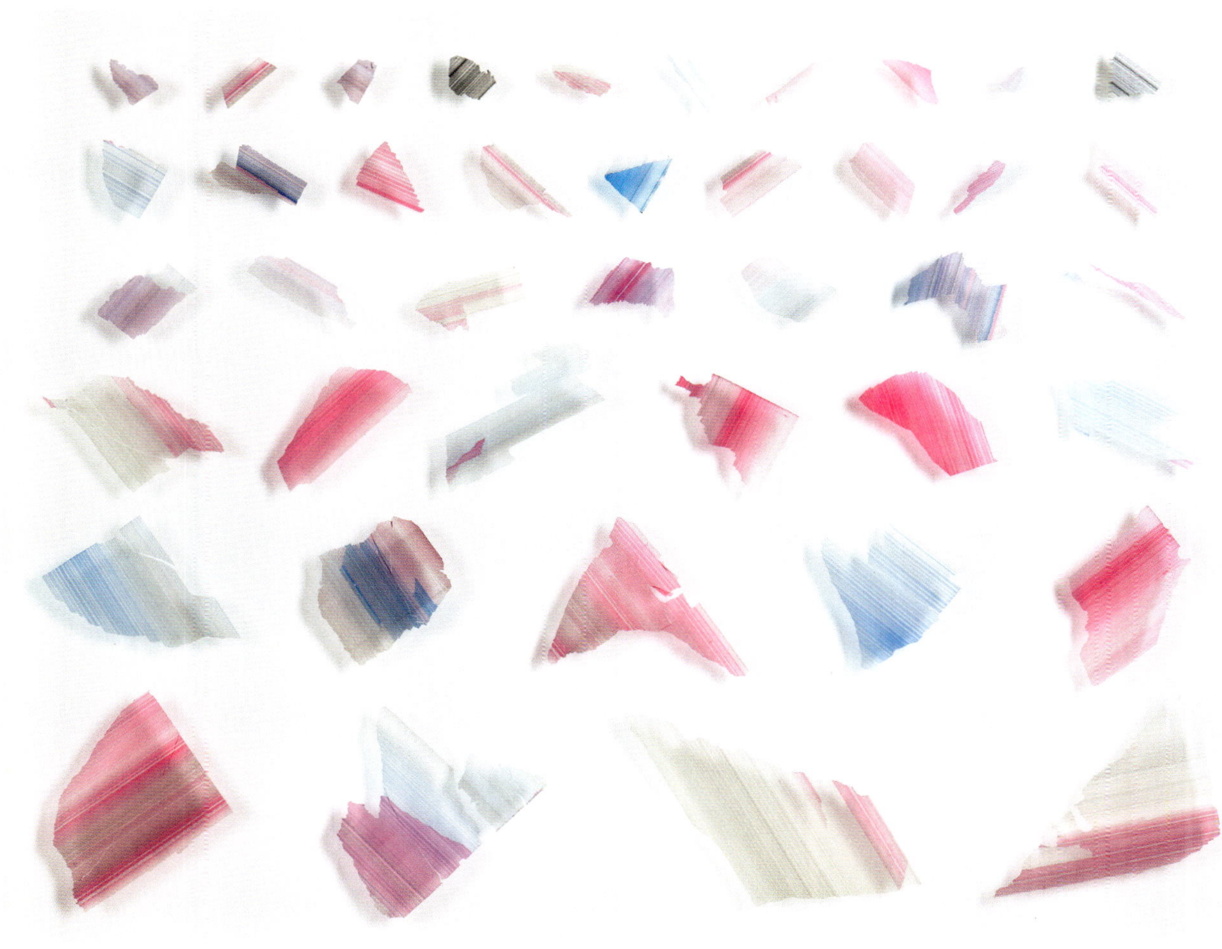

T/R.1001, Recycled Paint Fragments: Acrylic, Graphite + Acrylic Gel on Glass, 55 × 44 cm, 2022

T/R.1023, Recycled Paint Fragments: Acrylic, Graphite + Acrylic Gel on Glass, 86 × 109 cm, 2023

Following double page:
T/R.1026, Recycled Paint Fragments: Acrylic, Graphite + Acrylic Gel on Glass 44 × 55 cm, 2023

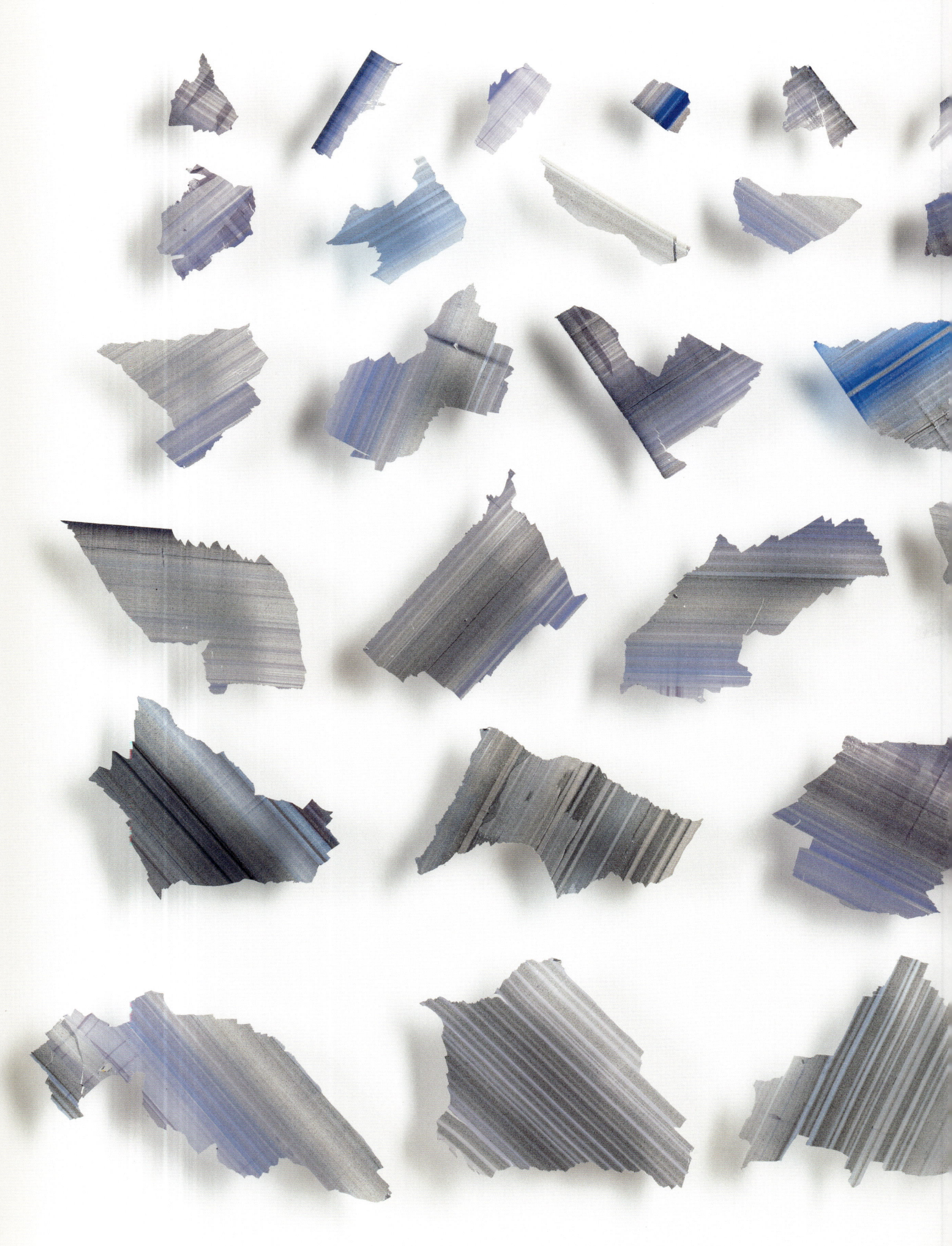

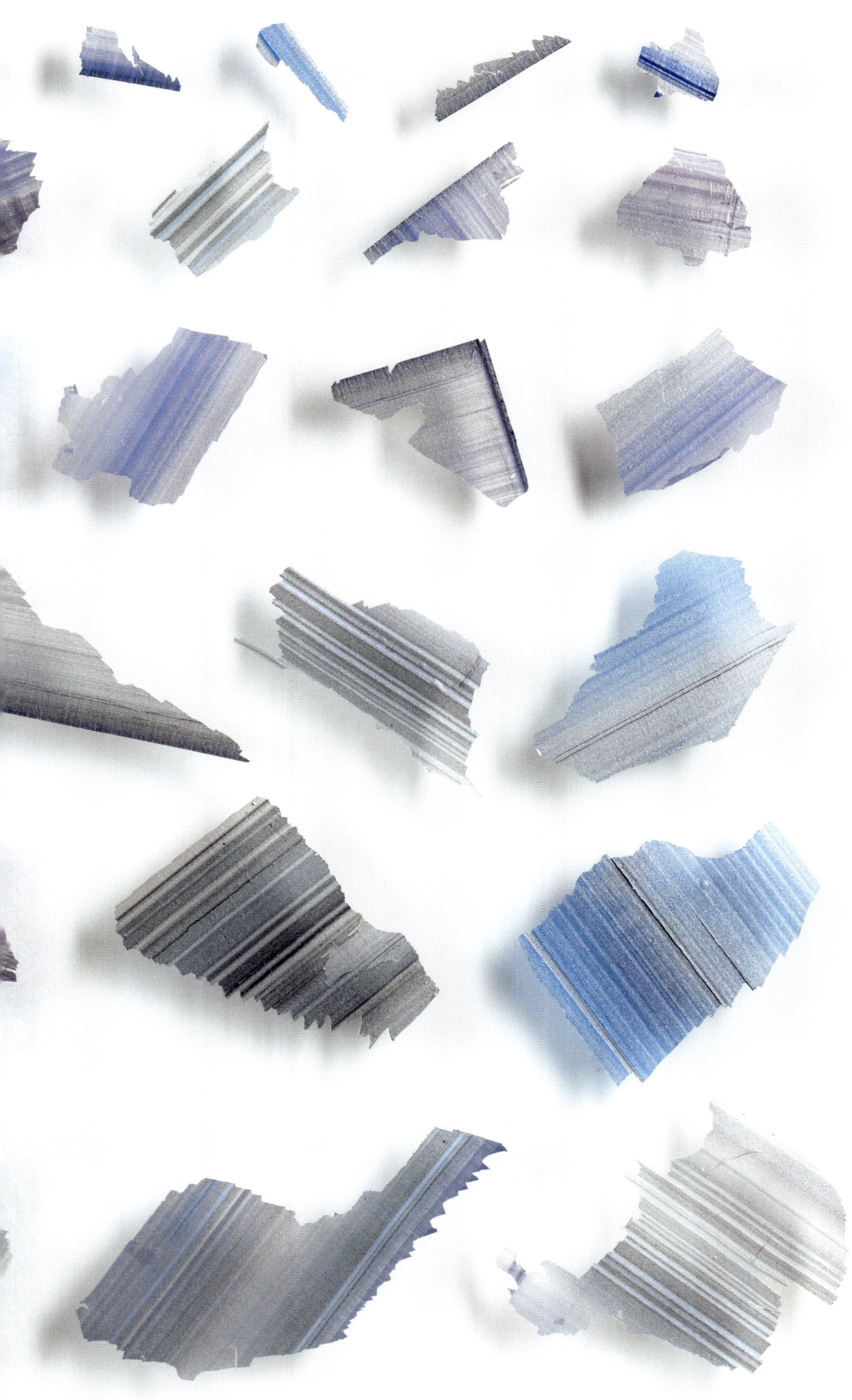

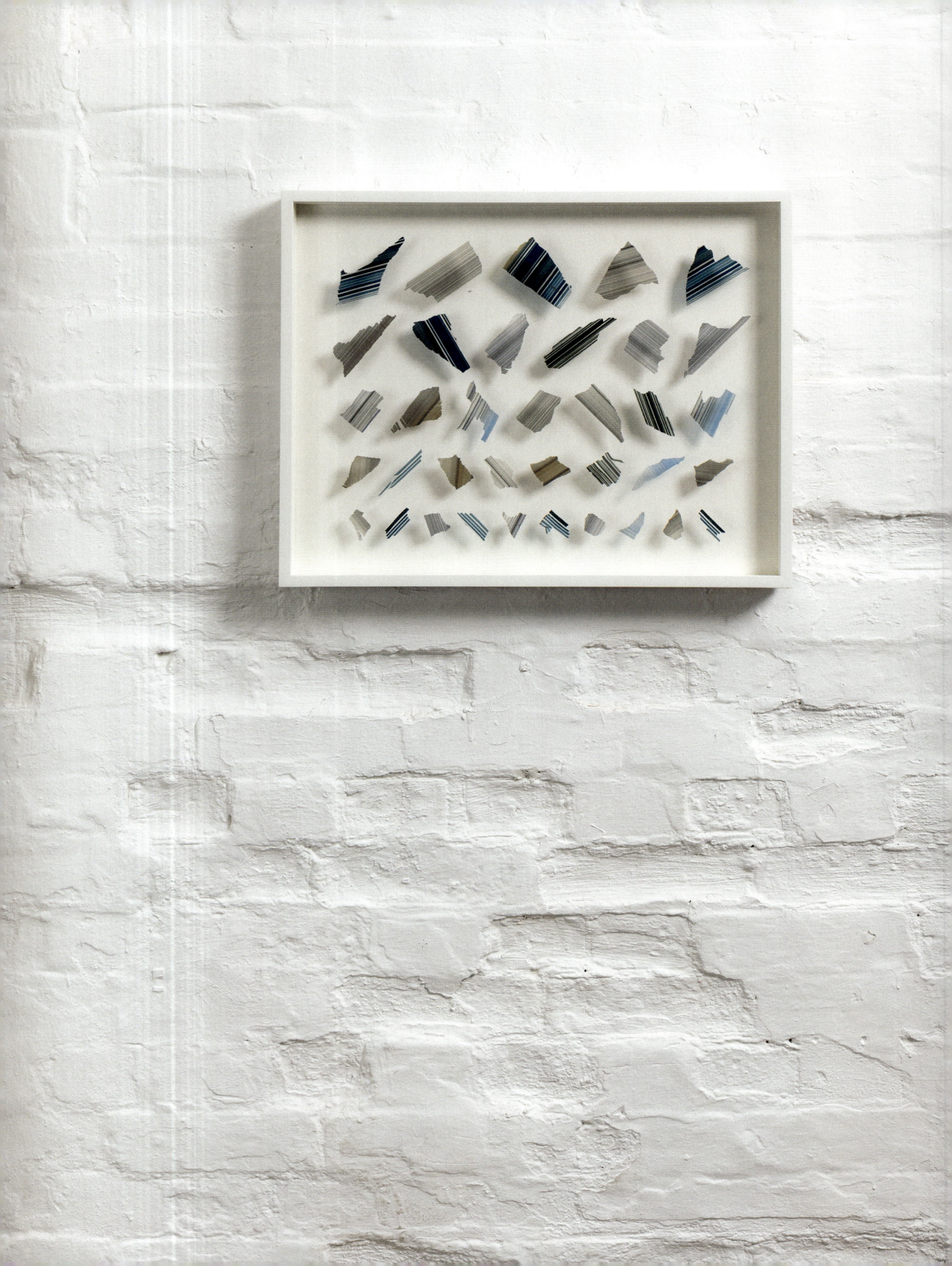

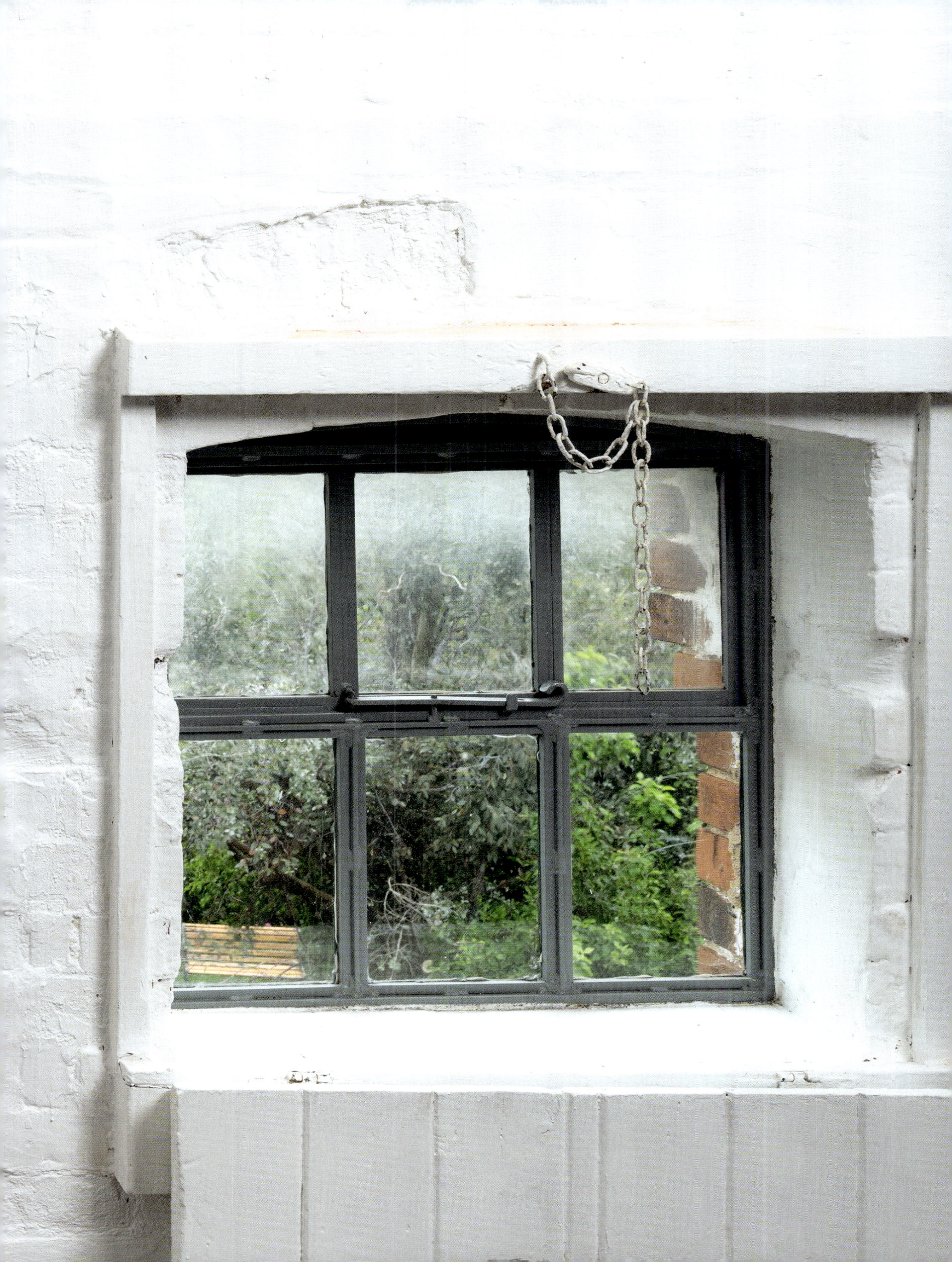

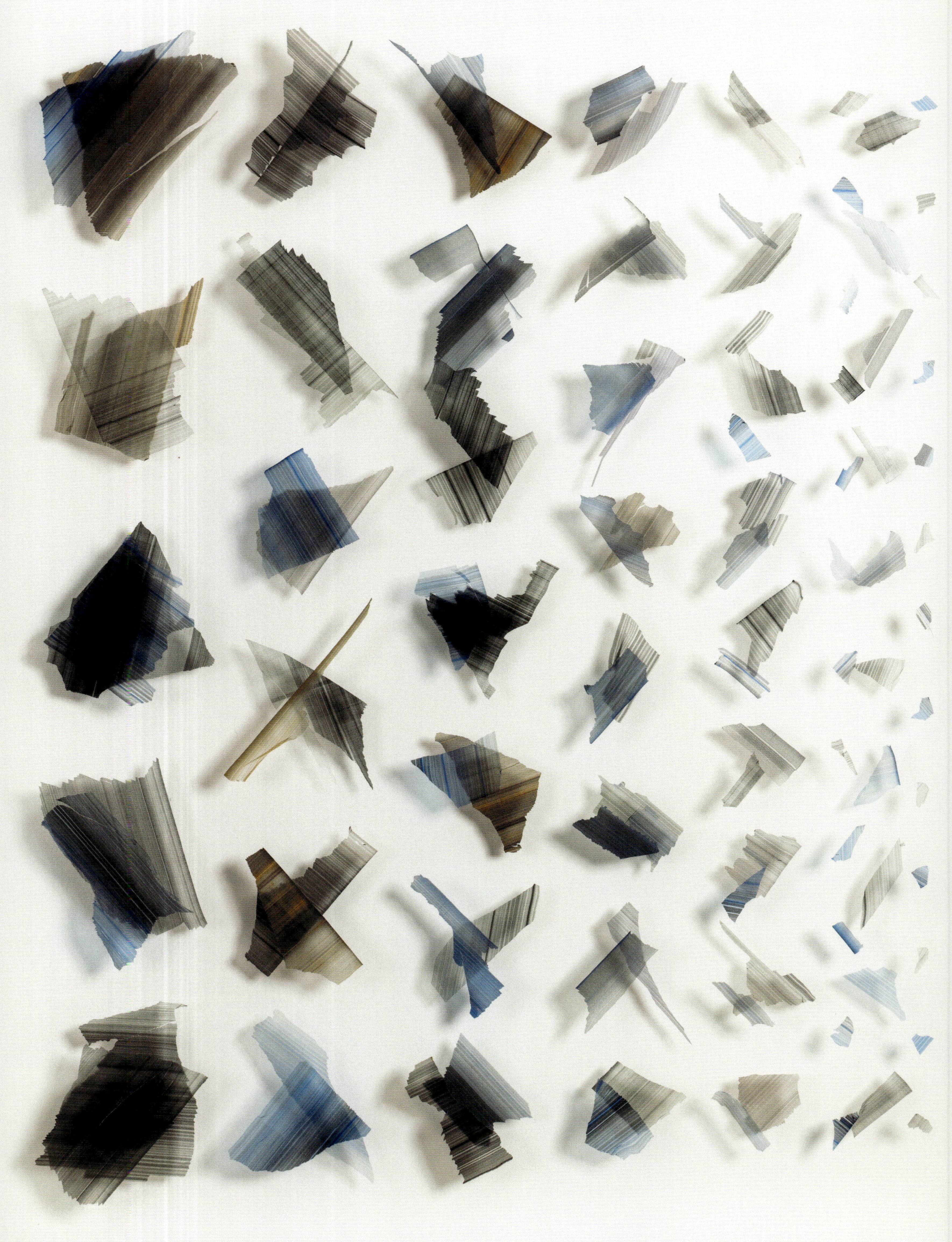

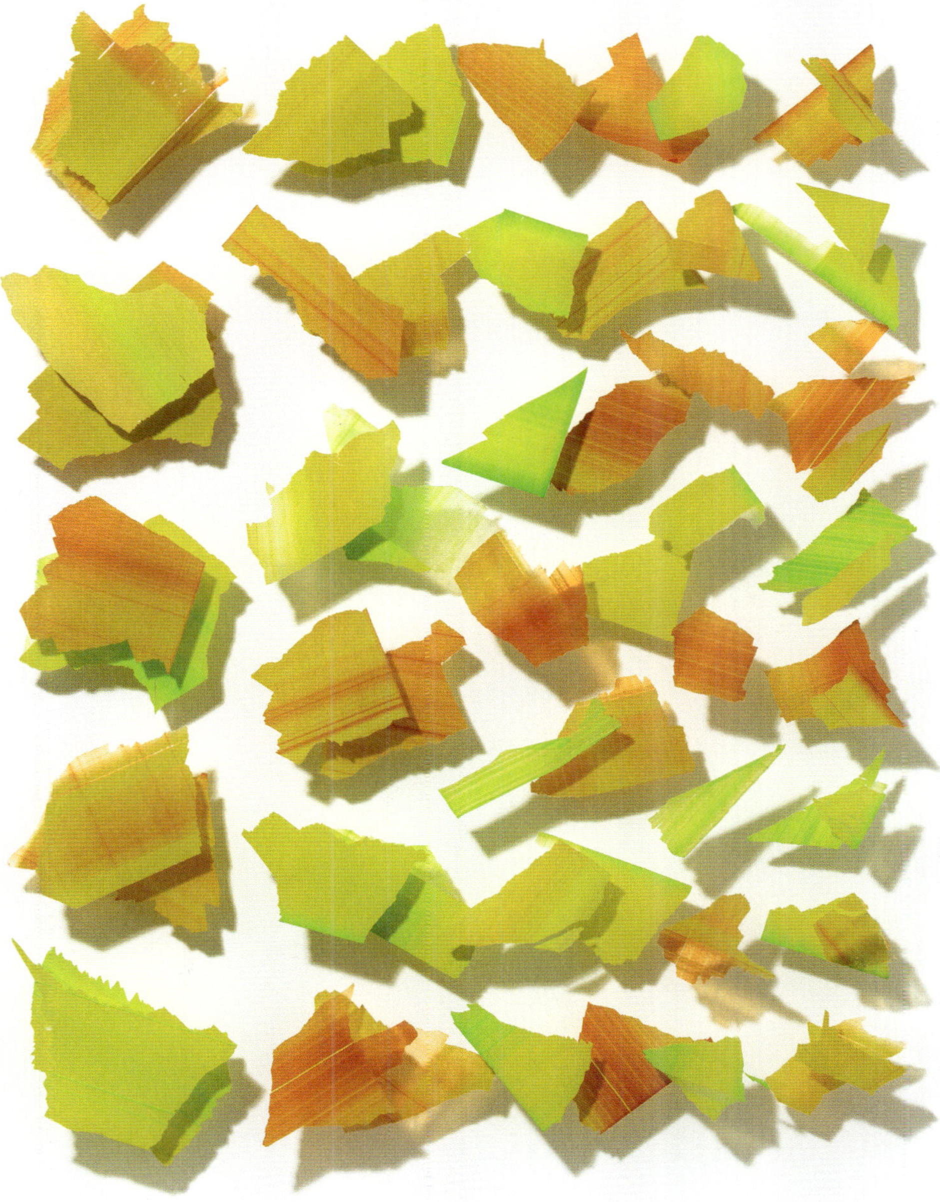

T/R.1045, Recycled Paint Fragments: Acrylic, Graphite + Acrylic Gel on Glass, 109×86 cm, 2024

T/R.1116, Recycled Paint Fragments: Acrylic + Acrylic Gel on Glass, 55×44 cm, 2025

Previous double page:
T/R.1050, Recycled Paint Fragments: Acrylic, Graphite + Acrylic Gel on Glass, 44×55 cm, 2024

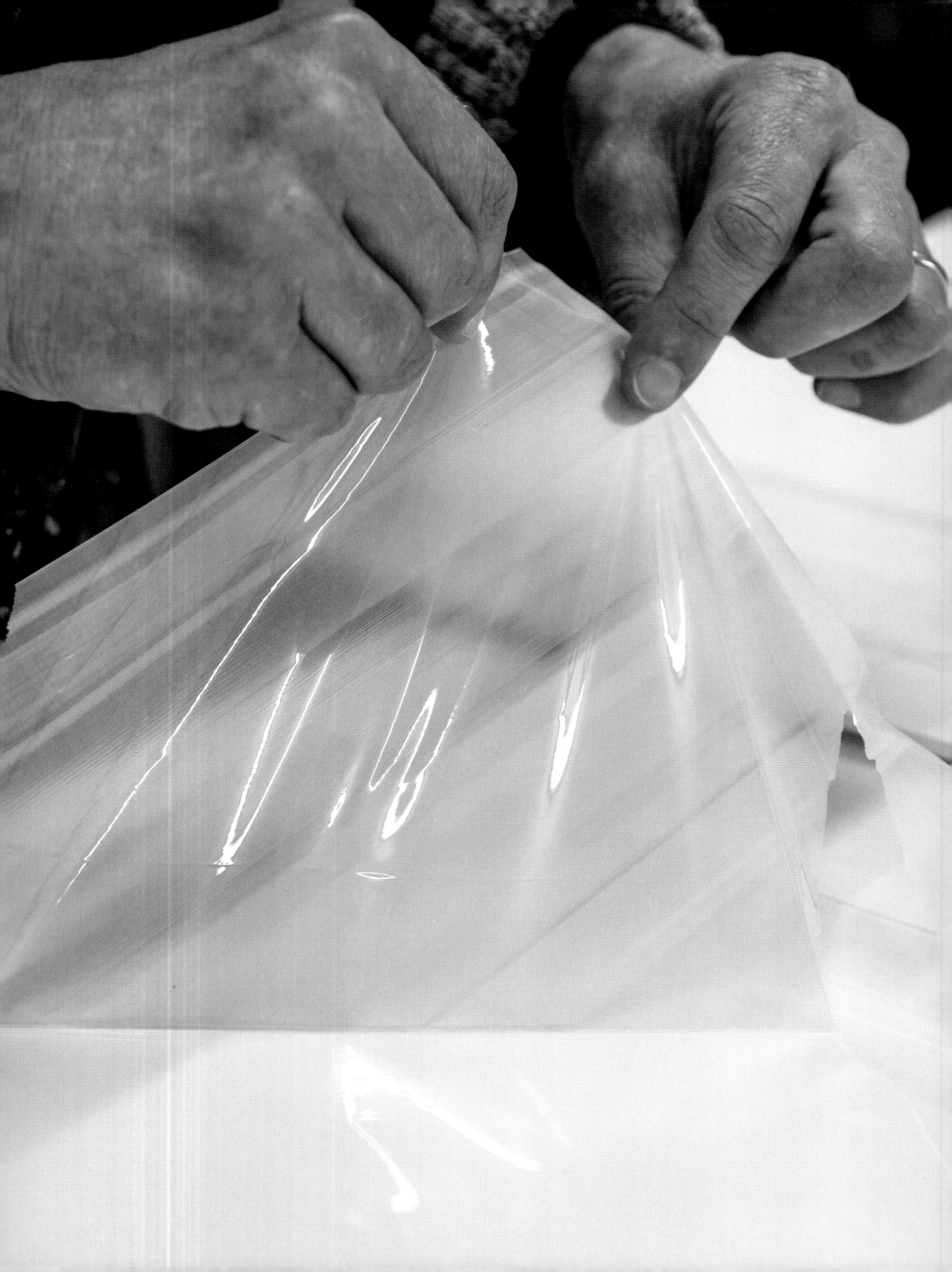

Biography

Eric Butcher
Born in Singapore, 1970
Lives and works in Oxfordshire, UK

1990-04
Corpus Christi College, Cambridge (BA Philosophy)

2000-01
Wimbledon School of Art, London (MA Fine Art)

2002
Art London: Visual Arts Development Award

2005-06
Curated *Definite Article*, Vertigo Gallery, London; Toomey-Tourell Gallery, San Francisco, USA

2007
Research Fellowship: The Arts Institute at Bournemouth

Research Fellowship: Centre for Art International Research (CAIR), Liverpool School of Art, Liverpool John Moores University, *Multiple Perspectives Fellowship*

2008-10
Artist in Residence, Benson-Sedgwick Engineering, London

2012
Curated *The Devil Finds Work for Idle Hands*, Toomey-Tourell Gallery, San Francisco, USA

2014
Co-curated *A Machine Aesthetic*, Gallery North, Newcastle; The Gallery, AUB, Bournemouth; Project Space Plus, University of Lincoln; The Gallery, Norwich University of the Arts; Transition Gallery, London

2017
Shortlisted for the Jerwood Drawing Prize 2017

2022
Shortlisted for the Derwent Art Prize

2023
Curated *Die Wat Spaart, Die Wat Heeft*, Galerie Robert Drees, Hanover, Germany

Co-curated *Perpetual Arrival*, Platform A Gallery, Middlesbrough

2024
Shortlisted for the Trinity Buoy Wharf Drawing Prize

Shortlisted for the Contemporary British Painting Prize

2025
Winner of the Evelyn Williams Drawing Award 2025

Winner of the RWA Academy Award 2025

Shortlisted for the Trinity Buoy Wharf Drawing Prize

Shortlisted for the John Ruskin Art Prize

2026
Curated *Obsessive Compulsive*, Nancy Toomey Fine Art, San Francisco, USA

Exhibitions

Solo exhibitions

2025
Shadow Archive, GPS Gallery, London

2022
An End Always has a Start, Saturation Point, London

2020
Sweet Heresy, Patrick Heide Contemporary Art, London

2018
Artificial Light, Nancy Toomey Fine Art, San Francisco, USA

2016
Data Capture, Patrick Heide Contemporary Art, London

2013
A Synthetic Kind of Love, Galerie Robert Drees, Hanover, Germany

2010
Material Witness, Toomey-Tourell Gallery, San Francisco, USA

2007
Honey Trap, Toomey-Tourell Gallery, San Francisco, USA

Static Interference, Vertigo Gallery, London

2005
Hanging Garden, Text + Work, the Art Institute at Bournemouth (text by James Barron)

Arte Fiera, Vertigo Gallery, Bologna, Italy

2004
Carbon Candy, Vertigo Gallery, London

2003
Arcs + Surfaces, Vertigo Gallery, London

2002
Cusp, Sarah Myerscough Fine Art, London (two-person with Rebecca McLynn)

2000
A Line of Enquiry, The Loading Bay, London

1999
The Antidote, The Loading Bay, London

1997
New Paintings, Concord Sylvania, London

The Painted Figure, Hirschl Contemporary Art, London (two-person with Gabriel Schmitz)

1995
Lingering in Chambers of the Sea, The Acorn Gallery, Liverpool

New Paintings, Gallery 28, Reading

1993
Coming Up for Air, Engert Haus, Munich, Germany

1991
Beata Clarissa, Corpus Christi College, Cambridge

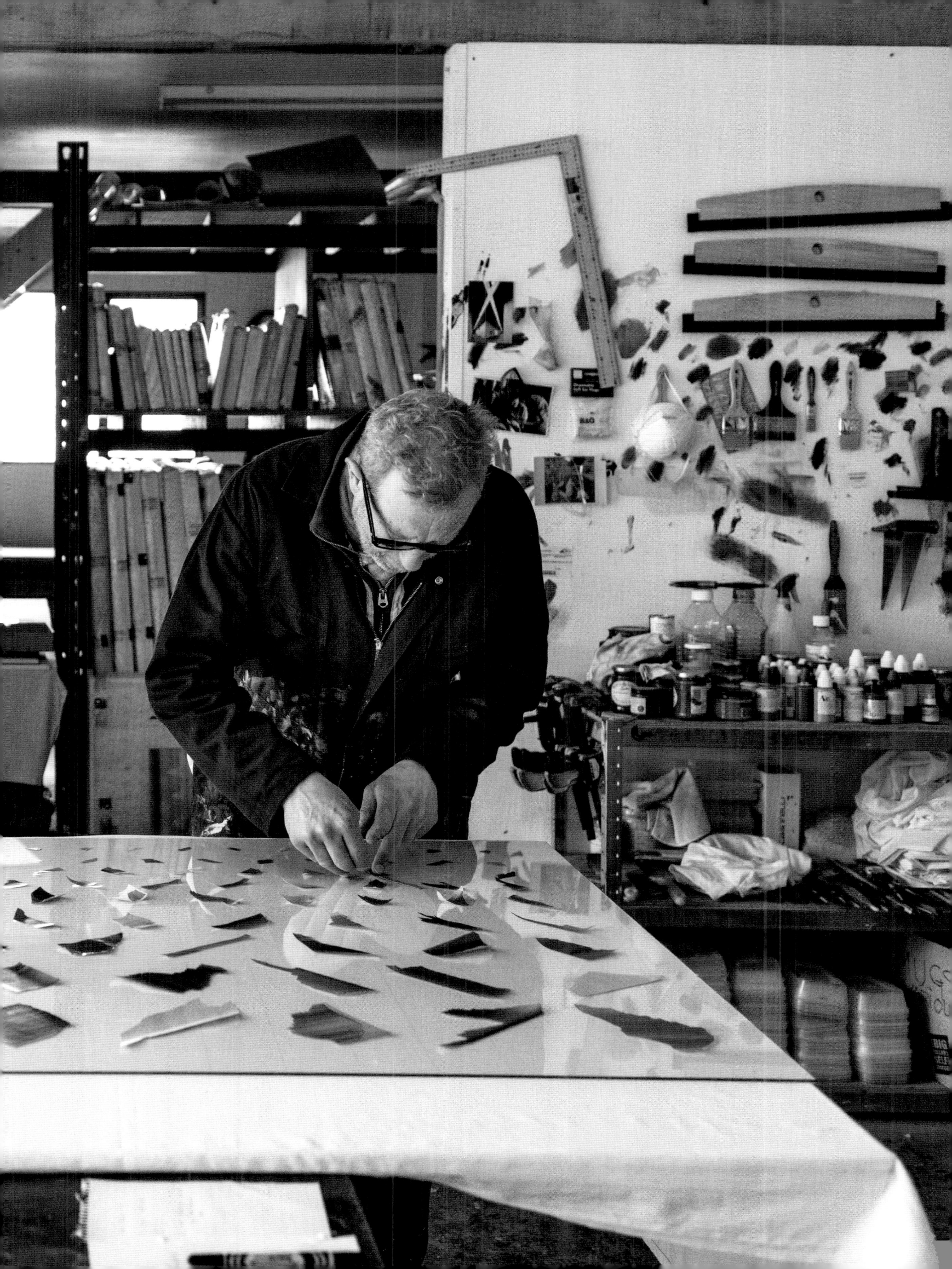

Exhibitions

Selected group exhibitions

2026
Obsessive Compulsive, Nancy Toomey Fine Art, San Francisco, USA

2025-26
Trinity Buoy Wharf Drawing Prize, Buoy Store, Trinity Buoy Wharf, London and Williamson Art Gallery & Museum, Birkenhead

2025
Painting – A Changed Environment, Messums, London

RWA Open Exhibition, Royal West of England Academy, Bristol

A Bell is a Cup Until it is Struck, BLOC Projects, Sheffield

Colour Rush, Poimena Gallery, Launceston, Tasmania, Australia

40 Dimensions, &Gallery, Edinburgh

RWA Biennial Open 2025: Paperworks, Royal West of England Academy, Bristol

John Ruskin Art Prize, Buoy Store, Trinity Buoy Wharf, London

2024-25
Contemporary British Painting Prize, BayArt Gallery, Cardiff; Thames-Side Studios Gallery, London; Huddersfield Art Gallery Curates at Yorkshire Artspace: Persistence Works, Sheffield

Trinity Buoy Wharf Drawing Prize, Buoy Store, Trinity Buoy Wharf, London; Salisbury Museum; Falmouth Art Gallery, Drawing Projects UK, Dundee; Manchester Waterside Gallery

2024
Group Exhibition, Patrick Heide Contemporary Art, Brussels, Belgium

Update #Summer, Galerie Drees, Hanover, Germany

Taking Time, The Cut, Halesworth

Royal Academy Summer Exhibition, Royal Academy of Arts, London (Curated by Cornelia Parker)

2023
Perpetual Arrival, Platform A Gallery, Middlesborough

I Want You to Panic, Zuleika Gallery, Woodstock

Curated at Dorfold: British Art Then and Now, Dorfold Hall, Cheshire

The New Accelerator, Ruskin Gallery, ARU, Cambridge

Die Wat Spaart, Die Wat Heeft, Galerie Robert Drees, Hanover, Germany

A Territory of Oneself, Zembla Gallery, Hawick, Scotland

2022
Accrochage // [akrɔˈʃaːʒə], Galerie Robert Drees, Hanover, Germany

Royal Academy Summer Exhibition, Royal Academy of Arts, London (Curated by Grayson Perry)

An Exhibition of Small Things with Big Ideas, White Conduit Projects, London

Derwent Art Prize, OXO Gallery, London

2019
Invited By, Galerie Robert Drees, Hanover

Everything but Canvas, Galerie Robert Drees, Hanover

2018
Intensity, House of St. Barnabas, London

Einsnullnull, Galerie Robert Drees, Hanover

2017
Jerwood Drawing Prize, Jerwood Space, London; East Gallery, Norwich; The Edge, Bath; Sidney Cooper Gallery, Canterbury; Vane Gallery, Newcastle-upon-Tyne

OVADA Seven Counties Open, OVADA Warehose, Oxford

Mardi Gras Requiem, Project Space Plus, Lincoln

2016
An Einem Tisch – Contemporary Geometrical Abstraction, Galerie Robert Drees, Hanover

Beyond Gravity II, Galerie und Kunstcabinett Corona Unger, Bremen

2014
Down to Zero, Patrick Heide Contemporary Art, London

(Detail), H Project Space, Bangkok, Thailand; Usher Gallery, Lincoln; Transition Gallery, London

2013-14
A Machine Aesthetic, Gallery North, Newcastle; The Gallery, AUB, Bournemouth; Project Space Plus, University of Lincoln; The Gallery, Norwich University of the Arts; Transition Gallery, London

2012
The Devil Finds Work for Idle Hands, Toomey-Tourell Gallery, San Francisco, USA

ReGroup, Red Space, London

2011
Raw, Pertwee, Anderson & Gold, London

Beyond the Commission, The Gallery, Arts University College Bournemouth

One Thing Leads to Another, Portland House, Malvern

2010
Über Flächen, Galerie Robert Drees, Hanover, Germany

2008
Ten, Toomey-Tourell Gallery, San Francisco, USA

2007
Meeting Place – Contemporary Art and the Museum Collection, Russell-Cotes Art Gallery & Museum, Bournemouth and the Arts Institute at Bournemouth

Underground, Shoreditch Town Hall, London (three-person with Roger Ackling and Simón Granell)

2005-06
Definite Article, Vertigo Gallery, London and Toomey-Tourell Gallery, San Francisco, USA, (with Roger Ackling, Marc Vaux and Cathy Wade)

2004
Surface, Vertigo Gallery, London

2003
Paperwork, Vertigo Gallery, London

30 x 30, Vertigo Gallery, London

2002
Wall to Wall, Sarah Myerscough Fine Art, London

1997
The Art Experience, The Atrium Gallery, London

1995
The Genitals are Beauty, The House of William Blake, London

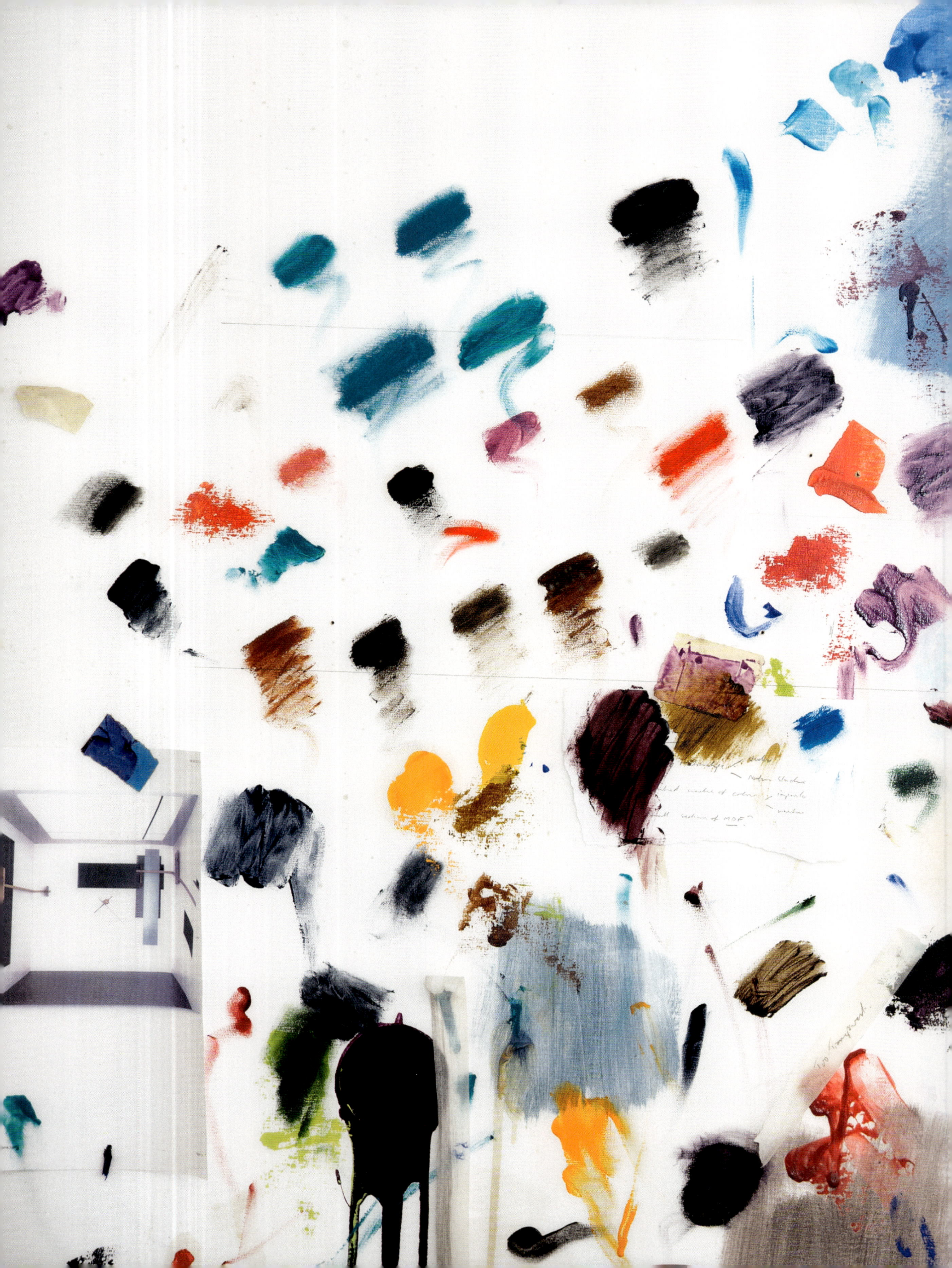

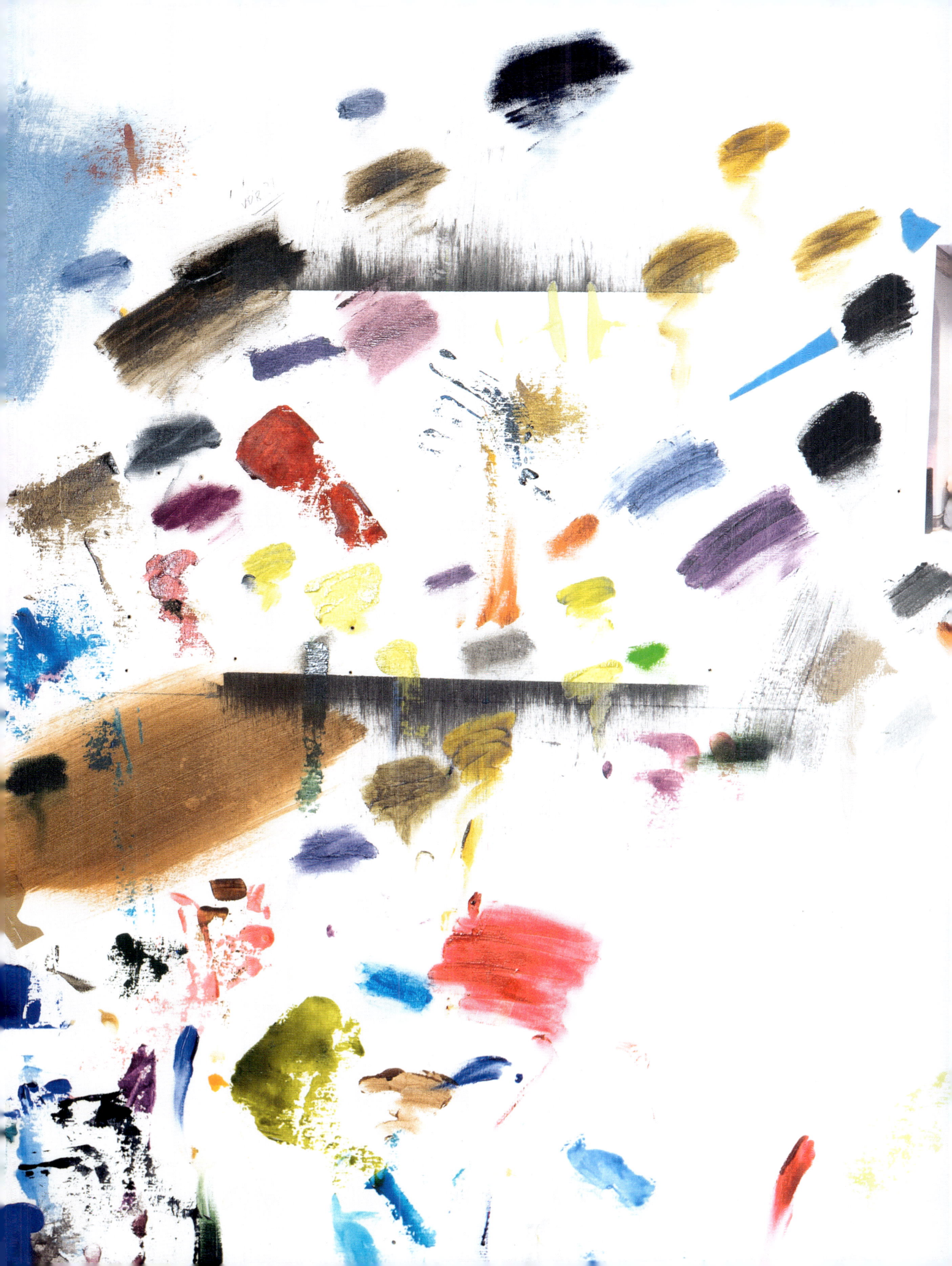

Bibliography

2025
Carey-Kent, Paul: *The Most Original Show of Frieze Week? Eric Butcher 'Shadow Archive'*, Artlyst, 18 October

Trinity Buoy Wharf Drawing Prize 2025 (catalogue), London

2024
Contemporary British Painting Prize 2024 (catalogue), Cardiff

Trinity Buoy Wharf Drawing Prize 2024 (catalogue), London

2023
O'Donnell, Annie: *Perpetual Arrival*, Saturation Point, London

Hughes, Tim: *Art to Make us all Panic*, Oxford Times, 11 May

Worst, Jörg: *Die Würde des Küchenschwamms*, Hannoversche Allgemeine Zeitung, 29 April

Spencer, Benet; King, Phil; Noga, Laurence; Blannin, Katrina & Steel, Jeffrey: *The New Accelerator* (catalogue), Anglia Ruskin University, Cambridge

2020
Carey-Kent, Paul (essay): Eric Butcher: *Richness in Rightness*, Time Trial (catalogue), London

Loader, Karen: *An Interview with Eric Butcher*, Saturation Point, London

French, Clare: *Sweet Heresy*, Saturation Point, London

2019
Schacht, Daniel Alexander: *Kurve, Gerade, Rechteck*, Hannoversche Allgemeine Zeitung, 1 February

Worat, Jörg: *Leinwand Bleibt Aussen Vor*, Cellesche Zeitung, 11 February

2018
Schacht, Daniel Alexander: *Einmal mit allen*, Hannoversche Allgemeine Zeitung, 31 August

Ed. Savage, Kim: *Eric Butcher*, Curated Selection, Art Maze Mag, Issue 9

2017
Heide, Patrick and Platzgummer, Verena (essay), *Eric Butcher*, Ten Years (catalogue), Patrick Heide Contemporary Art, London

Jerwood Drawing Prize 2017 (catalogue), London

2016
Müller, Felix: *Plastische Geometrie*, Hannoversche Allgemeine Zeitung, 13 September

2014
Riley, Travis: *A Machine Aesthetic*, Garageland, Issue XVI

Ed. Bracey, Andrew: (Detail) (catalogue), Transition Prints, London

2013
Krämer, Harald (essay): *Bildwerke, Bildwerke* (catalogue), Galerie Robert Drees, Hanover

Schacht, Daniel Alexander: *Echte Kraft, Künstliche Liebe*, Hannoversche Allgemeine Zeitung, 12 February

2010
Exley, Roy (essay): *Eric Butcher & the Aluminium Works*, Material Witness (catalogue), CAIR (Centre for Art International Research), Liverpool John Moores University, Liverpool

Baker, Kenneth: *Butcher Shines at Toomey Tourell*, San Francisco Chronicle, 13 March

Di Blasi, Johanna: *Farbexperimente in der Hannoverschen Galerie Drees*, Hannoversche Allgemeine Zeitung, 19 November

2007
Haldane, John (essay): *Underground*, Trimings, Lee (essay): *Loveslaves*, Sheldon, Julie (essay): *Process by Protocol*, Kovats, Tania (essay): *Digging, in Underground* (catalogue), CAIR (Centre for Art International Research) Liverpool John Moores University, Liverpool

Eds. Buckingham, Les and James, Stephanie: *Meeting Place – Contemporary Art and the Museum Collection* (catalogue, inc. essay Butcher, Eric: *Discoveries*), the Russell-Cotes Art Gallery & Museum, Bournemouth

Art at More London, The LG collection of Contemporary art, London (catalogue)

2005
Barron, James (essay): *Spaces, In, Out and Around*, Hanging Garden (catalogue), The Arts Institute at Bournemouth

Butcher, Eric (essay): *Objects and Surfaces*, Definite Article (catalogue), Vertigo Gallery, London. Reprinted (abridged) in Art & Architecture Journal, No. 63, Autumn 2005

2004
Packer, William (essay): *Eric Butcher*, Carbon Candy (catalogue), Vertigo Gallery, London

2003
Kingston, Angela: *New Paintings by Eric Butcher*, Shearn, Catherine: *A Conversation with Eric Butcher*, Arcs + Surfaces (catalogue), Vertigo Gallery, London

1995
Hughes, Ronnie: *Lingering in Chambers of the Sea*, The Big Issue, 22 March

1993
Zimmermann, Ingrid: *Ringen um Form und Transparenz*, Süddeutsche Zeitung, 1 June

Collections

Aviva PLC, London
Capital & Provident Management Ltd, London
Clariden Leu (Europe) Ltd, London
Crédit du Nord, Lille, France
Davis, Polk & Wardwell LLP, Madrid and Paris
Deutsche Rentenversicherung, Hanover
GMR Group, London
Hogan Lovells LLP, Houston, USA
Invesco, London
Kazakhmys PLC, London
Laborious, Hanover
LG Collection of Contemporary Art, London
Linklaters LLP, London and Brussels
Majestic Insurance Co, San Francisco
Mayer Brown International LLP, London
Meravis GmbH & Co. KG, Hanover and Hamburg
Munkenbeck – Marshall Architects, London
The Open University, Milton Keynes
Thomas Miller, London
Queen Elizabeth Hospital Cancer Centre, Birmingham
Schlumberger, London
Selescope, Paris
Société Générale, London
Summit Partners, London

Acknowledgements

The catalyst for this book was when my friend, the designer Thomas Manss, introduced me to Lucy Duckworth from Unicorn Publishing. That began a series of conversations between the three of us, out of which this book began to evolve. I'm enormously grateful to Thomas, who designed my previous book *Time Trial*, for his support and encouragement, not to mention the beautiful and measured design of this book. Similarly, Lucy contributed a huge amount of expertise, together with patience and good humour, ensuring the whole process remained vital and exciting throughout.

The first time Jonathan Watkins came to my studio to discuss my work, my head was spinning with problems and unanswered questions. Rarely had my practice been subjected to the rigours of such an incisive and enquiring mind. I was so troubled by some of the issues he raised that I was ready to give up making art there and then. I've wrestled with them ever since and continue to do so. They have deeply enriched my understanding of the complexities and implications of what I do in the studio. It was nothing short of an honour to receive Jonathan's insightful and thought-provoking essay for this publication.

I've known David Batchelor for 10 years. We don't know each other *very* well, but on the occasions we've met in his studio, we've always had very long, enormously stimulating and enjoyable conversations. One of the things I admire most about David is that while he's obviously extremely knowledgeable and erudite, he wears it lightly and his conversation is invariably characterised by warmth, generosity and good humour, all of which are in ample evidence throughout the conversation reprinted here.

Peter Abrahams has been documenting my work for 20 years. A brilliant artist in his own right, Peter brings decades of experience to what are invariably difficult objects to photograph. I have benefited from our detailed conversations about the intricacies of the work during our long photoshoots.

I am also deeply indebted to the multi-talented duo of Jon Barrett and Rosie May Giblett; Jon for his invaluable assistance in the studio, exhibition installation and anything relating to the mysteries of technology, Rosie for her expert sound recording and transcription of the conversation with David Batchelor. Both have been and continue to be a joy to work with.

Published in 2026 by Unicorn
an imprint of Unicorn Publishing Group
Charleston Studio
Meadow Business Centre
Lewes BN8 5RW
www.unicornpublishing.org

ISBN 978-1-917458-89-4
10 9 8 7 6 5 4 3 2 1

Designed by Thomas Manss
Colour origination by DawkinsColour
Printed in Italy by Printer Trento